"Berenson does a fine job of showing how . . . a host of smoke-and-mirrors accounting practices led to the latest bubble and its inescapable, if particularly devastating, pop."

—*Kirkus Reviews*

"This work will be of value to anyone who wants to understand why the economy has declined and will also provide thought-provoking reading for experts in the field."

—*Library Journal*

ALEX BERENSON graduated from Yale University in 1994, with degrees in history and economics. After working at *The Denver Post* and TheStreet.com, he joined *The New York Times* in 1999 as a business reporter specializing in financial investigative reporting. He lives in New York City.

THE NUMBER

THE
NUMBER

How the Drive
for Quarterly Earnings
Corrupted Wall Street and
Corporate America

ALEX BERENSON

RANDOM HOUSE TRADE PAPERBACKS

NEW YORK

2004 Random House Trade Paperback Edition

Copyright © 2003 by Alex Berenson

All rights reserved under International and Pan-American Copyright Conventions.
Published in the United States by Random House Trade Paperbacks, an imprint of
The Random House Publishing Group, a division of Random House, Inc., New York,
and simultaneously in Canada by Random House of Canada Limited, Toronto.

RANDOM HOUSE TRADE PAPERBACKS and colophon are
trademarks of Random House, Inc.

This work was originally published in hardcover by Random House, an imprint of The
Random House Publishing Group, a division of Random House, Inc., in 2003.

Library of Congress Cataloging-in-Publication Data
Berenson, Alex.
The number: how the drive for quarterly earnings corrupted Wall Street
and corporate America / Alex Berenson.
p.   cm.
Includes bibliographical references and index.
ISBN 978-0-8129-6625-1
1. Corporations—Accounting—Corrupt practices—United States.
2. Corporations—Accounting—Corrupt practices—United States—Prevention.
3. Financial statements—United States—Auditing. I. Title.
HV6769 .B467   2003   364.16'8—dc21   2002036950

Random House website address: www.atrandom.com

Book design by J. K. Lambert

FOR MY BROTHER DAVID,

A TRUE FRIEND

It is difficult to get a man to understand something

when his salary depends on his not understanding it.

UPTON SINCLAIR

Foreword

———

When a friend told me that he'd bumped into Mark Cuban at an airport and that Mark had happened to mention he was reading The Number *and liked it, I was thrilled. And when Mark offered to write a Foreword for the new edition of the book, I couldn't say yes fast enough.*

Mark is a genuine American success story, a middle-class kid from Pittsburgh who became a billionaire by out-hustling and outsmarting his competition. His gift for marketing has turned the Dallas Mavericks, who were woeful before he bought them in 2000, into one of the hottest franchises in professional sports. He's built and sold two successful technology companies.

But Mark also has a superb record as an investor—a record that has been overshadowed by his other achievements. His career in finance apparently started young. His mom remembers that, as a child, he would go to stamp shows with his dad, buying stamps on one floor and then flipping them for an immediate profit on another. On Wall Street, they call that riskless arbitrage.

That savvy lasted into adulthood. Unlike most other Internet entrepreneurs, Mark did not fall for the hype that surrounded the sector in *the late 1990s. At the peak of the technology bubble in 1999, he and partner Todd Wagner sold Broadcast.com, their publicly traded Internet company, to Yahoo, for $6 billion, a good deal for all Broadcast's shareholders. Then Mark sold most of the shares in Yahoo that he'd received in the deal, taking home more than $1 billion while most supposed Internet visionaries watched their fortunes crumble over the next three years. Not only did Mark avoid that fate, he actually profited from the collapse of Internet stocks by selling many of them short.*

And he wasn't shy about his belief that the Internet was overvalued. In April 2000, just as public enthusiasm for the Internet peaked, Cuban told a group of would-be entrepreneurs in Dallas that most Internet companies "won't even be in business in two years. . . . If they can't raise more and more money, they're toast. There's not three of them I would buy right now."

Today, Mark remains very cynical about the way Wall Street works, as you'll see in his Foreword. In fact, he's even more cynical than I am. I believe that the stock market is broadly efficient—that at any given time the Standard & Poor's 500 index might be 30 percent too low or 50 percent too high, but that in the long run it reflects the performance of the American economy. I don't think the overall market is a Ponzi scheme, as Mark says. But I do think that the part of the market Mark saw up close during the 1990s, the technology and Internet sector, looked a lot like a Ponzi scheme. Many investors did not care about the fundamentals of the companies they bought. They wanted only to grab a piece of what seemed to be a magic money machine. Their greed was aided and abetted by Wall Street professionals and corporate executives who had a moral and legal duty to restrain themselves but instead chose to feed the frenzy. Given what Mark saw firsthand, I'm not surprised he views Wall Street as nothing more than a machine to market stocks.

Some people may argue that Mark is a hypocrite for speaking so critically of a market that made him a billionaire. I don't think so.

Mark didn't create the madness of the late 1990s. He made money for the investors in Broadcast.com. And he never hid his decision to sell his stake in Yahoo. From everything I can see, Mark Cuban shoots straight. You may not like what he says, but you always know where he stands.

So I'm proud that Mark has agreed to write the foreword for the new edition of The Number. *I'd like to think that his endorsement is proof that the book accurately captures how Wall Street and corporate America really work. After all, I'm just a journalist. During the frenzy, I had my nose to the glass, but I wasn't part of the action. Mark was.*

Thanks, Mark.

—Alex Berenson, New York, N.Y., January 2004

In 1990, I sold my company, MicroSolutions—which specialized in what at the time was the relatively new business of helping companies network their computer equipment—to CompuServe. After taxes, I walked away with about $2 million. That was going to be my nest egg, and my goal was to protect it at all costs, and grow it wisely.

I set about interviewing stockbrokers and settled upon a broker from Goldman Sachs, Raleigh Ralls. Raleigh was in his late twenties, and relatively new to Goldman. But we hit it off very well and I trusted him. As we planned my financial future, I made it clear that I wanted my nest egg to be invested not like I was thirty years old, but as if I were sixty years old. I was a widows-and-orphans investor.

Over the next year I stuck to my plan. I trusted Raleigh, and he put me in bonds, dividend-paying utilities and blue chips, just as I asked.

During that year, Raleigh began asking me a lot of questions about technology. Because of my experience at MicroSolutions, I knew the products and companies that were hot. Synoptics, Wellfleet, Net-Worth, Lotus, Novell and others. I knew which had products that worked, didn't work, were selling or not. How these companies were marketed, and whether or not they were or would be successful.

I couldn't believe that I would have an advantage in the market. After all, I had read *A Random Walk Down Wall Street* in college. I truly thought that the markets were efficient, that any available knowledge about a company was already reflected in its stock price. Yet I saw Raleigh using the information I gave him to make money for his clients. He finally broke me down to start using this information to my advantage to make some money in the market. Finally after more than a year, I relented. I was ready to trade.

Notice I didn't use the word invest. I wasn't an investor. I just wanted to make money. The reason I was ready to try was that it was patently obvious that the market wasn't efficient. Someone like me with industry knowledge had an advantage. My knowledge could be used profitably. As we got ready to start, I asked Raleigh if he had any words of wisdom that I should remember. His response was simple: "Get long, get loud."

Get long, get loud. As we started buying and selling technology stocks, most of which were in the local area networking field that I had specialized in at MicroSolutions, Raleigh put me on the phone with analysts, money managers, individual investors, reporters, anyone with money or influence who wanted to talk technology and stocks.

We talked about token ring topologies that didn't work on 10BaseT. We talked about which companies were stuffing channels—selling more equipment to their distributors than the distributors really needed to meet the retail demand. We talked about who was winning, and who was losing. We talked about things that really amounted to the things you would hear if you attended any industry trade show panel. Yet after hanging up the phone with these people, I would watch stocks move up and down. Of course as the stocks moved, the number of people wanting to talk to me grew.

I remember buying stock in a Canadian company called Gandalf Technologies in the early 90s. Gandalf made Ethernet bridges that allowed businesses and homes to connect to the Internet and each other via high-speed digital phone lines called ISDN.

I had bought one for my house and liked the product, and I'd talked to other people who'd used it. They had decent results, nothing spectacular, but good enough. I had no idea Gandalf was even a public company until a friend of Raleigh's asked me about it. What did I think about Gandalf Technologies? It was trading at the time at about a buck a share. It was a decent company, I said. It had competition, but the market was new and they had as much chance as anyone to succeed. Sure, I'll buy some, and I would be happy to answer any questions about the technology: the market size, the competition, the growth rates. Whatever I knew, I would tell.

I bought the stock, I answered the questions, and I watched Gandalf climb from a dollar to about $20 a share over the next months.

At a dollar, I could make an argument that Gandalf could be attractive. Its market was growing, and compared to the competition, it was reasonably valued on a price-sales or price-earnings basis. But at $20, the company's market value was close to $1 billion—which in those days was real money. The situation was crazy. People were buying the stock because other people were buying the stock.

To add to the volume, a mid-sized investment bank that specialized in technology companies came out with a buy rating on Gandalf. They reiterated all the marketing mishmash that was fun to talk about when the stock was a dollar. The ISDN market was exploding. The product was good. Gandalf was adding distributors. If they only maintained X percentage of the market, they would grow to some big number. Their competitors were trading at huge market caps, so this company looks cheap. Et cetera, et cetera.

The bank made up forecasts formulating revenue numbers at monstrous growth rates that at some point in the future led to profits. Unfortunately, the bank couldn't attract enough new money to the stock to sustain its price. It didn't have enough brokers to shout

out the marketing spiel to entice enough new buyers to pay the old buyers. The hope among the "sophisticated buyers" was that one bank picking up coverage would lead to others doing the same. It didn't happen. No other big investment banks published reports on the stock. The volume turned down.

So I did the only smart thing. I sold my stock, and I shorted it to boot. Then I told the same people who asked me why I was buying the stock that I had shorted the stock. Over the next months, the stock sank into oblivion. In 1997, Gandalf filed for bankruptcy. Its shares were canceled—wiped out—a few months later. I wish I could take credit for the stock going up, and going down. I can't. If the company had performed well, who knows what the stock would have done?

But the entire experience taught me quite a bit about how the market works. For years on end a company's price can have less to do with a company's real prospects than with the excitement it and its supporters are able to generate among investors. That lesson was reinforced as I saw the Gandalf experience repeated with many different stocks over the next ten years. Brokers and bankers market and sell stocks. Unless demand can be manufactured, the stock will decline.

In July 1998, my partner Todd Wagner and I took our company, Broadcast.com, public with Morgan Stanley. Broadcast.com used audio and video streaming to enable companies to communicate live with customers, employees, vendors, anyone with a PC. We founded Broadcast.com in 1995, and we were well on our way to being profitable. Still, we never thought we would go public so quickly. But this was the Internet Era, and the demand for Internet stocks was starting to explode. So publicly traded we would become, and Morgan Stanley would shepherd us.

Part of the process of taking a new company public is something called a road show. The road show is just that. A company getting ready to sell shares visits big mutual funds, hedge funds, pension funds—anyone who can buy millions of dollars of stock in a single order. It's a sales tour. Seven days, sixty-three presentations. We often discussed turning up the volume on the stock. It was the ultimate "get loud." Call it Stockapalooza.

Prior to the road show, we put together an amazing presentation. We hired consultants to help us. We practiced and practiced. We argued about what we should and shouldn't say. We had Morgan Stanley and others ask us every possible question they could think of so we wouldn't look stupid when we sat in front of these savvy investors.

Savvy investors? I was shocked. Of the sixty-three companies we visited and four hundred plus participants I would be exaggerating if I said we got ten good questions about our business and how it worked. The vast majority of people in the meetings had no clue who we were or what we did. They just knew that there were a lot of people talking about the company and that they should be there.

The lack of knowledge at the meetings got to be such a joke between Todd and I that we used to purposely mess up to see if anyone noticed. Or we would have pet lines that we would make up to crack each other up. Did we ruin our chance for the IPO? Was our product so complicated that no one got it and as a result no one bought the stock? Hell no. They might not have had a clue, but that didn't stop them from buying the stock. We batted 1.000. Every single investor we talked to placed the maximum order allowable for the stock.

On July 18, 1998, Broadcast.com went public as BCST, priced at 18 dollars a share. It closed at $62.75, a gain of almost 250 percent, which at the time was the largest one-day rise of a new offering in the history of the stock market. The same mutual fund managers who were completely clueless about our company placed multimillion-dollar orders for our stock. Multimillion-dollar orders using *your money*.

If the value of a stock is what people will pay for it, then Broadcast.com was fairly valued. We were able to work with Morgan Stanley to create volume around the stock. Volume creates demand.

Stocks don't go up because companies do well or do poorly. Stocks go up and down depending on supply and demand. If a stock is marketed well enough to create more demand from buyers than there are sellers, the stock will go up. What about fundamentals? Fundamentals is a word invented by sellers to find buyers.

Price-earnings ratios, price-sales, the present value of future cash flows, pick one. Fundamentals are merely metrics created to help stockbrokers sell stocks, and to give buyers reassurance when buying stocks. Even the way profits are calculated is manipulated to give confidence to buyers.

I get asked every day to invest in private companies. I always ask the same couple questions. How soon till I get my money back, and how much cash can I make from the investment? I never ask what the PE ratio will be, what the price-to-sales ratio will be. Most private investors are the same way. Heck, in Junior Achievement we were taught to return money to our investors. For some reason, as Alex points out in *The Number*, buyers of stocks have lost sight of the value of companies paying them cash for their investment. In today's markets, cash isn't earned by holding a company and collecting dividends. It's earned by convincing someone to buy your stock from you.

If you really think of it, when a stock doesn't pay dividends, there really isn't a whole lot of difference between a share of stock and a baseball card.

Put your Mickey Mantle rookie card on your desk, and a share of your favorite non-dividend paying stock next to it, and let it sit there for twenty years. After twenty years you would still just have two pieces of paper sitting on your desk. The difference in value would come from how well they were marketed. If there were millions of stockbrokers selling baseball cards, if there were financial television channels dedicated to covering the value of baseball cards with a ticker of baseball card prices streaming at the bottom, if the fund industry spent billions to tell you to buy and hold baseball cards, I am willing to bet we would talk about the fundamentals of baseball cards instead of stocks.

I know that sounds crazy, but the stock market has gone from a place where investors actually own part of a company and have a say in their management to a market designed to enrich insiders by allowing them to sell shares they buy cheaply through options. Companies continuously issue new shares to their managers without asking their existing shareholders. Those managers then leak that stock to the market a little at a time. It's unlimited dilution of existing shareholders' stakes, dilution by a thousand cuts. If that isn't a scam, I don't know what is. Individual shareholders have nothing but the chance to sell their shares to the next sucker. A mutual fund buys one million shares of a company with your and your coworkers' money. You own 1 percent of the company. Six weeks later you own less, and all that money went to insiders, not to the company. And no one asked your permission, and you didn't know you got diluted or by how much till ninety days after the fact, if that soon.

When Broadcast.com went public, we raised a lot of money that certainly helped us grow as a company. But once you get past the raising capital part of the market, the stock market becomes not only inefficient, but as close to a Ponzi scheme as you can get.

As a public company, we got calls every day from people who owned Broadcast.com stock or had bought it for their funds. They didn't call because they were confused during our roadshow, were too embarrassed to ask questions and wanted to get more information. They called because they wanted to know if the "fundamentals"—the marketing points—they had heard before were improving. And the most important fundamental was "the number," our quarterly earnings (or in our case, a loss). Once we went public, Morgan Stanley published a report on our company, as did several other firms. They all projected our quarterly sales and earnings. Would we beat the number?

Of course, by law, we were not allowed to say anything. That didn't stop people from asking. They needed us to beat the forecast. They knew that if we beat the number the volume on the stock would go up. Brokers would tell their clients about it. The Wall Street Journal would write about it. CNBC would shout the good news to day traders and investment banks that watched their network all day long. All the volume would drive up the stock price.

Unfortunately, patience is not a virtue on Wall Street. Every day, portfolios are valued at closing price. If the value of your fund isn't keeping up with the indexes or your competition, the new money coming in the market won't come to you. It just wasn't feasible to wait until the number was reported by companies each quarter. The volume had to be on the stocks in your fund. To keep the volume about a stock up, and the demand for the stock increasing, you needed to have good news to tell.

Volume, the number, whisper numbers, insiders granting themselves millions and millions of options—these are the games that Wall Street plays to keep on enriching themselves at the expense of the public. I know this. I have tried to tell people to be careful before turning over their life savings and their financial future to someone whose first job is to keep their job, not make you money.

Until I read *The Number* by Alex Berenson, I never had a book that explained how the market truly worked that I could tell my friends, family, and acquaintances to read. I never had a book that would truly warn them that the market was not as fair and honest as mutual fund and brokerage commercials made them out to be. I may be a cynic when it comes to the stock market, but I am an informed cynic, and that has helped me make some very, very profitable decisions in the market.

If you are considering investing in the market, any part of it, or if you are considering giving your hard-earned money over to someone else to manage, please, please read *The Number* first.

—Mark Cuban, Dallas, Texas, January 2004

ONE OF MANY

January 22, 2001, 5:30 P.M. Darkness has settled over the East Coast, but the mood is sunny in the executive suites at the Islandia, New York, headquarters of Computer Associates. The world's fourth-largest independent software company has just released its quarterly earnings for the three months ending December 2000, and the report is a good one. Sales and profits are higher than Wall Street anticipated.

No one will benefit from the news more than Charles Wang, the chairman of Computer Associates, and Sanjay Kumar, the company's chief executive, good friends who have just bought the New York Islanders professional hockey team. Wang owns 30 million shares, more than $1 billion, of the company's stock. Kumar, a relative pauper, has about $200 million in Computer Associates shares. Those fortunes will grow the next day, as investors bid Computer Associates' stock up almost 6 percent.

After issuing the report, Computer Associates holds a conference call to discuss its results with the Wall Street analysts who follow the company. Kumar can't resist bragging. Although the software industry is in its worst downturn in a decade, his company has demonstrated its strength. "We're extremely pleased with the performance we pulled off," he says.[1]

If she had been on the call, that news would have come as a surprise to Mary Welch. Welch, a Computer Associates sales rep, had been fired by the company a week earlier, one of three hundred employees laid off as 2001 began. Like most of the fired employees, Welch was told she would not receive any severance pay, because she had been dismissed for poor performance. Yet she had received a positive job review only two weeks before. Welch and many other fired employees believed that Computer Associates wanted to avoid paying severance by disguising a company-wide cutback as individual firings. The layoffs were necessary because the company's sales had plunged in the December quarter, the fired employees claimed. "They did a mass layoff," Welch said.

At the time, Welch's complaints seemed nothing more than the gripes of a disgruntled ex-employee. After all, Computer Associates' financial statements showed that business had been better than ever in the December quarter, with sales up 13 percent and profit up almost one-third. Surely the company couldn't just make up its results.

But Mary Welch was right. Thanks to an audacious accounting trick, Computer Associates had found a way to rewrite its financial statements. The company had divorced the reality of its business, a business in decline, from the profit-and-loss picture it presented to Wall Street. Breaking the most basic conventions of accounting, it was rebooking sales and earnings that it had already reported.

Computer Associates was not a penny stock operating in the shadows of the market. It had eighteen thousand employees, tens of thousands of shareholders, and a market value of more than $20 billion, more than Nike or Federal Express. Yet no one—not the analysts paid to decipher the truth of Computer Associates' fortunes, not the accountants legally required to certify its books, not the mutual fund managers who bought its stock, and most certainly not the regulators who oversaw the U.S. securities markets—had blown the whistle on the company's accounting maneuvers.

There are fourteen thousand publicly traded companies in the United States. Expecting all of them to be honest is unrealistic. Like any town of fourteen thousand, the market is bound to have its share of grifters and shoplifters. But the deception at Computer Associates was dangerous precisely because it *wasn't* an aberration. By January 2001, all manner of companies were abusing accounting rules to mislead their investors, seemingly without fear of being caught. A strange madness had gripped the market. Even its most solid citizens were running red lights and breaking windows. And the police were nowhere in sight.

CONTENTS

Introduction

—

SYSTEM FAILURE

On Wall Street, not all numbers are created equal.

New home starts. The consumer confidence index. Retail sales. Overnight television ratings. Unemployment claims. PC shipments. Casino winnings in Atlantic City and the Las Vegas Strip.

The figures roll out every day from government agencies and industry trade groups and independent analysts. Watching them all is impossible; most speed by unnoticed.

But one set of numbers burns brighter than the rest. Every three months, publicly traded United States companies report their sales and profits to their shareholders. Those quarterly announcements are the lodestar that investors—and these days, that's most of us—use to judge the health of corporate America.

It makes intuitive sense that corporations must regularly tell their shareholders how much money they have made or lost. What's your weekly paycheck? Did you get a bonus last year? All in all, how much money did you make? You know the answer, without much trouble. Why shouldn't Exxon and General Motors?

They should, and they do. Every quarter they add up their sales and costs, and figure out where they stand. Then they tell the world, in press releases and conference calls and most important in reports that they file four times a year with the Securities and Exchange Commission, the federal agency that regulates U.S. stock markets. To be precise: Three quarterly reports, or 10-Qs, submitted to the S.E.C. within forty-five days after a quarter ends. One 10-K, the big one, the audited annual report, to be filed less than ninety days of the end of a company's fiscal year. Qs and Ks, in Wall Street shorthand.

Qs and Ks are monuments to numbers. Revenue. Selling, general, and administrative expenses. Operating income. Interest paid. Columns of huge numbers, eight, nine, or ten figures long, fall down the page in black and white to land with a bang disguised as a whimper at one small number: earnings per share.

Earnings per share is usually no more than a couple of bucks, an unprepossessing sum compared to the giant figures above. But its small size is deceiving. Multiply a dollar or two per share by hundreds of millions of shares, and you have real money. A stray penny on the 10 billion shares that General Electric has outstanding turns out to be $100 million.

Even within a profit report, not all numbers are equal. For traders and investors of all sizes, earnings per share is the ultimate benchmark of a company's success or failure. Has it risen from the previous quarter and the previous year? Has it met the "consensus"—the average estimate of the Wall Street analysts who follow the company? More than any other number, earnings per share determines whether a company's shares will rise or fall, whether its chief executive will be rewarded or fired, whether it will build a new headquarters or endure a round of layoffs.

On Wall Street, a place of little subtlety, earnings per share is known simply as "the number." As in "What was the number for Pfizer?" Earnings per share is the number for which all the other numbers are sacrificed. It is the distilled truth of a company's health. Earnings per share is the number that counts.

Too bad it's a lie.

Under the best of circumstances, the figures in a quarterly report—earnings per share most of all—are approximations, best guesses based on a thousand other best guesses. Earnings reports are about accounting, and the accounting that big companies use to measure their financial health has as much in common with the way you balance your checkbook as a five-alarm fire has with a backyard barbecue.

If you're like most people, your paycheck is your main source of income. Over the last few years, if you work for a publicly traded company, you may have gotten some stock options too. Those are nice, but the local grocery store prefers cash, so if you're wise, you won't figure options as income, either, until you cash them in.

Then there's the other side of the ledger: spending and saving. The distinction is usually clear, although the line blurs at your mortgage payment, since part of that is going to build equity in your home. Still, your personal accounting is relatively straightforward. You can easily compare how much you've earned and how much you've spent, because you get paid in cash and you spend cash (or use a credit card, which you pay off within a few weeks).

But big companies measure their costs and revenues in a very different way. Instead of simply counting the cash they are making and spending, they use something called "accrual accounting." Under accrual accounting, a company books revenue when it makes a sale, not when it actually receives the cash for the sale. It books an expense when it agrees to buy something, not when it actually pays. Accrual accounting also recognizes that companies invest in assets that will last many years, and it allows the companies to spread the cost of those assets over their life. For example, an airline doesn't expense the entire price of a new plane up front. Instead, it recognizes the cost of the plane over many years, as the aircraft's value "depreciates."

In theory, accrual accounting makes sense. Cash accounting can make companies appear to be losing money just when their business is ramping up and they're making lots of sales for which they'll be paid in the future.*

But what makes sense in theory can be abused in practice. Because they're not simply measuring cash inflows and outflows, companies need to make hundreds of assumptions to calculate their earnings each quarter. They must estimate everything from how much money they will earn on their pension funds to how quickly their assets will lose value.† With so many assumptions to make, even honest companies sometimes make mistakes. Those that want to cheat have an almost infinite number of ways to do so. They can book sales to customers who won't ever be able to pay them. They can hide ongoing, day-to-day expenses as investments in long-lived assets. They can shift research and development expenses to supposedly independent partners. They can make sham deals with other companies, swapping overvalued assets in a way that allows both sides to book a profit on the trade.

---

*For an example of why accrual accounting makes more sense than cash accounting to measure big companies' results, see Appendix 1.

†It may seem odd that companies can't know for certain something as basic as how quickly their assets will lose value. But consider this example: You and your neighbor buy identical new cars on the same day. You take good care of your car, regularly changing its oil and putting it in garages instead of parking it on the street so it doesn't get scratched. Your neighbor is much less conscientious. Three years later you have spent $1,000 more maintaining your car than your neighbor. But you figure that your car is worth $2,000 more than your neighbor's, because it's in better shape. The way you see it, you've saved $1,000. Your neighbor disagrees. He thinks the cars are worth the same. He thinks you've wasted $1,000 on unnecessary maintenance. Who's right? You may not be able to tell until the cars are sold. But if you were a public company, you would have to estimate your car's value every three months—and so would your neighbor. And those estimates would play an important part in determining your quarterly "earnings." Now, imagine that instead of owning one car, you own thousands of garbage trucks. If you underestimate how quickly those assets are losing value, either accidentally or deliberately, you will wind up overestimating your earnings. And it will be essentially impossible, until you actually sell the used trucks, for anyone to know what you've done.

Used properly, accrual accounting is about timing, not about creating profits where none exists. Over the long run, the profits that a company reports under accrual accounting should jibe with the cash it receives and spends. Over the long run, companies that make sales to customers who can't pay will have to admit that their clients are deadbeats. Over the long run, a company can't hide operating expenses as capital spending, because it will wind up with a balance sheet full of nonexistent assets. Over the long run, all the accounting and financial tricks in the world can't turn a failing business into a success.

But they can in the short run. And sometimes, with enough tricks, the short run can last a long time, long enough for executives to make tens or even hundreds of millions of dollars selling stock whose value has been inflated by pumped-up earnings.

—

Given the importance of the number, and the ease with which it can be manipulated, you might expect that investors would look at earnings per share with a skeptical eye. You might think they would carefully read the footnotes buried at the bottoms of Qs and Ks, and examine a company's cash flows to see whether its profits have any basis in reality.

But you'd be wrong. As a rule, before 2002, most individual and professional investors didn't worry much about accounting. As long as a major accounting firm certified that a company's financial statements were prepared according to GAAP, or "generally accepted accounting principles," shareholders took them at face value. Investors held as an article of faith that the quality of corporate financial reporting in the United States was better than anywhere else. Watched over by the Securities and Exchange Commission and independent accountants, American companies had no choice but to tell Wall Street the truth. U.S. markets were the fairest and most honest in the world.

Like most deeply held beliefs, this shibboleth overlooked inconvenient realities. The S.E.C. had never been given a budget large enough to check every financial statement for irregularities. Accountants had always had to balance their responsibilities to investors with their paychecks, which came from the companies whose books they audited.

Still, if history was any guide, investors had reason to be confident. The combination of mandatory corporate disclosure and federal oversight seemed to have worked since its creation in 1934. Sure, the concept behind the number—that public companies could precisely calculate their earnings each quarter—was a lie. But as long as companies prepared their financial statements in good faith, it was a white lie. Companies might not always be able to calculate their profits exactly, but if they made honest estimates they ought to be close. And for two generations they had been close. Aggressive accounting gimmickry had been uncommon, and overt fraud rare. Most financial statements were reasonably accurate. There had been exceptions, especially during the 1960s, but they never caused investors to question the markets' overall integrity. In fact, in some important ways, markets appeared to be growing fairer as the twentieth century progressed. Outright manipulation of individual stocks faded, and the S.E.C. aggressively pursued insider trading cases.

But as the bull market of the 1990s turned into a boom and then a bubble, a few regulators, short-sellers, and journalists warned that the accuracy of corporate financial statements, the core of the system, was slipping. Accounting gimmickry had grown widespread and increasingly dangerous, they complained. The number of earnings restatements soared in the late 1990s, and several big public companies admitted or were caught committing accounting fraud.

"We are witnessing an erosion in the quality of earnings and, therefore, the quality of financial reporting. Managing may be giving way to manipulation; integrity may be losing out to illusion," Arthur

Levitt, chairman of the S.E.C., said in a prophetic 1998 speech in New York. "Today, American markets enjoy the confidence of the world. How many half-truths, and how much accounting sleight-of-hand, will it take to tarnish that faith?"

But with the Nasdaq and Standard & Poor's 500 index setting new highs on what seemed a daily basis, Levitt's speech, and similar grumblings, were mostly ignored. Wall Street, the accounting industry, and corporate executives insisted the system of oversight and disclosure was as solid as ever. Most individual investors were inclined to agree, pouring money into mutual funds and their retirement accounts. Wall Street's complacency about the quality of earnings persisted even after the Nasdaq bubble burst in the spring of 2000—and, amazingly, even after Enron collapsed in the fall of 2001. By March 2002, the S&P 500 index, the most important barometer of the overall market, stood at 1,170, compared to 1,130 when Enron filed for bankruptcy in December.

To be sure, at 1,170, S&P 500 had fallen about 24 percent from its peak two years earlier. But that loss was concentrated in technology and telecommunications companies, which had been crushed by the slowdown in demand for computers and Internet services. Most other stocks had hardly fallen; many had risen from their levels of 2000. Considering that the United States had endured both a recession and a terrorist attack the previous year, stock prices in March 2002 reflected extraordinary investor confidence, a confidence seventy years in the making.

In a matter of months, that confidence disappeared. During the spring of 2002, dozens of cases of serious accounting gimmickry came to light at blue-chip, Fortune 500 companies. Qwest, a giant telecom company, said that it had improperly overstated its profits by $1.6 billion. Dynegy, an energy trader, admitted that it had inflated its cash flow by hundreds of millions of dollars. Bristol-Myers Squibb, one of the world's largest drug companies, acknowledged juicing its sales figures by encouraging its distributors to buy more product than they needed. I.B.M. was discovered booking profits from asset sales—which by their nature are one-time gains—as operating earnings. Every week seemed to bring another disaster, another S.E.C. or criminal investigation of accounting irregularities: Global Crossing. Computer Associates. Adelphia Communications. AOL Time Warner. Nvidia. Halliburton. Whole sectors of the market, most notably cable and telecommunications companies and energy traders, found themselves unable to sell new stock or bond issues at any price, so deeply did investors distrust their financial statements. Enron's auditor, Arthur Andersen, which had eighty-five thousand employees worldwide and a ninety-year history, broke apart and collapsed after being criminally indicted for obstruction of justice.

Then, at the beginning of June, Manhattan prosecutors indicted L. Dennis Kozlowski, the chairman of Tyco International, a huge conglomerate that for months had angrily denied allegations of accounting gimmickry, on criminal charges of sales tax evasion. (Prosecutors would later expand the charges, accusing Tyco's three top executives of stealing hundreds of millions of dollars from the company.) Tyco's stock, which had stood at $60 in December 2001, fell as low as $8. The drop cost investors $100 billion, more than the collapse of Enron. And on June 25, the telecommunications giant WorldCom admitted that it had outstated its profits by $4 billion. Less than a month later, WorldCom filed for Chapter 11, the largest corporate bankruptcy in history.

For many investors, the revelations at WorldCom and Tyco were too much to bear. The scope of the fraud at WorldCom was unprecedented, while the charges against Kozlowski put in high relief the greed that corporate chieftains had shown during the 1990s boom. Kozlowski had been one of the most highly regarded executives in the United States only a few months before, fawned over by Wall

Street analysts and the subject of a rave *Business Week* cover article in May 2001. Now he was being arraigned in a Manhattan courthouse among petty thieves and drug pushers. Could any chief executive or any financial statement be trusted? Was the spectacular growth that the U.S. economy and companies like General Electric had shown during the 1990s real or a mirage?

Between March and October of 2002, the Dow Jones industrial average fell more than 2,000 points. The S&P 500 dropped by about one-third, closing on October 9 at 777, its lowest level in five years. In seven months, $4.3 trillion in stock market wealth—$15,000 for every American—simply evaporated. From its March 2000 high, the S&P 500 had fallen nearly 50 percent, the worst bear market since the Depression.

The crash was particularly difficult for older Americans who had counted on stocks to finance their retirements. "I didn't want to become one of those doddering old professors who can never afford to leave," John Saxman, a Columbia University professor, said in July. "Now I'm sixty-three, and every time I try to think about a specific retirement date, I look at my quarterly reports and realize I can't."[1] But the pain was not confined to a few or a few million unlucky investors. U.S. economic growth, which had been very strong during the first quarter of 2002, stalled as companies pulled back on new hiring and new investments in plants and equipment. Osama bin Laden had hardly slowed the American economy; Dennis Kozlowski and Bernard J. Ebbers of WorldCom and Kenneth Lay of Enron brought it almost to a halt.

———

I first considered writing this book in the fall of 2001 when Enron collapsed. As a financial investigative reporter at *The New York Times,* I had seen plenty of bad accounting and corporate fraud. Still, I was stunned to see a company as large and supposedly as profitable as Enron implode in a matter of months. Sure, big companies had gone bankrupt before. But usually there were plenty of warning signs, and the problems were easy to understand, if not to fix. A labor war had destroyed Eastern Airlines; heavy debt from a hostile takeover had forced Federated Department Stores, the owner of Bloomingdale's and Macy's, into bankruptcy. Enron, however, had just disappeared. The assets that it listed on its books didn't seem to exist at all.

So I was taken aback when the market ignored Enron's collapse. As I began writing in the spring of 2002, I expected I would have to offer lots of specific examples to convince readers that the problem of bad accounting had become pervasive. But Tyco and Global Crossing and the rest of the rogues made that case beyond a reasonable doubt. The most important question now is not what happened at World-Com or Enron or Arthur Andersen or any individual company or accounting firm. It is why the system as a whole failed, why accounting and financial reporting at so many companies became criminally shoddy.

The answer has many threads. The ethical collapse of the accounting industry, vast increases in executive pay, and severe budget problems at the S.E.C. contributed to the crisis. The decline in Wall Street research, the extraordinary growth of mutual funds, and investors' insatiable demand for Internet stocks also played a part. Even the falling cost of trading stocks can be counted as an indirect cause. And in the final two-thirds of this book, I'll offer a comprehensive look at the changes of the last two decades.

But to truly understand what happened at the end of the 1990s, investors need to look back further than the beginning of the most recent bull market in 1982. The real answer requires a (brief) explanation of the history of accounting and Wall Street in the twentieth century, beginning with the boom and bust of the 1920s and the creation of the S.E.C. in 1934. For the seeds of the system's failure were present from the very start.

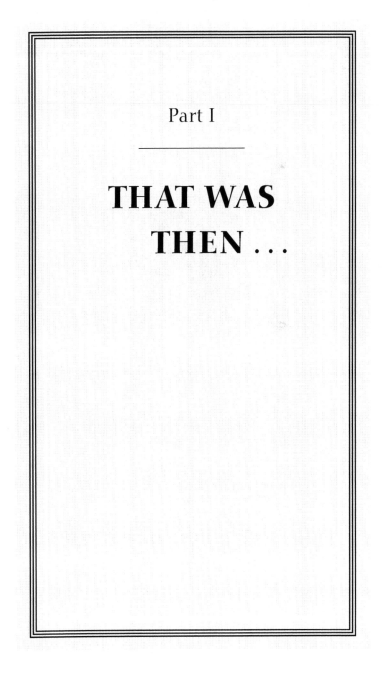

Part I

THAT WAS
THEN . . .

Chapter 1

—

BOOM AND BUST

It had been a very long week for J. P. Morgan Jr.

Morgan—the world's leading financier, the personification of Wall Street—had endured days of testimony before the Senate Banking and Currency Committee about his firm's misbehavior during the 1920s boom and the crash that followed. Under pointed questioning by Ferdinand Pecora, a hard-charging New York prosecutor who was the committee's chief counsel, Morgan admitted that he and many of his partners had not paid any taxes in 1931 and 1932, with the Depression at its worst. He acknowledged that earlier, at the height of the bubble, his firm had offered government officials the chance to buy shares in a hot new company at a below-market price. With 25 percent of all Americans unemployed, with banks failing and farmers starving, these revelations did not elicit great warmth. A generation later, *The New York Times* would call the inquiry "remarkable for its unfriendliness even in that year of bankers' general unpopularity."[1]

That year was 1933. And on the first day of its sixth month—Friday, June 1—at 10 A.M., in a Senate hearing room crowded with reporters and photographers, Morgan and his aides waited for another difficult day to begin.

Then the midget showed up.

The reason Lya Graf came to the Senate that day has been lost to history. Her employer, the Ringling Brothers and Barnum & Bailey Circus, was in town, but Graf had no obvious reason to make her way to the Capitol. Perhaps Ringling was looking for some easy publicity; a Ringling press agent named Charles Leef had accompanied her. Perhaps she just wanted to see Morgan in the flesh. If so, both circus and midget got their wishes. Ray Tucker, a reporter for the Scripps-Howard news service, saw Graf in the crowd outside the hearing room and pulled her in. "I'm going to introduce you to J. P. Morgan," Tucker said. And he did. Photographers swarmed and reporters rushed to capture every word of the not-very-interesting conversation between Morgan and Graf (Morgan: "I have a grandson bigger than you." Graf: "But I'm older.") Then Leef, the press agent, picked up Graf and popped her onto Morgan's lap.

In pictures of the incident, Morgan looks stunned and Graf amused, her arms spread wide.[2] Richard Whitney, the president of the New York Stock Exchange and a Morgan flunky, quickly sent Graf off, and Morgan recovered his composure.

But he could not recover his reputation. In a moment he was transformed from a powerful plutocrat to a confused old man. It is impossible to imagine Morgan's father, the original J.P., who had been America's central banker before America had a central bank, being caught in a similar indignity. Morgan Sr. ended market panics, steadied the economy, and saved Wall Street from itself; he did not truck with midgets, or senators. Morgan Jr. could not stop the crash of 1929 or end the Depression. He had tried and failed. For that Morgan might have been forgiven—the economic crisis was too big for any private citizen to fix—but he and his well-paid factotums had failed in a second, inexcusable way. They had failed to understand how serious the Depression had become and how much America now distrusted financiers and big business. And so Morgan and the rest of Wall Street's Old Guard had become nearly irrelevant to the bitter national debate over how to save capitalism from itself. Commentators wrote later that the incident had "humanized" Morgan, as if a man who treasured power and discretion, whose firm did not advertise or even put its name on its front door, wanted to be humanized. As if humanization was not the ultimate embarrassment.

A midget sat on J. P. Morgan's lap. It would be two generations before Wall Street and corporate America again ran so far amok during a boom or were so badly humiliated in the bust that followed.

—

A few years before that Friday morning, the nation's attitude toward Wall Street had been very different. In *Once in Golconda,* John Brooks summed up the peak of the frenzy as well as anyone ever has, in words eerily familiar today:

> Let us try, as best we can, to look at Wall Street as it was in August 1929, to catch its essentials. . . . Newcomers have arrived in great numbers. They are men and women who are sacrificing their own vacations, or else have simply chucked their jobs, to spend their days sitting, or more likely standing, in the brokerage customers' rooms watching the quotation board report the glorious news. . . .
>
> Many of those now crowding Wall Street have burned their bridges. They have thrown over their jobs on reaching some predetermined goal, a paper net worth of $50,000 or $100,000 or $200,000; they have bought expensive houses and mink coats for themselves or their wives, and look forward to lives of leisure and affluence. . . .
>
> All through the days, and long into the evenings, the talk, talk, talk goes on. There are tales of fortunes just made and of fortunes about to be made—above all, talk of fortunes. . . . There is talk about John J. Raskob's article in that month's *Ladies' Home Journal* entitled "Everybody Ought to Be Rich. . . ."

On the seventeenth the *Ile de France* and the *Berengaria* depart on transatlantic trips, the former eastward and the latter westward, each fully equipped for speculation with floating brokerage offices; when the *Berengaria* arrives in New York six days later, passengers tell of how every day the office on the promenade deck has been so mobbed that quotations had to be passed by word of mouth to passengers who couldn't get near enough. . . .

The madness had been a decade in the making. From a low of 63.90 in 1921, in the deep recession that followed the Great War, the Dow Jones industrial average had climbed steadily higher. By 1925 the Dow had more than doubled. After a pause in 1926, it leaped ahead again, finally reaching 381.17 on September 3, 1929. In eight years the Dow rose sixfold, by far the greatest gain in the history of the index up to that point.

In the generations since, economists and financial historians have exhaustively parsed the boom. Most have agreed broadly on its causes, from easy margin requirements that encouraged speculation to technological advances that spurred economic growth and brought electricity and cars to millions of Americans.* But there was at least one more factor in the decade-long rally, one less widely discussed. When the bull market began, stocks were *cheap*.

In the early 1920s, prudent investors usually stayed away from stocks, buying bonds instead. Many investors viewed the New York

---

*Essentially, an investor who buys on margin is borrowing part of the purchase price from his broker. If the stock rises, the investor's gains are multiplied, but if it falls even a little, the investor can face a "margin call" and be forced to put up more cash as collateral. If he can't, the broker can sell the stock—without the investor's consent—and use the proceeds to repay the loan. As a result, heavy margin borrowing can worsen market crashes, because it can result in forced selling at times when stocks are already falling.

Stock Exchange and its weaker cousin, the Curb Exchange, as little more than casinos. And they were right to be cynical. Trading on inside information was common, and stock manipulation widespread; stock prices would swing wildly on rumors of "bear raids" and "short squeezes."* "All the bubble blowers of other days, the moonshine promoters, green goods, and shell game men, financial pan-handlers and wildcat exploiters, and skin-game fakers . . . are now engaged in the stock selling game," a Pennsylvania congressman thundered in 1919.[3]

Nor could investors expect much protection from the authorities. State regulation was minimal; despite the congressional bluster, federal laws against stock manipulation hardly existed. The New York Stock Exchange, popularly known as the Big Board, functioned more or less as a private club, following its rules sporadically—usually when their enforcement would benefit its members. Even the press, that beacon of democracy and fair play, could not be trusted. Financial reporters from *The Wall Street Journal* and *The New York Times* were later discovered to have taken hundreds of thousands of dollars in bribes in return for pumping stocks in print.[4]

"Nearly all of those who traded in stocks frankly called themselves speculators," Benjamin Graham, the first and greatest stock analyst, wrote of the era in his memoirs. "They did not draw too fine a distinction between their financial operations and racetrack or other betting."[5] In fact, Graham recalled drolly, before the 1920s brokerage firms routinely handled bets on the outcome of presidential

---

*Short-sellers borrow stock and sell it, hoping to buy it back later for a lower price and profit from the decline. A short squeeze occurs when many shorts are simultaneously forced to return the stock they have borrowed, or "cover" their short positions. If there are not enough shares outstanding for the shorts to close out their positions, they can be forced into a ruinous bidding war for the few shares of stock that are available. In a full-blown squeeze, a stock's price can rise 50 or 100 points in a day.

elections for their clients, but "this genial practice was outlawed some years later when the stock exchange went all out for respectability."

A dearth of reliable financial information about companies contributed to the market's anything-goes nature. A few years before, Morgan Sr. had bemoaned the day when "all business will have to be done with glass pockets."[6] He need not have worried. The attitude of bankers and executives was that investors should cash their dividend checks and keep their questions to themselves. (In 1899, Henry Havermeyer, the president of the American Sugar Refining Company, was asked if he thought that corporations had the right to "offer stock to the people—to the whole community—and that the community then has no right to a knowledge of what the earning power of the stock is." In the best nineteenth-century robber-baron style, Havermeyer replied, "Precisely.")

The Big Board did not even require the companies it listed to report their profits to investors. It did make companies provide shareholders with a balance sheet listing assets and debts at least once a year.* Most companies went beyond that minimum, putting out an income statement at least once a year. But they often took the notion of an income statement quite literally, telling shareholders

---

*Balance sheets and income statements are the two most important pieces of financial information available to a company's shareholders.

The balance sheet explains a company's overall financial health. It reveals how much cash is available, the overall value of the company's assets, and how much of that value is available for shareholders after subtracting the company's debts and other liabilities.

The income statement explains how much money the company has made or lost over a specific period of time—usually either three months or a year. It details sales and expenses, which are generally broken into several categories, including taxes, interest, and overhead costs. What's left is the profit—or loss—available to shareholders for the period.

For more information on balance sheets, see Appendix 2.

how much money they had made or lost—and nothing more. At least one company, Pocahontas Fuel, offered investors only its balance sheet. Fewer than half the companies on the Big Board provided shareholders with full financial statements, including sales, interest costs, dividends and taxes paid, and one-time gains and losses.[7]

"It is not an exaggeration to say many corporate executives and investment bankers elevated opacity to a hallowed business principle," a trade group of financial analysts would later complain. "Information, such as it was in businesses beyond the railroads, was guarded jealously and understood to be emphatically private. Good information was almost by definition 'inside' information."[8]

So it is no surprise that many investors avoided stocks entirely as the 1920s began. But not every stock was rigged, and most companies were not frauds. The market's grime hid spectacular bargains in first-rate companies like U.S. Steel, which had been profitable and paid regular dividends through good years and bad. Their prices look almost absurdly low today.

The most basic measures of stock valuation are the dividend yield and the price-earnings (P/E) ratio. The dividend yield measures how much cash a shareholder receives each year, relative to the price of a share of stock. For example, if General Motors trades for $100 and pays an annual $4 dividend, G.M. has a dividend yield of 4/100, or 4 percent. The P/E ratio compares the price of a share to annual profits per share. If G.M. made $8 a share last year, it has a price-earnings ratio of 100/8, or about 12.5.

P/Es and dividend yields rise and fall with interest rates, economic growth, and investor confidence. But in general, low P/E ratios and high yields are a sign that stocks are cheap compared to alternative investments like bonds or real estate. Over the last century the average P/E of big American stocks has been about 15, and the average yield 4 percent. But that average figure has masked wild swings, and P/Es have rarely been lower, or yields higher, than they were in the early 1920s. General Electric, paying a dividend of $12 a share in 1921, could be had for $110, a yield of 11 percent. Overall, at a time when high-quality bonds paid 5 percent, the market's P/E ratio was below 10, and its dividend yield above 6 percent.[9]

With bargains like that at a time when the economy was growing solidly and inflation was quiet, stocks were all but certain to rise.

—

Rise they did, haltingly at first, then with increasing confidence as the decade progressed. And as companies like General Motors and Radio Corporation of America reported soaring sales and profits, investors realized something exciting about stocks that they had hardly understood before. As the economist Edgar Lawrence Smith explained in a 1924 book, *Common Stocks as Long-Term Investments,* a stock was not just a junior-grade bond that needed to pay a high dividend to compensate investors for its extra risk. Bonds paid fixed interest rates. But dividends on a stock were not fixed. They could rise as a company expanded and became more profitable. Bonds might offer safety, but stocks offered growth. In fact, if a company was growing quickly, it might be to shareholders' advantage to accept a low dividend now so that the company could reinvest its cash in its business and make much more money later.

Other economists and academics, such as Yale's Irving Fischer, seconded Smith's optimistic view. And investors saw for themselves how quickly companies could grow in a strong economy. Between 1915 and 1926, profits at the Computing-Tabulating-Recording Company (which later would change its name to International Business Machines) rose from less than $700,000 to $3.7 million, a fivefold increase.[10] C-T-R's dividend more than tripled, and its stock rose at a similar pace.

"During the postwar period, and particularly during the latter stage of the bull market culminating in 1929, the public acquired a completely different attitude toward the investment merits of common stocks," Graham wrote in 1934, in the first edition of *Security*

Analysis, his seminal work on stock valuation. (Graham, who at the time was managing money and teaching a class at Columbia University on investing, coauthored the seven-hundred-page book with David Dodd, a Columbia professor.) "The new theory or principle may be summed up in a sentence: 'The value of a common stock depends entirely upon what it will earn in the future.' "[11]

And as Graham noted sardonically, once that principle was established, investors could justify paying almost any price for a fast-growing company. Investors no longer needed to research the quality of a company's management, whether its stock was too expensive relative to its growth prospects, or whether a bond might be a better investment. "Making money in the stock market was now the easiest thing in the world. It was only necessary to buy 'good' stocks, regardless of price, and then to let nature take her upward course," Graham wrote. He was especially critical of investment trusts, the predecessor of mutual funds, which became very popular in the late 1920s.[12] "The investment process consisted merely of finding prominent companies with a rising trend of earnings, and then buying their shares regardless of price. Hence the sound policy was to buy only what everyone else was buying. . . . The original idea of searching for the undervalued and neglected issues dropped completely out of sight."

What was true for professional investors was doubly true for individuals. Americans in the 1920s had lived through repeated market panics and recessions so deep they would be called depressions today. They had watched the New York Stock Exchange close for four months in 1914, after war began in Europe. To the extent they had paid attention to the market at all, they had seen that it was a dangerous place for outsiders, a place where manipulation was rampant and outright fraud not uncommon. Yet, as the bull market progressed, it took a remarkably short time—years, not decades—for small investors to put aside their fears and plunge into the market. Millions of Americans enthusiastically bought stocks, and many sought out the fastest-growing, riskiest issues, such as R.C.A. and Electric Power & Light and Wright Aeronautical Corporation, which rose from $8 a share in 1922 to $280 a share in 1928.

If there was one moment that signaled the beginning of the transition from bull market to bubble, it was August 2, 1926. On that day the Dow Jones financial news service reported that Thomas Cochran, a Morgan partner, had said that "General Motors running at its present rate is cheap at the price, and it should and it will sell at least one hundred points higher."[13] For a man of the House of Morgan to tout a stock publicly was unusual, to say the least, and G.M. stock promptly rose 11½ points, or more than 6 percent. A few days later G.M. announced it would split its stock 3 for 2. Its shares surged again. The boom had begun.

It continued for the next three years, fueled by margin and easy credit and talk of a new era of prosperity. Americans should "regard the present with satisfaction and anticipate the future with optimism," President Calvin Coolidge said in December 1928.[14] Somewhere along the way, the public seemed to forget that investment was risky and speculation more so, that stocks could fall as well as rise. The games being played by market manipulators like Jesse Livermore and Michael Meehan became paradoxically reassuring. Wall Street might be a casino, but it was a casino rigged for the benefit of all its players, a money machine that would never stop giving. "Many speculators came to believe that a few powerful individuals were able to cause prices to rise and fall almost at will and that the Exchange would not prevent them from so acting," Robert Sobel, a financial historian, wrote in a chronicle of the era. "In large measure they were right."[15]

———

Were investors clamoring for companies with uncertain pasts but bright futures, companies whose shares could double one month and double again the next? Then Wall Street would give them what they wanted, and more, without looking too closely at what it sold.

Top-tier banks like Morgan had once hesitated to underwrite (a fancy word for sell) offerings of new or risky companies. Historically, the banks had been the most important gatekeepers against fraud, putting their reputations behind the stocks and bonds they sold. But as the boom progressed, the lure of high underwriting fees led the banks to lower their standards. By the late 1920s, even the most prestigious firms had succumbed to their own worst instincts and were pumping out dubious issues. The National City Company, a corporate forerunner of today's Citigroup, had sold Peruvian government bonds even though its own experts had warned that they might not be repaid. Goldman, Sachs poured out investment trusts whose main function appeared to be buying shares in other investment trusts. In less elevated circles that capital structure might have been called a Ponzi scheme. Lee, Higginson & Co., a reputable New York broker, sold almost $150 million in securities for Ivar Kreuger, "the Swedish Match King," without bothering to examine the Match King's books, which were utterly fictitious. "You Swedes are blockheads," Kreuger, perhaps the greatest con man of the twentieth century, told a friend. "You haggle about giving men money. But when I get off the boat in New York I find men on the pier begging me to take money off their hands."[16]

Kreuger was not alone. In 1924, investment banks and companies sold about $800 million in stock to the public. By 1929 stock sales had soared tenfold, to $8.2 billion.[17]

Along with the flood of new issues came a flood of accounting gimmicks, often invisible to investors until much later, that companies used to inflate their reported profits.[18] Like John Brooks's description of Wall Street's atmosphere in August 1929, many of the tricks will ring familiar to sophisticated investors today. Companies:

- hid ongoing expenses in large one-time charges;
- failed to account for losses that their subsidiaries had suffered, or passed money to subsidiaries that the subsidiaries then returned to them as profit;

- avoided accounting for their advertising expenses by claiming that advertising has a long-term brand-building effect and that spending on it should be treated like spending on a new factory, which will be valuable for many years and is not immediately expensed;
- wrote up assets and claimed that the assets' increased value represented a profit;
- understated depreciation and amortization charges;
- sold assets and pretended that the proceeds from the sales were actually profits from operations.

As ever, the chicanery was justified by its practitioners with the excuse that mere financial statements could not capture the brilliance of their enterprises. Talking to a Swedish diplomat, the Match King spoke for con men everywhere:

> We've chosen some new high priests and called them accountants. They too have a holy day—the 31st of December—on which we're supposed to confess. In olden times, the princes and everyone would go to confession because it was the thing to do, whether they believed or not. Today the world demands balance sheets, profit-and-loss statements once a year. But if you're really working on great ideas, you can't supply those on schedule. . . .
>
> The December ceremony isn't really a law of the gods—it's just something we've invented. All right, let's conform, but don't let's do it in a way that will spoil our plans. And someday people will realize that every balance sheet is wrong because it doesn't contain anything but figures. The real strengths and weaknesses of an enterprise lie in the plans.

The banks and investors who sent Kreuger $650 million during the 1920s and early 1930s might have disagreed. But without reliable, independently audited financial statements, without laws to compel disclosure and regulators to enforce those laws, investors had no way of knowing that Kreuger had lost hundreds of millions of dollars in his quixotic attempt to corner the world's match production. If they wanted to buy stocks, investors had little choice but to take companies' reported profits on faith.

—

So they did. And the bubble grew.

But the trouble with bubbles . . . the trouble with bubbles is that they don't last. Too bad, because they are so exciting before they burst. A few hundred dollars today turns into thousands tomorrow; and with margin and luck, those thousands turn into tens of thousands. The dice stay hot and the sevens keep coming, not for a night but for a year or two or three.

> *Hush thee, my babe, Granny's bought some new shares,*
> *Daddy's gone out to play with the bulls and the bears,*
> *Mommy's buying on tips, and she simply can't lose,*
> *And baby shall have some expensive new shoes!*

the *Saturday Evening Post* wrote in September 1929.[19] And bubbles don't seem like luck, not while they're happening. It seems only right that the optimists are winning and the whiners ground to dust. Bubbles are the home team running up the score in front of a cheering crowd, Studio 54 circa 1978, except without the velvet rope. Everybody gets in.

But bubbles never last. The dream of the boom is that every idea is a winner, that "it is only necessary to buy good stocks," that profits will always be higher tomorrow than today. The reality of business is false starts, dashed hopes, wasted effort, ruinous competition. Eventually the gap between fantasy and reality grows too big to ignore. Sometimes the bubble bursts because of an event outside the market, a war or oil embargo. Sometimes investors simply decide—seemingly all at once—that they would be better served buying bonds or real estate or anything but a stock trading at one hundred times earnings. Either way, the bubble bursts, badly.

The bubble of Morgan and Coolidge and R.C.A. and National City burst on Tuesday, October 29, 1929, eight weeks after the *Post*'s poem. The market had fallen through October and barely avoided chaos five days earlier, on Black Thursday, when stocks plunged in the morning and the Big Board closed its visitors gallery to prevent a riot. But the bulls still had hope. *The Wall Street Journal* explained optimistically on October 21 that "thousands of traders and investors have been waiting for an opportunity to buy stocks on just such a break as has occurred over the last several weeks." Even Black Thursday had ended ambiguously, with the market recovering after Morgan Jr. created a $20 million buying pool to support blue-chip stocks. Investors can buy good companies "with the utmost confidence," *The New York Times* told readers on October 28.[20]

Then came Black Tuesday. This time, no one could stop the panic. Investors who had bought on margin were forced to sell to repay their loans; buyers disappeared. The selling engulfed blue chips and speculative names alike. More than 16 million shares were traded on the New York Stock Exchange, a record that would not be surpassed for more than forty years.

—

By mid-November the Dow Jones average had fallen below 200, losing half its value in two months. The market rallied into the spring of 1930, regaining some of its losses, but the fever had broken. Investors could no longer pretend that stocks only went in one direction. Then calamity struck, as the United States slid into an economic crisis that worsened by the month. Unemployment soared; industrial production plunged; nervous consumers stopped spending. The economy fell into paralysis as fear fed on itself.

Most economists now believe the crash did not cause the Depression. A far more important factor was President Herbert Hoover's stubborn refusal to increase federal spending as demand elsewhere in the economy collapsed. Chaos in the banking system and ill-timed tariff hikes worsened the crisis. But those factors would only be understood later. At the time, many Americans blamed Wall Street for their misery. After all, business had seemed strong before October.

Throughout 1930 and 1931 the economy worsened and the market slid. By June 1932 the Dow had fallen to 41.22, its lowest level since 1897. As each month brought more bad news, as production collapsed and the unemployment rate rose to 25 percent—one in four adults out of work—the public's anger at Wall Street grew. It was easy to see the market's relentless decline as a plot to destroy the economy. Someone must be getting rich off the crash: speculators, short-sellers, communists, *someone*. Hoover threatened to take over the New York Stock Exchange if the Big Board did not take action to stop short-selling. One senator proposed a bill that would have made shorting a criminal offense. "Wall Street was like a trapped animal: what remained of its spirit was contained in a sullen, dangerous self-protectiveness," Brooks wrote later. On March 12, with his empire collapsing, Ivar Kreuger shot himself in the heart in a Paris hotel. "I have made such a mess of everything that I believe this is the best solution for all concerned," he wrote. "Good-bye now, and thanks."[21]

Such was the atmosphere in April 1932 when the Senate Banking and Commerce Committee opened a hearing into Wall Street with a grilling of Richard Whitney, the president of the New York Stock Exchange. The Senate's inquiry initially focused on the short-selling that Washington held responsible for the economy's woes. That line of questioning proved largely futile. But when the Senate turned its attention to the manipulation, deception, and greed that had run rampant during the 1920s, the show got much more interesting. For the next two years the hearings shined a harsh spotlight on the ways that securities firms and companies had profited during the boom.

The hearings also revealed some seamy corporate accounting tricks. (For example, the Insull Utility Investment Company, an electric power holding company, had used a variety of gimmicks to report a profit of $10.3 million to shareholders in 1930 while posting a loss of $6.5 million on its tax returns.) As the testimony flowed, the public's disdain for financiers reached new heights. Even Republicans, Wall Street's traditional allies, said they were disgusted with what they had learned. "If the turmoil in the courts and in the Congressional committees stops, changes, or modifies the great thimble-rigging game of Wall Street, the depression of the last four years will have been worth all it cost," wrote William Allen White, a Kansas newspaper publisher who was a powerful voice in the G.O.P.[22]

The arrogance and inflexibility that Wall Street displayed in the face of the revelations only made matters worse. Securities firms seemed to believe they had no responsibility to make sure that the stocks they sold offered a fair opportunity for long-term gains. In their view, they had done nothing more than meet the demand for new issues. Clarence Dillon, the senior partner at Dillon, Read, summed up the Street's attitude. Dillon said he believed his firm had done nothing wrong in taking three-quarters of the profits of the investment trust it had sold, even though it had put up only a fraction of the trust's capital. "We could have taken 100 percent," Dillon said. "We could have taken all that profit."[23] In another incident, Whitney, the president of the Big Board, was confronted in New York by two Senate investigators after he refused to forward a questionnaire from the Senate to members of the exchange. "You gentlemen are making a mistake," he said. "The Exchange is a perfect institution."[24] It was a line he would not be allowed to forget.

To be sure, investors had been greedy during the 1920s, and many had willingly overlooked flaws in the market as long as it was rising.

But not everyone who bought stocks was a speculator. Many investors had believed that stocks backed by first-tier firms offered some guarantee of safety—a belief encouraged by firms like Chase and National City, which had held themselves up as more responsible than no-name brokerage firms or bucket shops. "When you invest through The National City Company you have the benefits of its broad experience . . . [and] its willingness to analyze your situation thoughtfully before making recommendations," National City had cheerily advertised.[25] Now investors were discovering, not for the first time or the last, that they could not depend on Wall Street to protect them.

The hearings had their share of political grandstanding, but they also revealed serious problems with stock sales and trading and an urgent need for new laws. If securities firms could not police themselves, then the federal government would have to protect investors from fraud and manipulation.

For the first time, J. P. Morgan and his neighbors on Wall Street would—at least in theory—have a master.

Chapter 2

—

FOUNDATIONS

The Senate's hearings produced three laws: the Securities Act of 1933, the Glass-Steagall Act, and the Securities and Exchange Act of 1934. Together they gave the government broad new powers over Wall Street.

The 1933 Securities Act required companies to file "registration statements" with the government before they sold shares. Corporate executives, investment bankers, and auditors were legally required to make sure that the information in a registration statement was true and did not omit any important facts about a company's financial health. Glass-Steagall forced financial institutions like J. P. Morgan to choose between investment banking, such as selling stocks, or commercial banking, such as taking deposits and making loans. The 1934 Securities and Exchange Act created a new federal agency, the Securities and Exchange Commission, to oversee the securities business. The bill also:

- sharply limited short-selling;
- gave the Federal Reserve the power to set margin requirements for stock purchases, so that brokers would not be able to lend speculators 80 percent or 90 percent of the value of the shares they bought;

- forced directors and corporate executives to report purchases or sales of their companies' shares;
- required companies on the New York Stock Exchange to file audited annual reports of their sales and profits with the S.E.C.

Viewed one way, the new rules were radical. For the first time, corporate America and Wall Street were required to provide investors with complete, accurate information. But from another perspective, President Franklin D. Roosevelt had been quite conservative. Some New Dealers wanted more than disclosure rules. They wanted the federal government to have the final say on what stocks could be sold. "Demand must be gauged in advance by experts," Rex Tugwell, a Columbia University economist, wrote in 1932.[1] William O. Douglas, who would become the S.E.C.'s third chairman, complained that the 1933 law would not "control the speculative craze of the American public" and that it was "wholly antithetical to the program of control envisaged in the New Deal."[2] But that freedom was exactly the point. Even in the depths of the Depression, Roosevelt never seriously considered trying to take control of Wall Street. Investors would still be allowed to make their own mistakes. Disclosure, yes; central planning, no.

Morgan et al. did not exactly offer Roosevelt heartfelt thanks for his moderation. Despite the boom and bust, despite the revelations of insider trading and executive misbehavior, many Wall Streeters still believed that the market could regulate itself. Through 1933 and 1934, investment bankers went on a "capital strike," refusing to underwrite new stocks and bonds.[3] (The protest was made somewhat less effective by the fact that no one wanted to buy anyway.)

The New York Stock Exchange was hardly more cooperative. In 1935, led by Richard Whitney, the exchange overwhelmingly rejected as its president a reform candidate who had promised to work more closely with Washington. For the next three years, as the S.E.C. tried to tighten rules on trading and short-selling, the

exchange bucked the commission at every turn. The sparring continued until March 1938, when the Big Board disclosed that Whitney
had embezzled more than $1 million from it. The news left the
Exchange's reputation in tatters and gave it little choice but to accept
stricter oversight. "Wall Street could hardly have been more embarrassed if J. P. Morgan had been caught helping himself off the collec-
tion plate at the Cathedral of St. John the Divine," the *Nation*
wrote.[4] One month later, Whitney pled guilty to fraud charges. He
would serve more than three years in Sing Sing.

Facing a serious threat of a federal takeover, the exchange replaced
most of its directors and hired William McChesney Martin as its
president. Martin, who did not drink, smoke, or gamble, was Whitney's antithesis, a sober man for a sober time. "He does not belong to
any of the swanky New York clubs, does not fraternize with powerful bankers and promoters, . . . and aside from his time in the
theatre, the tennis court, and church, he spends most of his spare
moments in his room as a student," one appreciative reporter wrote.

But for the S.E.C., Whitney's ouster was a Pyrrhic victory. Under
Martin, the exchange did make some minor rule changes, but its
basic structure remained intact. More important, by focusing so
closely on the Big Board, the S.E.C. lost the chance to take greater
control over corporate governance and accounting standards.*

The commission was aware that strong, uniform accounting rules
would be crucial if investors were to compare financial statements

---

*Corporate governance is the boring but very important discussion of the way
companies are run. The structure of public companies inevitably creates a gap
between the people who own a company's assets, a.k.a shareholders, and the people
who control those assets, a.k.a executives. The trick is to make sure that executives
act in the interest of shareholders. Unfortunately, without a large block of shares, no
single shareholder has the power to hold executives accountable. Over the years,
governance experts have suggested various solutions to this problem, such as giving
executives lots of stock options so their financial interest is theoretically aligned with
that of the company. Unfortunately, the fixes have often made matters worse. (More
on this in Chapters 3 and 7.)

from different companies. And the agency knew that accountants often buckled to pressure from their corporate clients and signed off on gimmicks that distorted profit reports. In December 1936, James Landis, the S.E.C.'s second chairman, had complained that accountants' "loyalties to management are stronger than their sense of responsibility to the investor."[5] Three years later, after leaving the commission, Landis would be more blunt: "What is really needed is a good spanking for the accountants as a whole."

Douglas, who followed Landis as chairman, asked the S.E.C.'s chief accountant to prepare a study of accounting practices as a first step in making them more conservative and consistent. "The Commission must be the pacesetter in the accounting field," Douglas said at his inaugural press conference.

But the study languished, and the fight with Whitney consumed Douglas's attention. Within a few months, the agency had backed off its plans for stricter oversight of accounting. "One need only recognize that the principles of the science of accounting are in a state of flux . . . to be hesitant in wresting guardianship from the hands of the profession," commissioner George Mathews wrote in 1938.[6]

At its moment of maximum influence, the commission had allowed Whitney to set its mission for it, with enormous long-term consequences. For most of the next two generations the agency would define its role narrowly, focusing on the exchanges and small-scale stock fraud instead of watching out for systemic problems with accounting or corporate governance.

———

Too bad, because accounting had plenty of systemic problems that needed fixing.

Despite its importance to capitalism, accounting exists almost in a vacuum. Its past has hardly been studied; historians have inexplicably focused on Napoleon and Stalin instead of Arthur Andersen and Luca Pacoli, the Italian monk who in the late 1400s wrote *Summa*, the first treatise on bookkeeping. As lovable as investment bankers, as charismatic as insurance agents, accountants "walk in the shadow of virtual anonymity. So discreet are they that at times it seems as if their aim were to become a disembodied function, almost without a proper name," *Fortune* wrote in 1932, and not much has changed.[7]

Yet accounting deserves more attention than it has received. Accountants are the plumbers of capitalism, unappreciated but vital to the system. The transition to an industrial economy during the nineteenth century meant that businesses could no longer easily finance themselves. To build a railroad line or expand a factory, entrepreneurs had to raise capital from outside investors, and those outside investors needed reliable financial information to decide where to put their money. But the proto-accountants of the era quickly discovered that calculating a factory's profit was much more difficult than figuring out the financial position of small stores or farms that were run more or less on a cash basis. For those firms, accounting was easy: Total up the income received over the course of a year, subtract the expenses, and end up with profit. On the other hand, factory owners were constantly buying new machines, investments that might take years to pay off. At the same time the equipment that they had already installed was slowly wearing out. So they might be making profitable sales at a time when they seemed to be burning through cash—or they might apparently be making money but in reality not be covering the costs of replacing their machines.

Accountants in Britain and the United States grappled with these issues throughout the nineteenth century. Progress was hardly smooth. An 1844 letter to a U.S. accounting journal complained that the writer had received forty-three different answers to a question he had previously posed in the journal. "How strange that no two of your correspondents agree, either in details or in practical results," the writer said, calling accountants "lamentably deficient."[8]

But by century's end, accountants had found solutions to most of the questions. Companies would have to take charges for "depreciation" to measure the falling value of their assets. Their books would be kept on an "accrual" rather than a cash basis, with expenses and revenues booked when they were incurred rather than when cash was actually received or spent. Perhaps the most important innovation came in 1880, when Charles Ezra Sprague created the template for the modern balance sheet. Sprague explained that a company's assets must always equal its liabilities, including its equity. "What I have . . . equals what I owe plus what I am worth," Sprague wrote—a formulation that seems obvious now but was a breakthrough at the time.[9]

These nineteenth-century accountants did not always know the best way to balance the books. But they were clear, clearer than they have ever been since, that they owed their allegiance to investors, not to management. The reason is simple: The United States depended on Britain for much of its capital, and many of the first American accountants were British, sent over by British banks and insurers who wanted to protect their investments. They were paid by, and answered to, their countrymen, not the American companies whose books they audited.[10] For the first and only time, accountants did not have to worry about being fired for doing their jobs too well. As one auditor proclaimed in 1896:

> The professional accountant is an investigator, a looker for leaks, a dissector, and a detective in the highest acceptation of the term; he must have a good knowledge of real estate, machinery, buildings, and other property. His business is to verify that which is right and to detect and expose that which is wrong; to discover and expose facts which exist, whether they be plainly expressed by clear and distinct records or whether they be concealed by the cunning knave or hidden under plausibly arranged records or as is frequently the case omitted from the records entirely. . . . He must interpret, rearrange, and produce in simple but distinct form, self-explanatory and free from mysteries of bookkeeping, the narrative of facts. . . .
>
> He is the foe of deceit and the champion of honesty.[11]

But this halcyon state did not last. By the end of the century the U.S. stock and bond markets had developed enough that American companies no longer needed British capital. Instead of depending on a few large investors, companies began to raise money from smaller investors who had no choice but to take their financial statements on faith. Sure, investors could still ask that companies have their books certified by outside accountants, but those accountants would be hired by and paid by the companies themselves. No longer would an accountant be truly independent.

A century later, accountants still face the tension of serving two masters. But instead of owning up to the problem and accepting that strong rules are necessary to mitigate it, accountants have chosen to pretend that the conflict doesn't exist and fought repeated efforts to make them answer to an independent regulator. Despite reams of evidence to the contrary, they have insisted that their own ethics and professionalism will ensure that they fulfill their responsibilities to investors.

—

Simultaneously, in a stroke of what can only be called genius, accountants have managed to define those responsibilities so narrowly that they are basically meaningless.

Throughout the first decades of the twentieth century, accounting trade groups argued that accounting was an art, not a science, and that they needed flexibility to make the best judgments for different situations. "Accountancy never was or could be an exact science, and every profit or loss . . . is in very substantial measure an expression of opinion," the *Journal of Accountancy* wrote in 1912. More than pride underlay this dogma. If accounting was merely a matter of working through a step-by-step checklist, then companies might replace accountants with lower-paid clerks, as had happened in the railroad industry after the Interstate Commerce Commission required uniform reporting procedures.[12]

This argument for flexibility was widely accepted, not without reason. After all, complicated accounting questions sometimes had more than one solution. But in winning the right to exercise independent judgment, accountants had escaped the responsibility to make sure the financial statements for different companies would truly be comparable. One accounting firm might encourage companies to write off losses from problem accounts very quickly, while a second allowed more leeway.

At the same time, individual firms refused to take professional responsibility for their supposedly independent judgments. Management, not auditors, had the duty to ensure that a company's financial statements offered an honest presentation of its results, accountants said.

"The primary responsibility for the selection of principles and the scope of disclosure must remain that of the directors and officers of the corporation," the American Institute of Accountants said in 1931. All accountants were required to do was make sure that a company had properly followed the accounting rules it chose to use. Auditors could certify financial statements even if they thought a company had used the wrong accounting treatments, as long as they believed the company had acted in good faith, the A.I.A. said.

So accountants had the upside of being professionals without the downside. They insisted on the right to exercise independent judgment, but they also refused to take responsibility for the effects of their decisions. They weren't exactly clerks, but they weren't "the foe of deceit and the champion of honesty," either. And they certainly weren't independent.

The passage of the securities laws and the creation of the S.E.C. did little to change this dynamic. By requiring audited financial statements for many companies that had never had them before, the 1934 law created a huge new appetite for accountants' services. But the industry's main concern for most of the 1930s seemed to be limiting the potential for lawsuits created by the legislation. "A.I.A. members spent what appears to have been an inordinate amount of time debating terminology; for example, would the use of the term 'examination' rather than 'audit' or 'report' rather than 'certificate' be helpful in limiting the profession's legal liability?" Gary John Previts and Barbara Dubis Merino wrote in *A History of Accountancy in the United States: The Cultural Significance of Accounting.*[13]

By 1939 the disclaimers had reached absurd heights. One auditor said that it could make "no representation whatsoever that there are no liabilities or obligations . . . which are not shown in the books of the company." Translation: Don't blame us if you find out the company owes a couple of hundred million dollars it didn't mention. We're just the accountants.

———

While Whitney and the S.E.C. were chasing each other's tails, and accountants acting as heroically as might be expected, investors were delivering their own verdict on stocks. It was not a happy one.

After the panic lows of 1933, prices slowly recovered, along with the economy, through the middle of the decade. But they remained far below their 1929 highs, and investors remained bitter about their losses, as Whitney discovered in 1935 when he toured the nation to tout the virtues of stock ownership.[14] Fred Allen, a well-known radio host, joked that Whitney's campaign would feature a young man telling his father that "I knew you didn't have the rent, Daddy, so I took a dollar out of my bank to play the stock market. I made a million dollars in ten minutes!" A few months later the exchange drew more jeers when it proposed appointing a "czar" who could help it regain the public's trust.

The last straw for many small investors came in 1937 and 1938 when stocks lost almost half their value as the economy fell into its deepest trough since the early 1930s. By then a generation of investors had learned that stocks were too risky to own. Bonds might pay only 2 or 3 percent, but at least they offered a guaranteed return and a good night's sleep. What difference did the S.E.C.'s protection make if the market kept falling?

"On summer days on Wall Street, things were so quiet that, walking down that famous canyon, all you could hear through open windows was the roll of backgammon dice," one veteran investment banker would recall a generation later.[15] In April 1939, only 20 million shares changed hands on the Big Board, not many more than had traded on Black Tuesday alone. By 1941 the number of individual shareholders had fallen to about 5 million, half the number of 1929.[16]

The situation grew even worse after America entered World War II. In April 1942, with the war going badly, the Dow fell as low as 92.92, half its 1937 level and one-quarter its pre-crash peak. And as Washington mobilized the economy for World War II, Wall Street's role in financing business all but disappeared. Companies essential to the war received loans from the federal government; others had little hope of raising capital. New issues of stock and debt plunged to $1 billion in 1942, one-tenth their 1929 levels.[17] Stocks in the United States seemed headed for oblivion.

—

Beneath the surface, though, there were reasons for optimism.

Even as individual investors turned away from the market, a small group of academics and money managers started to think critically about the best ways to value stocks. Over the next several years, they would create the foundations on which modern stock analysis is still based, and form the two great camps of investing, growth and value.

The process began in 1934 when Graham and Dodd wrote *Security Analysis*. The genius of *Security Analysis,* the investors' bible, is that it combines philosophy and practice. The book teaches investors both how to think about what a stock is worth and how to comb through financial statements to find hidden values—and hidden traps. Graham was the quintessential value investor, looking for out-of-favor companies with steady earnings and dividends. He is sometimes accused of being too skeptical of growth stocks and of focusing too much on balance sheets and not enough on the income statement. In fact, Graham's analysis was more nuanced. All else being equal, he favored companies with growing sales and profits, and he spent considerable time in *Security Analysis* explaining how to read income statements. Three years later, in *The Interpretation of Financial Statements,* his second book, he would write, "It is only in the exceptional case that book value or liquidating value plays an important role in security analysis.* In the great majority of instances the attractiveness or the success of an investment will be found to depend on the earning power behind it."

But having just lived through the bubble and bust, Graham believed that investors put too much weight on short-term earnings trends, especially if they were strongly positive. "We cannot be sure that a trend of profits shown in the past will continue in the future," Graham wrote. "The law of diminishing returns and of increasing competition . . . must finally flatten out any sharply upward curve of growth. There is also the flow and ebb of the business cycle, from which the particular danger arises that the earnings curve will look most impressive on the very eve of a serious setback."[18] Further, Graham warned, "There is no method of establishing a logical relationship between trend and price. This means that the value placed upon a satisfactory trend must be wholly arbitrary, and hence specu-

---

*Book value is the value of a company's assets as stated on its balance sheet, after deducting liabilities. In theory, book value represents the amount of money likely to be available to shareholders should a company be liquidated. In reality, companies are not usually liquidated unless they are losing money and have no prospect for a turnaround—and under those circumstances, their assets usually sell for much less than the values at which they are listed on the company's book. Even so, book value is an important measure of a company's worth.

lative, and hence inevitably subject to exaggeration and later collapse."

So Graham focused on stocks where he could, as he later put it, "get the future for free." His favorite companies had steady or growing earnings and hard assets greater than the value of their shares. With stocks in the doldrums at the time the first edition was published, he had little difficulty finding candidates, since many companies were selling for less than the cash they had on hand. As the markets recovered, the great bargains would disappear, and it would become harder to find companies that were extremely cheap and still had good managements and strong growth potential. Even so, Graham's disciples, including Warren Buffett—a student of Graham's at Columbia University—continued to have success seeking out companies with solid balance sheets that had been ignored by the market. *Security Analysis* remains in print today, almost seventy years after its first edition.

In 1938, four years after *Security Analysis* first appeared, John Burr Williams, a doctoral student at Harvard, tried to answer the question Graham had asked four years earlier: How should investors value future earnings? In *The Theory of Investment Value,* Williams argued that stocks were no more or less valuable than the future cash they produced for their shareholders, usually in the form of dividends. "A stock is worth only *what you can get out of it* . . . A cow for her milk, a hen for her eggs, and a stock, by heck, for her dividends."[19]

Williams's theory, which became known as the dividend discount model, makes intuitive sense, and it offers strong support for investing in growth stocks. A company with rapidly rising dividends will be worth much more over time than one whose payouts are flat or declining. Unfortunately, actually putting the model into practice is difficult, because it depends crucially on three variables. First, investors need to figure out what future dividends will be. Then they need to determine how sure they are of their predictions. Finally, they must figure out how much to "discount" the future dividends. Discounting is necessary because a dollar received tomorrow is worth less than a dollar in hand today. But there is no magic formula to determine the discount rate for a particular stock. It depends on both interest rates and how certain investors are about a company's growth prospects.

As a result, Williams's model can be used to justify almost any price for a stock. Increase the estimate of future dividends or lower the discount rate, and voila—shares that seemed expensive are suddenly cheap. Of course, careful investors can try to keep their estimates reasonable, but the model lends itself to easy optimism. Further, as Graham and his disciples pointed out over and over, the faster a stock is growing, the harder it is for investors to predict its future. A railroad that has earned $12 a share for the last decade will probably earn $12 a share for the next few years as well. But what about a company whose earnings have grown from 50 cents to $2 in five years? Will it grow at the same rate for the next five, and earn $8 a share at the end of that time? What if economic growth slows or new competitors emerge?

Nonetheless, at least Williams provided an intellectual framework for valuing stocks based on their future cash flows. And his model was not *inherently* aggressive; investors who wanted to use it conservatively could simply plug in a high discount rate to account for the natural uncertainty of future dividends.

Over the next few years, other money managers and analysts picked up on the threads laid by Graham and Williams. A group of analysts, including Graham, began to meet monthly in New York at the apartment of Helen Slade, a New York doyenne who served as a patron for the fledgling fraternity of analysts. Then, in 1945, Slade founded *The Financial Analysts Journal,* which became the center of sophisticated debates over the best way to pick stocks as well as to create portfolios that would outperform the overall market while minimizing risk. The golden age of Wall Street research—such as it was—was fast approaching.

—

Even accounting began to improve, at least a little. In 1938, police discovered a massive fraud at McKesson & Robbins, a big drug company traded on the New York Stock Exchange and audited by Price Waterhouse. Executives at McKesson had embezzled more than $18 million, hiding their theft by creating a fake division. The fictitious unit represented almost one-fifth of McKesson's total assets, but Price Waterhouse somehow had managed to miss the fact that it didn't exist. (Clues to the fraud included a shipment that supposedly had been sent from Canada to Australia—by truck.)

The scope of the fraud, and the fact that it had involved Price Waterhouse, the most prestigious accounting firm, led the S.E.C. to open a high-profile investigation of McKesson's collapse. With heavy press coverage, the investigation quickly turned into a referendum on accounting and auditing practices. "The entire profession was, in effect, on trial," one accounting historian later wrote.[20] Regulators and investors did not take long to reach a verdict, especially after accountants explained at the hearings that audits did not have to include any inspection of real inventories. An examination of a firm's records was good enough. Accountants were *professionals*, not customs inspectors. They couldn't be expected to dirty their shoes in the field.

Faced with this attitude, the public and the S.E.C. could be forgiven for wondering why accountants existed at all. To the untrained eye, checking to make sure a company's inventory is real certainly seems like an auditor's job. The New York attorney general argued that accounting as a whole had "fundamental weaknesses" that needed to be addressed. The industry had little choice but to respond. In 1939 the American Institute of Accountants issued new guidelines for auditing, requiring accountants to confirm that inventory and sales really existed. The new rules also required that auditors make sure a company's internal financial controls were correct before relying on them.

Perhaps more important, the hearings put the accounting industry on notice that investors and regulators expected accountants to be more than rubber stamps for management. Although the hearings did not result in new federal rules governing accountants, they did raise the S.E.C.'s interest in accounting standards. Over the next several years the commission repeatedly jawboned accounting firms to protect investors better. In 1946, the S.E.C. accused accountants of allowing wholesale gimmickry at smaller publicly traded companies whose financial reports did not have to be filed with the commission. And in 1948, when an accounting standard-setting committee proposed allowing companies to set aside reserves for future losses without having to specify what those losses would be, the S.E.C. threatened to take for itself the authority to set accounting standards, though it did not follow through.

The broader political climate during the 1940s also encouraged conservatism in financial statements. With a war on and a Democratic president, companies had no interest in appearing to make too much money. Auditors were, as always, glad to bend to their clients' wishes. For once, though, companies wanted to make their profits look smaller, not larger.

———

So Wall Street had, in small but appreciable ways, changed for the better by the late 1940s. To the public, though, it was still 1933. A 1948 poll by the Federal Reserve found that 90 percent of Americans were opposed to buying stocks.[21] Asked why, about half said they were unfamiliar with stocks as an investment, while the rest said equities were "a gamble" and "not safe."

In hindsight, the irony is immense. In 1949, American stocks were as safe an investment as they would ever be. With Europe and Asia digging out from the war, the United States had the world's dominant economy. Foreign competition hardly existed for companies like

General Electric. After having suffered through the Depression, industrial America was lean and efficient—the bloat of the 1960s and 1970s had not yet set in. At the same time, with foreign competition weak, many American industries had tacitly organized themselves into highly profitable cartels. The average big industrial company had a return on capital of 18 percent, an amazingly high figure.[22]

The overall economic picture was equally bright. Employment was high, and consumers had just begun a post-Depression and post-war spending spree that still hasn't ended. The number of new homes built in 1949 topped 1 million for the first time ever. The Federal Reserve had kept interest rates low, so high-quality bonds were paying less than 3 percent. About the only worry was inflation, which had crept up slightly but was hardly an immediate threat. Meanwhile, the creation of the S.E.C. and the work of Graham and other analysts had helped level the playing field for individual investors. Disclosure rules were stronger and accounting standards more uniform than they had been a generation earlier. Audited financial statements could be had at S.E.C. offices or directly from companies. Small stocks could still be manipulated, but big companies were too closely watched and too widely held for a single market operator to dictate their price. The markets may not have been fair, but they were far fairer than they had been a generation earlier.

Yet stocks were dirt cheap, cheaper than they had been when the 1920s bull market began. The Dow Jones industrial average fell as low as 161 in 1949, less than half its level two decades earlier and only 60 percent higher than it had stood in 1906. The average big stock sold for six times its annual earnings and paid a dividend of almost 7 percent. U.S. Steel, with earnings of $5.39 a share and a dividend of $2.25, traded as low as $21, giving it a P/E ratio of 4 and a dividend yield of 11 percent.

Put another way, $1 invested in stocks in 1949 bought 16 cents of corporate earnings, 7 cents of cash dividends, and the chance to share in the growth of the world's dominant economy. $1 invested in bonds bought not quite 3 cents of interest at a time when the risk of inflation, which is death to bonds, was rising.

A bear market is the opposite of a bull market. Wall Street has no word for the opposite of a bubble, but it should. Because what happened over the course of the 1940s, especially toward the end of the decade, was the opposite of a bubble. It was not exactly a bust. A bust is the end of a bubble, not the opposite. And it was not exactly a bear market, because stocks were not falling. They just were not rising, when in retrospect it is obvious that they were a screamingly good investment.

But bubbles and antibubbles, for lack of a better word, have one thing in common: Neither lasts forever. Eventually smart investors, small and large, see that stocks are too cheap not to buy. They hold their noses, ignore the conventional wisdom, fight their fear, and get back in. As one investor told the *New York Post* in 1950, "The salesman showed me in black and white how much better I would have been if I had bought his [mutual] fund instead of keeping my cash in the bank."[23]

—

And so on June 14, 1949, the second great bull market of the twentieth century began. By the end of that year the Dow had risen to 200. Three years later it stood at 290. After a lull in 1953, the market soared 44 percent in 1954, one of its best years ever. On November 17, 1954, the Dow finally cracked its 1929 highs, and jubilation and concern mixed on Wall Street. Were the gains real? Or was another crash coming? The public's lingering mistrust of the market spurred two congressional investigations of the nascent boom. Ben Graham patiently explained the mysteries of high finance to the Senate Banking and Currency Committee:

SENATOR: Could you explain some terms to us? Could you tell us what is meant by profit taking?

GRAHAM: Well, profit taking is very simple. It means that people who have a paper profit in their shares realize that paper profit by selling . . .

SENATOR: Is that similar to a sell-off?

GRAHAM: Well, a sell-off is simply a decline, presumably temporary, in the market, for any number of reasons. Profit taking may be the reason advanced, or a war scare, or something that happens in this committee room or anything else.

SENATOR: Or a technical adjustment is another term?

GRAHAM: The technical adjustment is very likely related to profit taking.[24]

(One can only imagine that Graham was trying to keep a straight face by this point. He knew as well as anyone that "profit taking" and "technical adjustments" were, and still are, Wall Street jargon for "I have no idea why the market went down today.") Meanwhile, Harvard economist John Kenneth Galbraith, for the first time but not the last, warned of another 1929. But the boom had only begun. The Dow ended 1959 at 679, more than triple its level in 1950. It was the best decade ever for U.S. stocks.

And somewhere along the way, investors forgot that they hated Wall Street. To the contrary: At a time when the Soviet Union was the United States' mortal enemy, George Funston, the new president of the New York Stock Exchange, declared the Big Board a center of "people's capitalism," as if every American had a moral obligation to buy stocks. "The way to fight communism is through American prosperity," Funston said. "We're trying to broaden the basis for share ownership and thus strengthen the basis of democracy."[25] At the same time, brokerage firms, led by Merrill Lynch, reached out to the growing market of middle-class Americans who wanted to save for their retirements and their children's educations. In the late 1940s, Merrill had begun to run six-thousand-word newspaper ads explaining "What Everybody Ought to Know About the Stock and Bond Business." The advertisements introduced millions of Americans to stocks.[26]

Of course, Funston's slogans and Merrill's education campaigns might have met a less friendly audience had stocks not been soaring. As it was, the publicity came at a perfect time. The market's rise attracted new investors who put fresh cash into stocks, causing the market to rise and attracting new investors . . . et cetera, ad infinitum. Surveys by the New York Stock Exchange showed the number of Americans who owned stocks steadily rising during the 1950s. In 1952, about 6 million Americans, one in sixteen adults, owned stocks. By 1961, 17 million did.

The modern market—large, liquid, and of great importance to Main Street—had been born.

Chapter 3

BUBBLING UNDER

Bear markets have villains. Bull markets have heroes. Bull markets *need* heroes, living talismans to be rubbed for luck. And as the 1960s dawned and stocks continued their rise, Gerry Tsai became the first hero of the post-crash bull market. Traders and investors scrambled to follow his moves. He was the heir to the manipulators of the 1920s, a man with the power to make stocks dance.

Even better, Gerry Tsai was no mere stock operator on the fringes of the market and the law. He was a mutual fund manager, one of a new breed of professional investors whose importance had soared during the 1950s.

Mutual funds had first become popular during the 1920s boom, when they were known as investment trusts. Run by full-time managers, the funds theoretically offered small investors the chance to own a diverse basket of stocks at low cost. But they had performed pitifully during the bust, and as Wall Street fell into its post-crash doldrums, they faded into insignificance.

Then the market turned. Seeing the chance to win a new generation of investors, fund companies recruited sales representatives to peddle their funds for commissions that could run as high as 8.5 percent. Sometimes the funds were sold in multi-year investment plans, with all commissions paid up front, an arrangement that meant that new shareholders could lose half of their first year's investment to commissions. (Eventually, the S.E.C. discouraged that practice.) But what was bad for the investor was good for the salesman; by the late 1950s, tens of thousands of Americans had signed up to sell mutual funds part-time. "Elementary and high school teachers would try to sell fund plans to parents of students, and clergymen would do the same for members of their congregations. . . . High-pressure tactics were the rule."[1]

The tactics worked. In 1950 there were fewer than 100 mutual funds, with 939,000 accounts and $2.5 billion in assets. A decade later there were 161 funds, with 4.5 million accounts and $17 billion under management.[2]

As the funds grew, so did their influence and the attention they received. By the early 1960s no manager was better known than Tsai, who had run the Fidelity Capital Fund since its inception in 1957. Tsai was a risk-taker personally and professionally; his hobbies included helicopter flying, at least until he crash-landed in the Hudson River.[3] On Wall Street he made his name buying fast-growing "glamour stocks" like Xerox and Polaroid. At a time when most investors hardly traded, Tsai rotated his portfolio quickly. Most important, he beat the market, cementing his reputation at the end of 1962, when he gained 68 percent in three months. By then, "many people seemed to believe he possessed mystical powers of the Orient (he was born in Shanghai) which somehow enabled him to perceive the future. . . . Rumors that TSAI IS BUYING! and TSAI IS SELL-ING! . . . usually caused a desperate scramble to follow his lead," *Institutional Investor* magazine wrote.[4] *Institutional Investor* also noted that *Newsweek* and other magazines, which should have known better, had, inevitably, referred to Tsai as "inscrutable." In fact, Tsai was "eminently scrutable. . . . His gaze, furthermore, is not blank, but rather animated, and when the occasion warrants, stern and cutting," *Institutional Investor* noted.

Scrutable or not, Tsai—and his imitators—would be a major factor in a surge of aggressive accounting during the 1960s that presaged the much more serious problems that followed a generation later.

—

In theory, the rise of mutual funds should have been a boon for Wall Street. Run by professional, full-time managers, the funds should have been immune to the frenzies that swamped individual investors. They could even have been a force for better corporate governance. No longer would shareholders be powerless; a few large funds could together control 20 percent or more of a company, enough to have a credible threat of ousting its management if they chose.

But the explosion in funds was as much curse as blessing. The sad truth is that most investment professionals do not know much more—either about the individual stocks they own or the broad market—than smart individual investors. There are exceptions. Some managers, especially those with decades of experience, really have learned how to take the market's swings in stride. Some have uncanny success at finding obscure companies that are fast-growing, or cheap, or both. Some have spent so much time investing in one sector that they know it as well as any chief executive does. A few can look at a company's financial statements and sniff out hidden values or hidden fraud.

A handful of managers puts those skills together, combining an eye for value with an understanding of industry cycles and an intuition about the truth of financial statements. They talk to competitors, suppliers, distributors, retailers. They read trade magazines. They are the first to hear that the senior vice president for sales has quit, and the first to find out why. They spend weekends reading 10-Ks, not golfing with management. They are unafraid to stand apart from the crowd or suffer through periods when they trail the averages.

But most fund managers do not have the brains or the courage to be independent. The average manager knows enough about the stocks he owns that he doesn't look foolish to his equally busy boss, or to a reporter who calls on a day when the Dow is down 3 percent. He knows the hot products in his companies' pipelines. He remembers what earnings were for the last two quarters and what they are supposed to be for the next two. He sees management at conferences twice a year; he recognizes the CEO, chief financial officer, maybe a couple of divisional heads. And that's about it. Not bad for a guy keeping track of 150 companies, a guy who has to make a morning presentation in St. Louis to the brokers selling his fund and have dinner in Detroit at an auto industry conference.

The average manager spouts the happy lingo that all fund managers pick up when they make their first trade. He is looking for "growth at a reasonable price," for stocks that are "on sale," for managements with "bench strength," and companies that are "leaders in their space." But does he have any real insight, either into the stocks he owns or the market's overall action? Does he actually *know* anything?

No.

In fact, many academics argue that investors, both professional and individual, are simply wasting their time by trying to beat the market. Their theory, known as the efficient market hypothesis, holds that stock prices always incorporate all the information that is known about a company at any given time. No single investor, however wise, can outsmart the collective intelligence of tens of millions of people.

Put another way, the efficient market hypothesis is that the market is always right. Prices change only in response to new information about a company's prospects, and new information is by definition unknowable before it happens. Investors who seem to be beating the market are actually just getting lucky or taking on extra risk.

If the efficient market hypothesis is true, then the mutual fund industry shouldn't exist. Small investors would be far better off giving their money to index funds, which are "passively managed" and simply follow indexes like the S&P 500. Index funds are cheaper to run than actively managed funds, so unless professional managers can beat the market as a group (presumably by outsmarting individual investors, their collective competition), small investors shouldn't pay for active managers. And, in fact, index funds do beat actively managed funds. The S&P 500 has outperformed the average fund in fifteen out of the last twenty years, and that figure doesn't include the upfront sales charges that most funds charge.[5] Between 1981 and 2001, the average fund trailed the S&P 500 by more than 3 percentage points a year; the S&P 500 rose 14.9 percent annually, the average fund only 11.5 percent. Yet the mutual fund industry continues to grow, and index funds remain only a small part of it. Mutual funds may be dead in theory, but they are very alive in fact. Efficient market theory has little influence on the way people actually invest.

So is the theory correct? I personally don't think so. Outperforming the market is hard, and the more one trades, the harder it is, because trading is expensive. But just because most investors lag the averages does not make beating them impossible. Warren Buffett has consistently outperformed the S&P 500 for the last forty years, and he is not alone. And it is notable that, like Buffett, many of the investors with great long-term records either studied with or worked for Ben Graham. "I'm convinced that there is much inefficiency in the market," Buffett said in a 1984 speech about "The Super-Investors of Graham and Doddsville." "Market prices are frequently nonsensical."

(But there is a second, "weaker" version of the theory supported by lots of research. The weak version argues that the future direction of a stock can't be predicted simply from its previous price movements. In other words, technical analysis, a.k.a. charting, is a joke. Chartists have all sorts of fancy names for the squiggles that stocks create as they rise and fall: the "head and shoulders," the "double-top," the "false bottom." But anyone who listens carefully to a chartist will eventually discover that his prophecies are always the same: If a stock is going up, it will keep going up, unless it stops going up, in which case it will go down for a while. At that point it may start to go up again, or maybe keep going down. If the stock is going down, the prediction will be the same, in reverse. The fact that so many investors take technical analysis seriously is strong evidence that the market may not be so efficient after all.)

—

Another big plus that funds supposedly offer, the ability to fight for better corporate governance, also turns out to be largely fictional. A fund can't control a company through 5 percent ownership, or 10 percent. Only if it launches a serious takeover attempt—or spends years publicly pointing out managements' flaws—will its complaints be taken seriously. And mutual funds are not interested in takeover battles or drawn-out fights with companies. As fund managers will gladly explain, they're paid to pick winning stocks, not run companies. If they dislike the way a company is run or have questions about its accounting, they usually just sell and move on. With so many stocks to choose from, why get stuck with the losers?

At the same time, funds are saddled with perverse incentives that can actually raise their risks to individual investors. First off, when individual investors buy a stock, they are putting their own savings at risk. Fund managers aren't, so they may be more willing to take chances than the individual investors they supposedly represent. Further, with so many funds competing for investors' attention, the only way for a fund to stand out is with exceptional returns. Not good returns. Exceptional returns. Buying out-of-favor companies and waiting for the market to see their hidden value doesn't stand out. Beating the market by 2 percent—or even 3 percent or 5 percent—a year doesn't stand out, not until you've done it for a decade or so.

What stands out? Buying companies whose sales are growing 50 percent a year, whose profits are doubling, and whose stock is tripling. Financial magazines look for managers who can do that as eagerly as *Vogue* searches out new supermodels. The tale of the heroic fund that has tamed the beast of the market and racked up 100 percent annual returns is guaranteed to move copies.

So returns mean press, and press means new investors. And because a fund's management fees are usually calculated as a percentage of its total assets, new investors mean more money for the fund company—and the manager. But to have a chance of exceptional returns, a manager must almost always take on exceptional risk. He may be naïve and not understand the risk he's taking. He may be cynical and figure it's not his problem if he loses. Either way, he has every reason to make big bets on high-growth companies.

Unfortunately, novice investors often don't understand fund managers' hidden motives. In fact, they are usually taught to think of funds as safer than stocks, because funds are diversified. Owning just one or two stocks is inherently risky; your savings can disappear overnight if a company has an unexpected crisis. Owning a fund eliminates that possibility.

But the incentives that encourage fund managers to take big risks also encourage them to buy stocks that rise and fall together. To get great returns, a fund needs to own stocks that tend to move in tandem. Having one stock that rises while another falls won't do the trick. So in the real world, funds are often less diversified than they appear to be, and they can fall as quickly as they rise. Individual investors rarely learn that unfortunate fact until it's too late.

—

The fund industry's hidden dangers would not be exposed until the end of the 1960s. But the broad market showed unmistakable signs of speculation much earlier. The market's rise during the 1950s had far outstripped growth in corporate profits and dividends. As a result, by 1960 the average big stock had a price-earnings ratio of 20 and a dividend yield of 3 percent. Stocks were no longer the once-a-century bargain they had been in 1949. By historical averages they were somewhat expensive—although not absurdly overvalued.

Yet at a time when caution was appropriate, the same investors who had avoided stocks a decade earlier suddenly piled in. As in the 1920s, a few good years turned fear into greed. Almost one in four potential investors in a 1959 New York Stock Exchange survey said the main reason to buy a stock was "opportunity for quick profit."[6] By 1960, the sturdy blue-chip companies that had led the Dow and S&P 500 higher during the 1950s began to fall out of favor. The market's new leaders were smaller, less seasoned companies with more potential—and more risk. With the digital age just beginning and the federal government throwing billions of dollars into space and defense research, companies like Texas Instruments and Honeywell soared. As early as 1959, one professional investor mocked Wall Street's infatuation with technology and defense companies:

Take a nice little company that's been making shoelaces for 40 years and sells at a respectable six times earnings. Change the name from Shoelaces, Inc., to Electronics and Silicon Furth-Burners. In today's market, the words "electronics" and "silicon" are worth 15 times earnings. However, the real play comes from "furth-burners," which no one understands. A word that no one understands allows you to double your entire score. Therefore, we have six times earnings for the shoelace business and 15 times for the electronics and silicon, or a total of 21 times earnings. Multiply this by two for furth-burners, and we now have a score of 42 times earnings for the entire company.[7]

In 1954 investors were so unfamiliar with the concept of growth stocks that *The Wall Street Journal* found it necessary to describe what one was: "The good growth company, experience shows, may pay out only a small part of its earnings in cash dividends, using the rest for research, development of new products, and expansion. . . . The plowed-back earnings should bring larger earnings power."[8]

Now growth stocks needed no explanation. With investors looking for the next Motorola or Xerox, Wall Street's burgeoning research community began to seek out stocks with strong growth potential. While quarterly earnings reports were still rare, in 1955 the S.E.C. had required semiannual earnings reports. (Between 1946 and 1953 the commission required, oddly, that companies report their sales but not their profits every quarter.) The increased flow of financial information contributed to investors' interest in earnings and in analysts' projections. Membership in the Financial Analysts Foundation surged from three thousand in 1951 to eleven thousand a decade later.[9] Some analysts became minor celebrities. In 1962, *Newsweek* profiled six of the "most influential on Wall Street: Men who know the companies, know the market—and often know the future." One of the six touted Montgomery Ward as the next Chrysler (he was right, but not the way he meant), while another joked that "stocks are basically like sex—timing is everything." For the first time, companies could be penalized if they did not meet analysts' expectations.

It would not grow into a monster for another generation, but the cult of the number had been born.

—

The good times paused in 1962, when a heavy-handed attempt by President Kennedy to restrain steel prices caused the Dow to skid 28 percent in six months. But after the Cuban Missile Crisis ended in October, the market began another broad rally. New investors rushed to join in as the stocks climbed higher. "Young and middle-aged investors now felt they had gone through the fire and survived. To a generation that had not known the pains of a truly severe panic and crash, the 1962 experience seemed frightening, but quite bearable," market historian Robert Sobel wrote.[10] By 1965 more than 20 million Americans owned stocks, a rise of 4 million in four years. Investors eagerly watched the Dow close on 1,000; the four-digit barrier seemed sure to fall in 1966.

As the market grew more frenzied, investors became focused on the earnings magic of a group of fast-growing companies called conglomerates. Their decade-long rise and fall would offer proof, if any was needed, that the reforms of the New Deal had not fundamentally changed the market. Investors remained irresistibly attracted to companies that appeared to show strong profit growth. And S.E.C. or no S.E.C., accountants and investment bankers were willing to help companies commit what was essentially legalized fraud to create that growth.

The conglomerates first became popular in the late 1950s. They specialized in taking over other companies and increasing their profits, supposedly with superior management. The trend started with Litton, a defense contractor that increased its sales from $15 million in 1956 to almost $1 billion by 1964 by getting into shipbuilding and dozens of other businesses. Many other companies followed; the most aggressive of all was Ling Industries, which became Ling-Temco and then Ling-Temco-Vought. L-T-V increased its sales from $7 million in 1958 to $3.8 billion in 1969. Its earnings grew from 83 cents a share in 1960 to $5.56 in 1967.[11]

By the end of the 1960s, L-T-V was the fourteenth largest industrial company in the United States, and nine other conglomerates were in the top 200. L-T-V's chairman, James Ling, and the other "conglomerateurs" had become the first genuine business celebrities since Henry Ford and the industrial barons of the early twentieth century. General Motors and U. S. Steel were lethargic bureaucracies, out of step with a nation that increasingly celebrated individual dissent. Conglomerateurs were the rebels of the Fortune 500. They flaunted their wealth; Ling built a $3 million Dallas mansion that included a $14,000 marble bathtub, and he publicly took inspiration for his business tactics from Marshal Erwin Rommel, the brilliant desert commander of World War II.[12] Never mind that Rommel had fought for the Germans. The war was over. The conglomerateurs were new managers for a new era. Their results proved their strategy.

But those results were a myth, a miracle of accounting that had nothing to do with real-world business acumen. Any company with a high price-earnings ratio can cause its earnings to rise simply by buying another company whose stock is cheaper than its own.* The only management skills the conglomerateurs needed were a high stock price and a steady supply of cheap companies to buy.

Finding those takeover targets became more difficult as the 1960s progressed. Many obvious candidates had already been bought; others were trying to become conglomerates themselves. To keep the acquisition binge alive, conglomerates relied on accounting and financing gimmicks to hide the cost of their takeovers. By the middle of the decade they had discovered ways to make acquisitions for what seemed to be no cost at all. Under the accounting rules in place at the time, these gimmicks were not considered a violation of generally accepted accounting principles, much less fraud. But they should have been. They hid the conglomerates' liabilities and vastly overstated their income.

It should come as no surprise that accountants had little interest in stopping them. Following its favorite strategy of death by delay, the accounting industry had debated better ways to account for mergers since 1960. In December 1966 the Accounting Principles Board—the industry's standard-setter—proposed a change that would

---

*Suppose Conglomerate XYZ has net income of $10 million, with 10 million shares outstanding, for earnings of $1 a share. Suppose also that it has a price-earnings ratio of 40, a price of $40, and a total market value of $400 million. Its target is Company ABC, which also has income of $10 million, 10 million shares outstanding, and earnings of $1 a share. But ABC has a price-earnings ratio of only 15, a price of $15, and a market value of $150 million. XYZ buys ABC for $20 a share in an all-stock deal, issuing 0.5 share of XYZ stock for each share of ABC stock. Presto! The new XYZ-ABC now has 15 million shares of stock outstanding and earnings of $20 million, or earnings of $1.33 a share. Without making its business more efficient, XYZ has increased its per-share earnings by 33 percent. If its stock follows, XYZ will rise to $53.33, thanks to the simple magic of acquisition accounting.

have made the conglomerates' favorite trick much more difficult. Faced with opposition from accounting firms and conglomerates, the board backed off.[13] Two years later a study by the American Institute of Certified Public Accountants also proposed tighter rules.*

By then the conglomerate boom had just about peaked. The problems with merger accounting were obvious, and many investors had realized that conglomerate profits were inflated. The end came in 1969, when the market plunged, making it hard for conglomerates to issue the debt or stocks they needed for new acquisitions. A conglomerateur who runs out of acquisitions is a very unhappy conglomerateur. He's stuck managing the companies he has already bought, which are all too often third-rate companies in slow-growth industries. Winners buy; losers manage. Worse, the skills that make a successful conglomerateur—salesmanship, impatience with details, and a huge ego—are more or less the opposite of the skills needed to successfully manage a company.

The highest flier fell hardest. By 1969, L-T-V reported a loss of $10.69 a share. James Ling was asked to seek other employment, and L-T-V rapidly undid his acquisition spree. Still, L-T-V's loss reached $17.18 a share in 1970. The company's stock fell from $169 in 1967 to $7 three years later. From 1969 to 1971 the stocks of ten major conglomerates fell an average of 86 percent.[14]

The accounting industry took no action to tighten the rules on merger accounting until August 1970, when the Accounting Principles Board made a change so weak that it was derided as irrelevant by several of its members. The foot-dragging meant that "billions of dollars of economic activity was accounted for in a manner that almost literally everyone knew was an inadequate and some-

---

*The AICPA was the successor to various industry trade groups. Accountants like creating, merging, and disbanding trade groups almost as much as they like legal disclaimers.

times downright misleading method," A. A. Sommer, a lawyer and future S.E.C. commissioner, wrote in 1970.[15]

But what did Sommer expect? The conglomerates had no interest in rules changes that would hurt their reported profits, and the conglomerates were very good clients of the accounting industry. In *The Go-Go Years,* his tale of the market in the 1960s, the inimitable John Brooks summed up the mysteries of conglomerate accounting with a phrase only a *New Yorker* writer could get away with:

> Another effect was to confuse everyone concerned, and it cannot be said that the confusion was always entirely accidental; often enough it was plainly intended to throw dust in the eyes of the average investor with his tunnel vision trained on the bottom line. By following conservative practices and their consciences, accountants could have prevented most of this jiggery-pokery; they did not.[16]

Neither did the mutual fund industry. In fact, quite the reverse. Managers such as Gerry Tsai, who wanted earnings growth and did not particularly care where it came from, were early and avid supporters of the conglomerates, ignoring the obvious red flags raised by their accounting gimmicks.

In the introduction to *The Money Managers,* a 1969 book that profiled nineteen top institutional investors, "Adam Smith" (the pseudonym for George J. W. Goodman, a money manager) wrote that managers now "live in the Age of Performance. Performance means, quite simply, that your portfolio does better than the others. If the market goes up, the performance portfolio goes up more. If the market goes down, the performance portfolio goes down less."[17]

The theory sounded reasonable. Who wouldn't want a fund that rose more than the market on the way up and lost less on the way down? But between 1949 and 1968, stocks had fallen more than

20 percent only once, in 1962. In that environment, only one kind of performance mattered—the kind on the way up. Smith said as much as few sentences later: "Most of these professionals no longer think of their mission as preserving capital. They think of it as *making money*. Those are two sharply different states of mind." (Italics in the original.) And so by the late 1960s, Tsai and his imitators had gravitated to conglomerates, computer and electronics companies, and the newest trend stocks of all, franchisers. With inflation rising and the Vietnam War escalating, the rest of the market was stagnant, or worse.

Did fund managers understand the games the conglomerates were playing? The question is almost irrelevant. If they didn't, they should have. Professional money managers are paid to divine whether earnings growth is real or manufactured. Those who ignore aggressive accounting are guilty of cynicism, stupidity, or both.

Cynicism and stupidity paid off for a while. In 1965, Gerry Tsai quit Fidelity to start his own company. Investors poured $270 million into his new Manhattan Fund, which gained 40 percent in 1967. The Enterprise Fund, run by Fred Carr, who favored mini-conglomerates and other tiny over-the-counter stocks, gained 117 percent that year and 45 percent the next. "Essentially, we are traditional, conservative, long-term investors," Carr said.[18] To prove it, his Beverly Hills offices were filled with classic books on investing and business, bought—in Carr's words—"by the yard from a Santa Monica bookstore."

In 1969, when the bull market ended, fund shareholders discovered what the owners of investment trusts had found out forty years earlier: Diversification is no protection against loss if that diversification consists of owning a diverse group of second-rate stocks. The Manhattan Fund fell 13 percent in 1969 and 37 percent in 1970, compared to a loss of 8 percent for the S&P in 1969 and a gain of 4 percent in the index the next year.

The Enterprise Fund skidded 25 percent in 1969, and Fred Carr resigned.[19] Other go-go funds also went down down. (Tsai landed on his feet, though, selling his fund company to CNA Financial of Chicago for about $30 million. In the 1980s, he would repeat the pattern, twice more making deals that worked out better for him than his shareholders. "With Gerry, you don't bet the horse, you bet the jockey," one person who knew him said. "You invest when Gerry invests, and get out when he does.")[20]

The antics of a manager named Fred Mates proved the dangers of the Age of Performance. During 1968, the Mates Fund racked up a 154 percent return, the year's best, but the fund's gains had as much to do with accounting as stock picking. Mates bought stock directly from small companies at a deep discount in exchange for a promise not to sell it for several years.[21] Mates would then value the stock in his portfolio at almost its full market price, much more than he had paid, resulting in an instant paper profit. Of course, Mates could not actually sell his shares for the price he claimed they were worth, but as long as his shareholders did not ask for their money back, he didn't have to.

Then in December 1968 the S.E.C. banned trading in Omega Equities, a "mini-conglomerate" that made up one-fifth of Mates's portfolio. Many of Mates's shareholders tried to redeem their shares, but so much of his portfolio was made up of untradable stocks that he could not raise the cash he needed to pay them back. He had to ask the S.E.C. for permission to lock up his fund while he unwound his positions. When Mates finally allowed shareholders to redeem their shares and get their money out in June 1969, his fund was almost 50 percent lower than it had been six months earlier, with more losses to come.[22]

It was no longer possible to distinguish the shepherd from the wolves. Either way, mutual fund shareholders were being fleeced.

—

What was the S.E.C. doing during all this? Not enough.

The S.E.C.'s power had peaked in the late 1930s, when William O. Douglas, the agency's third commissioner, had famously compared it to a shotgun kept "behind the door—loaded, well-oiled, cleaned, ready for use—but with the hope it would never have to be used."[23] When the Japanese bombed Pearl Harbor, the S.E.C. suddenly became irrelevant. From its creation in 1934, the agency was housed in prime real estate at 1758 Pennsylvania Avenue, just down the street from the White House. After World War II began, the S.E.C. was exiled to Philadelphia. It came back to Washington after the war, but it never regained its prestige and importance. By 1959 its own chairman would call it "a wartime casualty."[24] Its staff steadily shrank. In 1941 it had 1,723 employees; by 1947 it was down to 1,200. And in 1955, with markets much more active than a decade earlier, the commission had just 666 employees. It could hardly hope to oversee hundreds of thousands of accountants, mutual fund sales-people, brokers, and analysts.

So the S.E.C. stuck to easy game, going after the small-scale stock promoters who inevitably popped up as the bull market gained speed. The agency also spent considerable time investigating the American Stock Exchange, the successor to the Curb Exchange and then as now the market where bad stocks go to die. But for cases more complicated than simple fraud, the S.E.C. hardly existed at all.

The commission's performance on systemic issues was also spotty. The agency largely left accountants to their own devices, and it took little action to regulate the fast-growing research business. Most important, it did not instill in the executive suites—of conglomerates, of investment banks, of mutual fund companies, of accounting firms—any fear that it was watching out for fraud. At a party to cele-brate the S.E.C.'s twenty-fifth anniversary in 1959, William Douglas, by then a Supreme Court justice, made known his dissatisfaction with the agency's direction:

An early speaker had mentioned the big drive on "boiler rooms," the covert switchboards where a bevy of high-powered salesmen worked over sucker lists for sales of securities. . . . When it came my turn, the hour was late and I made it short. I said, "The main difference I see between the old S.E.C. and the new one is that we put in prison a much higher type of person."[25]

The shotgun had grown rusty from disuse.

Under President John F. Kennedy the agency revived, bulking up both its budget and its payroll. By 1964 it had fifteen hundred employees and an aggressive new chairman, Manuel Cohen. Unfortunately, Cohen was forced to devote much of his energy to sparring with the commission's bête noire, the New York Stock Exchange, as the S.E.C. began a decade-long effort to cut the costs of trading Big Board stocks. The S.E.C.'s action against the exchange was important and ultimately successful, but it distracted the commission from other systemic problems. The commission never took a firm stand on merger accounting and never really got a handle on the go-go mutual funds. In his 1982 book, *The Transformation of Wall Street: A History of the Securities and Exchange Commission and Modern Corporate Finance,* Washington University law professor Joel Seligman explained the commission's lack of enthusiasm for accounting:

> By requiring the same agency to regulate public utility holding companies, the investment company (mutual fund) industry, all national securities markets, all interstate broker-dealers, as well as corporate disclosure, corporate governance, (and) accounting . . . Congress created an extraordinarily broad mandate that all but ensured that significant portions of it would be largely ignored. . . .
>
> Lacking commissioners with training or interest in the accounting field, the S.E.C.'s Office of Chief Accountant, consistently underfunded and understaffed, has not made studies of leading accounting problems, and has rarely proved able to attract outstanding theorists.[26]

The problem would not go away.

—

Despite James Ling and his fellow conglomerateurs, and Gerry Tsai and Fred Carr and Fred Mates and the rest of the swinging stock-pickers, the 1960s never became a full-fledged bubble. No one has ever quite explained why. Perhaps the S.E.C.'s lingering influence kept the big investment banks from pushing the limits of speculation and hype. Perhaps Wall Street research, supported by investors instead of investment bankers, remained honest enough to keep a lid on the worst accounting gimmicks and overvalued companies. Perhaps Tsai and the rest of the go-go managers did not control enough assets to push the market into hyperdrive.

Or maybe the reason had nothing to do with Wall Street. Maybe investors had memories of 1929 somewhere deep in their collective unconscious. Maybe the Vietnam War spoiled the carefree atmosphere necessary for a mania and kept the market from becoming the singular national focus it had been forty years earlier. More prosaic, maybe inflation and rising interest rates kept valuations under control. In any case, the frenzy that touched the conglomerates and the go-go funds did not fully consume the rest of the market, much less the nation as a whole.

So the bear market, when it came, did not come as a crash. The Dow reached an intraday peak of 1,001.11 on February 9, 1966, before falling more than 20 percent the rest of the year. It turned back up in 1967 and made one more run at 1,000 in 1968 before sliding about 30 percent by 1970. It would not close above 1,000 until 1973.[27] There were no panics, no brokers jumping out of buildings, and anyway the nation had other things on its mind. Probably as a result, Wall Street survived the end of the bull market essentially unchanged, escaping the calls for new regulation it had faced a generation earlier.

By 1971, Benjamin Graham, seventy-seven and in the middle of his sixth decade as an investor and analyst, had grown disgusted. The markets seemed to have learned nothing from 1929. As he discussed the boom and bust in initial public offerings during the 1960s, Graham wondered whether investors could be protected from themselves. He sounded almost despairing:

> The speculative public is incorrigible. In financial terms it cannot count beyond three. It will buy anything, at any price, if there seems to be some "action" in progress. It will fall for any company identified with "franchising," computers, electronics, science, technology, or what have you, when the particular fashion is raging. Our readers, sensible investors all, are of course above such foolishness. But questions remain: Should not responsible investment houses be honor-bound to refrain from identifying themselves with such enterprises, nine out of ten of which may be foredoomed to ultimate failure? . . .
>
> Could and should the S.E.C. be given other powers to protect the public? . . .
>
> Should every prospectus . . . carry some kind of formal warranty that the offering price for the issue is not substantially out of line with the ruling prices for issues of the same general type already established in the market?
>
> It will be difficult to impose worthwhile changes in the field of new offerings, because the abuses are so largely the result of the public's own heedlessness and greed. But the matter deserves long and careful consideration.[28]

The matter did not receive long and careful consideration. The 1960s proved that the reforms of the 1930s were no match for a sustained bull market. Although there was no bubble, the 1960s showed that one was more than possible. But absent a crash, the public did not much care. Accountants, mutual fund managers, investment bankers, and corporate executives continued on their merry way.

Chapter 4

—

THE DEATH
OF EQUITIES

Some cities and states and towns just seem to have more than their share of fraud. Long Island is notorious for penny stock swindles. Biotechnology and computer scams have flourished in Utah, of all places. And during the 1980s Colorado was fertile soil for boiler rooms—high-pressure brokerage firms that sell worthless stock over the phone. (It has since cracked down.)

Then there's southern California. Maybe the shadow of Hollywood tints truth and fiction beyond recognition. Maybe crooked executives believe they can do what they please since a continent separates them from Wall Street. Maybe the sunshine triggers a criminal giddiness. Or maybe it's just coincidence. But a disproportionate number of the financial scandals of the last generation have blossomed in the land of the lotus eaters. The collapse of Lincoln Savings & Loan, Charles Keating's bank, cost taxpayers $3.4 billion; other California S&L failures cost tens of billions more. Barry Minkow came from the San Fernando Valley to fleece bankers and investors of several million dollars while he was still a teenager. And movie accounting is notoriously corrupt.

Before Keating or Minkow, though, there was Stanley Goldblum, the granddaddy of southern California scam artists. Goldblum's company, Equity Funding, was not the biggest financial disaster to emerge from the bear market of the early 1970s. That honor belonged to Penn Central, which when it filed for bankruptcy in 1970 was the largest railroad in the United States. But the audacity of the Equity Funding scheme, which was probably the largest outright corporate fraud since McKesson a generation before, grabbed the public's attention, and more than any company Equity Funding came to symbolize the go-go years and the sour bust that followed.

By all accounts, Stanley Goldblum was not a very nice man. A large, short-tempered weightlifter, Goldblum enjoyed using his bulk to intimidate his employees and other adversaries. His secretaries called him God,[1] and when he was asked once what he would do if a board member opposed him, he said, "Get a new director." Goldblum became chairman of Equity Funding in 1969, after Michael Riordan, the company's founder, died in a mud slide at his Los Angeles home. Equity Funding sold life insurance, with a gimmick; it allowed customers to borrow against the value of their insurance policies in order to buy mutual funds. In the insurance industry this plan qualified as a major innovation, though it actually amounted to little more than buying stocks on margin. Equity Funding expanded quickly. It first sold shares to the public in 1964, raising $600,000; in 1969 it joined the New York Stock Exchange.

After Goldblum took over, Equity Funding's growth accelerated. Its earnings rose from $1.67 a share in 1969 to $2.81 in 1972, as it bought several other insurers. *Fortune* magazine called it the fastest-growing diversified financial company in the United States.[2] Then Ray Dirks, an insurance company analyst, got a tip that many of Equity Funding's policies were fakes. Dirks flew to Los Angeles to confront Equity Funding, though not before passing the story along to a couple of his clients. As the rumor spread, Equity Funding's stock plunged, the S.E.C. opened an investigation, and Dirks tipped *The Wall Street Journal.* Within weeks the company collapsed, admitting massive fraud. Besides creating hundreds of millions in fake life insurance policies, Equity Funding had printed counterfeit stock certificates and carried them on its books as its assets. "Publicly held companies do not lose money," Goldblum had told an Equity Funding executive vice-president in 1969, and he meant it. By 1972 the company had become so dependent on fake revenues from fake policies that it needed a separate, hidden office to create them.

Goldblum wound up with an eight-year prison sentence, but the S.E.C. and the Big Board seemed less concerned about the scam than the fact that Dirks had told his clients about it. In April 1973, while Equity Funding unraveled, the Big Board formally accused Dirks of failing to follow "good business practice" and threatened to suspend him for life from the exchange. The S.E.C. opened its own investigation into Dirks's actions. The idea that analysts should be encouraged to perform independent research and follow up on tips apparently did not occur to the commission. (Both inquiries dragged on for several years but Dirks was ultimately cleared.)

Equity Fund's disintegration further irritated shareholders already smarting from the end of the bull market. How had a New York Stock Exchange–listed company fooled accountants and regulators for years? Why were authorities chasing the guy who'd blown the whistle instead of the executives who'd run the scam? Why did Equity Funding's auditors go to the company, rather than the S.E.C., when Dirks presented them with evidence of the fraud? In *The Great Wall Street Scandal,* his recounting of the fraud, Dirks sounded a familiar litany of concerns:

> The Equity Funding scandal indicates, as nothing else ever has, that audited statements are not always what they seem to be. What the Equity Funding scandal tells America's stockholders is that the certification of corporate figures in the annual reports they receive may very well be meaningless. . . .
>
> There is the question of the pernicious philosophy of Wall

Street . . . a philosophy that encourages and even demands
"performance" by corporations. . . .

[The S.E.C.] is hobbled, first, by political realities, and second, by the literally impossible task of policing the colossal
securities industry with a staff of 1,700 people—a total that
includes every clerk-typist. . . .[3]

Dirks also had harsh words for his fellow research analysts. Several major firms, including Smith, Barney (now Salomon Smith Barney, a unit of Citigroup) and Lehman Brothers, had recommended
Equity Funding.[4] Dirks complained that analysts copied one another's reports and too often were intimidated by management.

—

The Equity Funding scandal, along with chicanery at the conglomerates and the Penn Central bankruptcy, produced the most serious
criticism of the accounting industry since the McKesson hearings a
generation earlier. Summing up the general mood, a *New Yorker* car-
toon featured an executive introducing an accountant with a wink
and saying, "In examining our books, Mr. Matthews promises to
use generally accepted accounting principles, if you know what I
mean."[5]

In an effort to head off outside scrutiny, in 1971 the AICPA, the
industry's trade group, set up a blue-ribbon committee to review the
conglomerate accounting fiasco. The committee, led by former S.E.C.
commissioner Francis Wheat, found that the Accounting Principles Board, the industry's standard-setter, did not have sufficient
independence to do its job and should be abolished. In place of the
industry-controlled APB, the Wheat Committee recommended . . .
a new industry-controlled board. But there were big differences
between the old APB and the new Financial Accounting Standards
Board. First, the former had three words in its name; the latter had
four. Second, the APB's directors had been picked by the industry;

the FASB's directors would be chosen by something called the Financial Accounting Federation, whose members would be chosen by the industry.[6]

Somehow the Securities and Exchange Commission accepted the Wheat Committee's proposal as a great improvement, and the FASB was born in 1973. It quickly became obvious that the new board was as weak as its predecessor. One accounting expert predicted soon after the FASB's creation that the board's dependence for funding on its parent industry meant that its members would be "goldfish in a bowl of sharks."[7] The next twenty-nine years bore out that depressing forecast. For most of its existence the FASB's main mission seemed to be to avoid the wrath of the Big Eight accounting firms, not to crack down on aggressive accounting.*

Not surprisingly, the creation of the FASB did not blunt criticism of the industry. So in 1974 the AICPA created yet another fact-finding group. This one, led by Manuel Cohen, who had retired as chairman of the S.E.C. in 1969, was asked to consider whether accountants and investors had different expectations for what an audit "can and should reasonably expect to accomplish." Given that mandate, and the fact that the Cohen commission had been created and funded by the AICPA, a whitewash was inevitable.

Only it wasn't. In a report released in 1978, the commission blamed accountants for abdicating their responsibilities. "The public accounting profession has failed to react and evolve rapidly enough to keep pace with the speed of change in the American business environment. . . . In general, users [investors] appear to have reasonable expectations of the abilities of auditors and of the assurances they can give. The burden of narrowing the gap falls primarily on audi-

---

*The Big Eight were the eight major accounting firms that dominated the profession from the 1960s through the late 1980s: Arthur Andersen, Arthur Young, Coopers & Lybrand, Ernst & Whinney, Deloitte Haskins & Sells, Peat Marwick, Price Waterhouse, and Touche Ross.

tors and other parties," the commission wrote. The committee also sharply criticized the industry for not budgeting enough time or resources to conduct thorough audits. Fifty-eight percent of auditors had admitted signing off on financial statements without carrying out all the work necessary to check if they were accurate, the commission said. It recommended creating a new and truly independent group to set standards in place of the FASB, and tightening standards for audits.

Meanwhile, the Senate subcommittee that oversaw accounting had come to an even harsher conclusion. In a 1976 report, the committee found that

> the traditional public image of The Big Eight accounting firms as impartial and objective experts is not founded on fact. . . . As political partisans and purveyors of nonaccounting services, they become loyal agents of the clients which employ their services. . . .
>
> It appears that The Big Eight firms are more concerned with serving the interests of corporate managements who select them and authorize their fees than with protecting the interests of the public.[8]

A political and business consensus for greater supervision of accountants seemed to be forming. In 1978, Congressman John Moss, chairman of the House subcommittee that oversaw the securities industry, introduced legislation to create an independent federally chartered commission to oversee accountants. The bill would also have increased the potential liability of accountants for bad audits.[9] The legislation would have been the most important strengthening of the securities laws since the New Deal.

But the push for reform wilted as quickly as it had gathered strength. The Moss bill didn't even get out of the House. Most of the

Cohen Commission's recommendations were never implemented. By the late 1970s memories of Equity Funding, Penn Central, and the conglomerates had faded. Without fresh scandals to stoke the public's outrage, Congress had little appetite to take on the Big Eight, who were powerful, unified, and opposed to federal oversight. Broader political currents also aided the accounting industry. At a time when trucking, airlines, and telecommunications were being deregulated, lawmakers were loath to put heavy new restrictions on a historically unregulated business. The S.E.C. also backed away from imposing tougher rules. The commission "has proven to be pretty much of a paper tiger in its role as an accounting overseer. . . . The commission just muddles along, issuing rules, fanning controversies, never taking a firm stand on anything," one observer wrote in 1981.[10]

Instead of federal oversight, investors would have to settle for "peer review" of the industry. Every three years the major accounting firms would check each other for quality and freshness. Holding back giggles, the Big Eight claimed they would scrutinize one another as closely as any outside agency. "A tough, gutsy, no-nonsense process, that's the way we see peer review," the managing director of Touche Ross said.[11] Never mind that any firm that looked too closely at a competitor ran the risk of getting the same treatment when its turn came. Not surprisingly, for the next twenty years no firm ever found serious problems with another during a peer review. Once again accountants had dodged serious regulation. In 1980, the chairman of Price Waterhouse could not resist gloating over the industry's victory:

> As recently as a year ago, it seemed that the accounting profession would continue to face strong criticism for an indefinite time. . . . As we enter the new decade, however, there are many signs that a sense of balance may soon be restored. . . .

We can now turn our full energies to the issues that are of genuine concern: inflation, capital expansion, government accountability, and the expansion of our responsibilities to serve the needs of clients and the public.[12]

It was nice to know that, as always, Price Waterhouse and its peers were putting the public first.

—

While accountants were quietly battling Washington, the securities industry was very publicly in the midst of its most wrenching decade since the 1930s.

After 1970, as the Vietnam War wound down and inflation eased, the market began a two-year rally. By 1973 the Standard & Poor's 500 index had hit an all-time high of 120.24, about 10 percent above its 1968 peak. Then the 1973 oil embargo reignited inflation and dealt the U.S. economy a blow that lasted a decade. Watergate and Nixon's impeachment added to the trauma. From January 1973 to October 1974 the S&P 500 fell 48 percent, the biggest slide in a major U.S. index since the Depression. The index did not permanently recover until 1983.

Frustrated by their losses, millions of Americans quit the market. In 1970, 31 million Americans owned stocks, the most ever.[13] In 1975, about 25 million remained. After two decades of growth, the mutual fund industry also slipped into reverse. From 1972 through 1974 investors redeemed more shares than they bought. Total mutual fund assets fell from $57 billion in 1972 to $38 billion three years later.

But as May 1, 1975, approached, the bear market was not the securities industry's only concern. For almost two centuries the brokerage firms that formed the nerve center of capitalism had ignored the free market's most basic requirement, price competition. From its creation in 1792 the New York Stock Exchange had set minimum commissions that brokers were allowed to charge to trade its stocks. (The irony here is almost too obvious to mention. Wall Street has always loved free markets, except when they might cut its fees. Today, when even real estate agents are being forced to compete on price, the 7 percent commission charged by big investment banks for initial public offerings remains sacrosanct. Goldman, Sachs and Merrill, Lynch will compete on service, on reputation, on the size of their trading desks, on everything but price. Don't even ask.)

Besides being anticompetitive, the fixed commissions discriminated against institutional investors making large trades, since they did not allow for volume discounts. In other words, brokers charged investors one hundred times as much to buy 20,000 shares as to buy 200, a far greater spread than the difference in the cost of executing the two trades.[14]

As mutual funds and other institutional investors became a bigger part of the market in the 1950s and 1960s, fixed commissions came under pressure. Trading of Big Board stocks trickled onto regional exchanges where commissions could be negotiated. In response, the exchange tried to tighten rules that barred its members from trading its stocks in other markets. By 1968 both the S.E.C. and the Justice Department had opened hearings into fixed commissions and the Big Board's efforts to protect them. Faced with the possibility that its members might actually have to compete with one another, the Big Board hyperventilated that market-rate commissions would lead to "possible chaos." The exchange never seems to have considered the idea that lower commissions might actually encourage trading.

The Big Board's huffing and puffing could only delay the inevitable. In 1973 the S.E.C. announced that the Big Board would have to deregulate all commissions in May 1975. Smaller brokerage firms, which had the most to lose from competitive commissions, went into hysterics. One witness at an S.E.C. hearing told the commission that May 1 "is a great holiday in Russia. And Russia has said there is no need to fight democracy. It will burn itself out. Well, commissioners, you have the candle and the matches, and it will be a short fuse."[15]

Moscow had no comment. But if the Soviets hoped that competitive commissions would cause chaos in the streets, they were sadly disappointed. Commissions dropped, but trading volume rose enough to make up the difference. Some small brokerage firms went bankrupt, and the price of a seat on the Big Board fell. But after losing money in 1973 and breaking even in 1974, the exchange's members were collectively profitable for the next six years.

At first the commission cuts went mainly to institutional investors, which wasn't surprising. But over time, commissions fell for individual investors as well. Between 1976 and 1980 the market share of discount brokers, who charged commissions far lower than full-service brokers like Merrill, Lynch, rose from 1 percent to 6 percent.[16] By making trading cheaper, lower commissions lured millions of individual investors to the market, and encouraged institutional investors to put more of their assets in stocks. In the midst of a grinding bear market, those effects were muted. But when the next bull market began, cheaper commissions gave it a notable boost.

—

Though fears about May Day were overblown, the second half of the 1970s were no better than the first for stocks. As oil prices soared, inflation rose, and American manufacturers lost ground to competition from Japan and Europe. After a sharp rally in 1975 from their 1974 lows, stocks moved sideways during the rest of the decade, which meant in inflation-adjusted terms they fell. The 1,000 mark, which was first touched in 1966, seemed a steep psychological barrier for the Dow Jones industrial average; the Dow would move above 1,000, then drop back a few months later.

By the late 1970s, fear of inflation consumed the markets. Essentially, high inflation is evidence that the economy is growing more quickly than is sustainable in the long run. Below 2 to 3 percent a year, inflation is largely invisible, but it can have severe negative effects above that level. It destroys the value of bonds and causes economic distortions as consumers and businesses try to hedge against it. Its most virulent form is hyperinflation, when prices increase tenfold or even one hundredfold in months, wiping out the life savings of people who have put their nest eggs into bonds or low-interest savings accounts. (Usually, those people are the most risk averse, the least financially knowledgeable, and the least financially secure.)

The United States had never experienced hyperinflation. But other industrialized countries, most notably Germany during the early 1920s, had, with devastating political and economic effects. With inflation at 13.3 percent in 1979, the highest level in U.S. history, policymakers decided to restore price stability using the only tool guaranteed to work: high interest rates. High rates and tight credit cripple the economy by forcing consumers and businesses to cut back on borrowing. In turn, lower demand reduces the ability of businesses to raise prices or workers to demand higher pay. Eventually, inflation falls, rates can be lowered, and the economy can grow again. But the process is extremely painful.

Between 1979 and 1982 the Federal Reserve's chairman, Paul Volcker, raised the short-term interest rates that the Fed charged banks as high as 18 percent. In turn, the prime rate, the interest rate that banks charged their best borrowers, hit 21.5 percent. The double-digit interest rates threw the economy into its sharpest recession since World War II. Stocks swooned again. In August 1982, the Dow Jones average stood at 777, not much higher than its level two decades earlier. In inflation-adjusted terms, the Dow had fallen 75 percent. The Standard & Poor's 500 fell as low as 102, compared to its high of 106 in 1968.

To be sure, the 1970s were not the 1930s. The economy did not slide into depression. After Watergate the public's anger and cynicism were focused on Washington, not Wall Street. And most investors did not abandon the market; the number of Americans who owned stocks inched up during the second half of the decade. By 1980 it topped 30 million, just shy of its all-time 1971 high. Mutual fund assets also crept higher after 1975.

But by the end of the decade, investors could not help but notice that stocks and bonds had badly trailed other assets during the 1970s. Real estate, oil, commodities, gold, *stamps*—all had outrun financial assets. In 1979, *Business Week* proclaimed "the death of equities." Market historian Robert Sobel called his 1980 book about the bull run from 1949 to 1968 *The Last Bull Market.* "It is probable that there never again will be anything quite like this last bull market," Sobel wrote.

—

Pessimism about inflation and the course of the U.S. economy ran so deep that investors failed to notice that the market had, for the third time in the twentieth century, gotten cheap. While stocks had stagnated, a decade of inflation had pumped up corporate profits. The S&P 500 index traded at nine times earnings, well below its historic ratio and about the same level as 1950; many industrial stocks traded at much less. AT&T, trading for $51, had earnings of $8.55 and a dividend of $5.40, giving it a P/E ratio of 6 and a dividend yield of nearly 11 percent. Stocks were not the slam dunk in 1982 that they had been in 1950, because bond yields and interest rates were higher, and the United States economy was not nearly as dominant. But if inflation were to break and interest rates fall, the low valuation of stocks meant that the market might have a long way to run.

And by 1982, Paul Volcker's iron grip had already begun to subdue inflation. Though it didn't appear so at the time, broader geopolitical and technological trends had also turned to favor the United States. The Soviet Union was near collapse, and though Japan appeared on track to become the world's leading economic power, its dominance would be short-lived.

The greatest bull market in history was about to begin.

Over the next eighteen years the Dow Jones industrial average and the S&P 500 would both rise fifteenfold. The Nasdaq composite index would rise thirtyfold. And a few technology stocks would rise one-thousandfold or more, making millionaires of investors lucky enough to buy them early and smart enough to hold on.

The market's rise was not solely responsible for the breakdown in accounting standards that took place over the next twenty years. Changes in the accounting industry drove the Big Eight (soon to become the Big Six, then the Big Five) to new lows of cravenness. Massive increases in executive pay, fueled by stock options, gave CEOs powerful new incentives to cheat. The Republican Party, with an assist from the Democrats, starved the S.E.C. of the resources it needed to crack down on financial fraud. Performance-happy mutual funds became enormously influential and enormously focused on short-term earnings growth. Wall Street analysts forgot the word *sell*. And individual investors indulged their worst speculative instincts.

But it seems safe to say that the market's rise started the dominoes falling. If Wall Street's history proves anything, it is that investors of all sizes examine financial statements much less closely when stocks are rising. Without the bull market, nothing else that followed makes sense.

Part II

. . . THIS
IS NOW

Chapter 5

COUNTDOWN

In Wall Street's version of heaven, the strip clubs don't have covers and every month is January. Stocks have a century-long record of strong performance at the beginning of the year when investors inject their Christmas bonuses into the market and look for stocks knocked down by year-end selling. In hell, on the other hand, the calendar always reads October. The beginning of fall is historically miserable for stocks, for reasons that are less clear. And in purgatory it's perpetually August. August is the month when capitalism's relentless engine slows, when any trader or investment banker with a choice leaves behind the sweating streets of New York for the expensive breezes of the Hamptons. August is the month when nothing happens.

Yet the last and greatest bull market of the twentieth century started on a warm and muggy August Tuesday in New York.[1] With the economy sputtering and inflation subsiding, interest rates on short-term Treasuries had fallen from 13 percent to less than 9 percent during the summer of 1982. Still, stocks remained depressed, and long-term interest rates were stuck at more than 12 percent, not far from the all-time highs they had reached in 1981. Investors wanted a clear signal that inflation was beaten.

On August 17, 1982, they got it, not from a better-than-expected report on the consumer price index or a sudden drop in oil prices, but from an economist who had earned the sobriquet Dr. Doom for his gloomy—and accurate—predictions on interest rates and stocks. Henry Kaufman, the chief economist at Salomon Brothers, was bearish no longer. With the economy weak and inflation falling, long-term rates would fall below 10 percent by year-end, Kaufman said.

Traders like to say that no one rings a bell at the bottom, but Kaufman came as close as any strategist ever has. And investors, both bond and stock, listened. By the end of trading Tuesday, rates on three-month Treasury bills had fallen a half-percentage point, a huge move, while the Dow Jones industrial average had jumped almost 5 percent. It was the biggest point gain ever for the Dow, though not the largest in percentage terms, and the second-heaviest trading day ever, with almost 93 million shares changing hands.* One analyst called the market "a hungry dog grasping for a ragged bone—declining interest rates."[2]

The economy remained weak through the end of 1982, with unemployment near 10 percent and the budget deficit swelling under the weight of President Ronald Reagan's tax cuts. But with help from falling oil prices and cheap imports, inflation was fading. As a result, long-term interest rates, which are intimately tied to inflation, fell steadily during the mid-1980s. Lower rates made borrowing cheaper for businesses and consumers. The economy and corporate profits couldn't help but improve; stocks, which appeared cheap once rates dropped, couldn't help but rise. By the end of 1982 the Dow Jones

---

*The heaviest day ever had come a year earlier when Joe Granville, at the time one of Wall Street's best-known stock strategists, told his clients to "sell everything." During the 1970s, Granville became famous for the accuracy of his bearish calls; unfortunately, he never accepted that the bear market had ended. For the next two decades, as stocks soared, he would prophecy doom again and again, becoming little by little the market's cranky, slightly unhinged uncle.

industrial average had once again crossed 1,000, gaining almost 40 percent in four months. This time the four-digit mark would hold for good. In 1983 the Dow gained another 20 percent. And after a pause in 1984, the rally steamed ahead for three more years.

—

As the bull market gained strength, public attention focused on a group of financiers who were making big profits by taking over companies with borrowed money. The corporate raiders, as they became known, came to symbolize the excesses of the 1980s; history's verdict on them has not been kind. According to movies like *Wall Street* and books like *Den of Thieves,* raiders ripped apart companies for fun and profit.

The truth is more complicated. The 1970s had been bad for American business. The malaise persisted into the early 1980s. American manufacturers continued to lose ground to Japan and Europe, and the hulks of big conglomerates scattered the corporate landscape. Even established companies fell into the conglomerate fad, taking over businesses unrelated to their core operations. Coke owned Paramount, the movie studio; Mobil inexplicably bought Montgomery Ward, the retailer, in 1976.

But where many investors saw only bloat and bad management, the raiders saw value. America's corporate giants might be badly run, but that didn't mean they were bad investments. In fact, the early raiders had a lot in common, in substance if not style, with Ben Graham and other gurus of value investing. Graham and his disciples had always encouraged investors to think as if they were the owners of a business, not merely shareholders in it. In his 1984 lecture on "The Superinvestors of Graham-and-Doddsville," Warren Buffett explained:

> While they differ greatly in style, these investors are, mentally, always *buying the business, not buying the stock.* A few of them

sometimes buy whole businesses. Far more often they simply buy small pieces of business. . . . But all exploit the difference between the market price of a stock and its intrinsic value.[3]

By the early 1980s the "intrinsic value" of many public companies, as measured by their earnings, dividends, or hard assets like real estate or oil reserves, dwarfed their prices. They were irresistible targets for raiders, who maximized their returns by putting up only a small equity stake and borrowing the rest.* (Hence the term *leveraged buyout,* or LBO.) With stocks so low, raiders could easily pay the interest on the bonds they used to finance their acquisitions, even after offering shareholders a hefty takeover premium.

Some early leveraged buyouts produced huge profits. In 1982 a partnership run by William E. Simon, President Nixon's Treasury secretary, bought Gibson Greeting Cards for $80 million—including just $1 million of its own cash. By 1984, Simon had taken Gibson public again, making $200 million.[4] Looking back on the buyout boom, the author and former investment banker Charles Morris would write in 1999:

> Academics love talking about efficient markets. The experience of the early 1980s, however, suggests that markets more often react like mules—they eventually get where they're supposed to be, but at their own pace, and they sometimes have to be hit with an ax handle to get started. The mispricing of American stocks persisted through most of the first half of the 1980s, to the point where it was hard for an LBO to go wrong.[5]

---

*Federal tax rules also encouraged raiders to load up on debt and skimp on equity. Interest payments on debt were (and are) a pre-tax expense for companies, while dividend payments on stock come out of after-tax income. Raiders argued that in the early 1980s many companies were "underleveraged," with too little debt and too much equity. As a result, they paid more in taxes than they needed to.

LBOs profoundly changed corporate America, forcing executives to pay more attention to their shareholders and their stock prices. In 1985, for example, Mobil spun off Montgomery Ward and refocused on the energy business. "It was a diversification that never worked," one analyst said when Mobil announced the spin-off. "But until the pressure on Big Oil from people like Boone Pickens [a prominent raider], Mobil was not that concerned about the lack of performance at Ward."[6] Being an employee of a company under attack by a raider was no fun. But capitalism is famously, in the words of the economist Joseph Schumpter, a process of "creative destruction." By forcing companies to run more efficiently, the buyout boom spurred the renaissance of the American economy in the 1980s and 1990s.*

Unfortunately, in the long run, the raiders were too successful for their own good. As stock prices rose, the great bargains of the early 1980s disappeared. The raiders were forced to target marginal companies or pay high prices for good ones. Michael Milken and Drexel Burnham Lambert, who controlled the market for the high-interest bonds that raiders used to finance their takeovers, happily abetted this foolishness, since their fees were paid up front and in cash. By 1988 the raiders were paying prices so high that they had no margin for error. When the economy sputtered in 1989, the junk bond market shattered. Dozens of companies that had been bought with

---

*It is harder to defend management-led buyouts, where CEOs bought out their own shareholders with borrowed money. In those cases, executives essentially profited from their own incompetence. If they really knew how to run their companies more efficiently, they should have done so before their buyouts on behalf of all their shareholders—not afterward for their own benefit.

It is also hard to defend "greenmail," the practice of a raider taking a minority stake in a company and then demanding that he be bought out at a premium to its market price in return for his agreement not to start a takeover fight. In that case, the only beneficiary is the raider, who makes a few million dollars and disappears, leaving the company's previous shareholders no better off than they were before.

high-yield bonds failed to meet their interest payments and were forced into bankruptcy.

Neither Drexel nor Milken survived the downturn. They had attacked corporate America and made billions of dollars along the way; when the economy and market turned against them, they had few allies. In February 1990, with the junk market crumbling, Drexel filed for bankruptcy. Two months later, Milken pled guilty to six minor charges and paid $600 million in fines. He served two years in jail. Surveying the wreckage, James Grant, the editor of *Grant's Interest Rate Observer*, said, "On Wall Street there is a rule that every good idea must be driven into the ground like a tomato stake. Junk bonds were good ideas that became dangerous ones."[7]

But the cheers that went up when Milken went down obscured a crucial change in corporate finance that the LBO boom had caused. CEOs, always interested in maximizing the odds of their own survival, had learned a lesson from the raiders. High stock dividends were no longer a sign of strength. They had become a bull's-eye, a sign that a company was generating cash that could be used to finance a hostile takeover. To make themselves less attractive to raiders, companies cut back on dividends. In 1983 the typical S&P 500 company paid out 47 percent of its earnings each year. In other words, a company that made $1 per share returned 47 cents to its investors and kept the other 53 cents to reinvest in its business. By 2000 the average dividend payout had fallen to 25 percent of earnings. Many companies paid no dividends at all.

CEOs promised that lower dividends would benefit shareholders. Companies would either reinvest their profits or spend them on stock buybacks, which are taxed at a lower rate than dividends. But the decline of dividends had an unexpected side effect, enabling companies to play accounting games much more easily. Stock buybacks are often announced with fanfare, then trail off. Dividends, though not guaranteed, represent a strong promise from a company to its investors. Shareholders notice if a company cuts back on its dividend checks or, worse, misses a payment. But a company can't pay dividends unless it has cash on hand.* So dividends function as a sort of quarterly lie detector, limiting the leeway of companies to abuse accounting rules and inflate their profits. A company that is paying half or more of its reported income as dividends needs to generate cash, not just paper profits. Otherwise its bank account will quickly run dry.

Before the 1990s, "dividends were the primary means that firms had to show that earnings were real. Investors care(d) little about how firms defined their earnings as long as hard cash flowed," Jeremy J. Siegel, a Wharton finance professor, later wrote.[8] But thanks to Milken and his raiders, the connection between earnings and dividends faded, opening the way for companies like Enron and World-Com to report billions of dollars in profits while paying out minuscule dividends, or no dividends at all.

———

In 1987, though, Wall Street had more pressing concerns than the long-term consequences of the death of dividends. After bottoming in 1985, interest rates had crept higher for two years; with the U.S. trade deficit swelling, the dollar had plummeted against the yen and European currencies. The federal budget deficit was rising, and the United States appeared to be losing its advantage in information technology, its last bastion of strength, to Japan.

Yet in the first eight months of 1987, the Dow Jones industrial average rose 40 percent, topping out at 2,722 on August 25. In five years the Dow had more than tripled. The market's rise had far outstripped the growth in corporate profits, and as a result the price-earnings ratio of the S&P 500 had more than doubled in five years.

---

*Of course, a company can also borrow the money to pay its dividends—if it can find a willing lender. But that trick is unlikely to work for more than a couple of quarters. In the long run, banks and bondholders will look hard at a company that isn't generating enough cash to meet its dividend requirements.

By the summer of 1987 the P/E ratio of the S&P 500 hit 23, its highest level in at least fifty years. Journalists and some market strategists raised the specter of 1929, wondering if the bull market had become a bubble.

Over the next two months the Dow sank about 480 points. Then came Monday, October 19. As 600 million shares changed hands on the New York Stock Exchange, double the previous record, the Dow fell 508 points, almost 23 percent. It was far and away the biggest single-day point drop ever, and the second largest percentage drop, nearly twice as big as Black Thursday in October 1929. Forty stocks fell on the Big Board for every one that rose. The market makers who traded stocks on the Nasdaq simply refused to answer their phones and honor the prices they had offered. For much of the day, investors couldn't even be sure what prices were; the electronic "tape" of trades on the New York Stock Exchange fell more than two hours behind. The chairman of the Big Board, John Phelan, said it was "the worst market I have ever seen in my lifetime or would hope to see again."[9]

In the days to come, many investors would worry that the crash presaged a new depression, citing the eerie parallels between 1929 and 1987. Wall Street executives and traders wondered if their entire industry might melt down. Securities firms depend on low-interest loans from banks for the cash they use to trade stocks each day. The severity of the crash had cost some firms so much money that they would have had to liquidate their stock positions and close their doors if their loans were called. Those liquidations, in turn, would put a new wave of heavy selling pressure on a market that was already reeling. And what if small investors panicked? Between 1980 and 1987 the number of individual investors had risen from 30 million to almost 50 million. Stock mutual funds had grown even faster; the number of fund shareholders had jumped from 6 million to 21 million, and assets from $44 billion to $180 billion. A flood of individual stock sales, or fund redemptions, might strain Wall Street beyond its limits. "One word is operative out there now," a trader said. "Fright."[10]

In the white-knuckle days that followed, the Federal Reserve acted quickly to stem the risk that the crash would cause the banking system to seize up. The Fed cut interest rates and flooded commercial banks with cash so that they would not have to call their loans to securities firms. Meanwhile, individual investors stayed calm. Only a fraction of fund shareholders redeemed their shares.

Over the next few months it became clear that 1987 was not 1929. The crash hardly touched the economy, which grew solidly in 1988. And the market began to recover almost immediately. By October 1989 the Dow had set a new all-time high. In two years all the damage from the crash had been undone.

The market's swift recovery caused a critical change in investors' psyche. Stocks suddenly looked bulletproof, especially to investors who had begun buying stocks after 1982 and never seen a prolonged bear market. Although the Dow and S&P and Nasdaq might fall, and might even fall hard, they would recover their losses soon enough. Investors who stepped up when the picture appeared bleakest would be amply rewarded for their courage. Growing confidence in the Federal Reserve's ability to manage the economy paralleled, and contributed to, this new view of the market. First the Fed had tamed inflation; now it had dealt with a 500-point drop in the Dow. The economy was in good hands, and as long as the economy grew, stocks would rise.

Wall Street's rapid turnaround after a mild bear market in 1990 reinforced that optimism. In the months after Iraq invaded Kuwait in July, oil prices surged and stocks slipped 20 percent. But after the United States forced Iraq out of Kuwait, markets quickly regained their losses. In April 1991, the S&P and Dow set new records. A bear market was no longer something to be feared; it was a buying opportunity. Reminiscing in 1996 about the crash and its aftermath, one mutual fund manager said, "If you had held on, a year later you would have been ahead, and two years later well ahead. Seven years later you would have made a bloody fortune. People have learned their lesson. What you see now is when stocks go down, people are in there buying."[11]

———

As the 1990s began and the memory of the crash faded, a familiar pattern emerged. Through the 1980s the bull market's biggest winners were value stocks—the companies with low price-earnings ratios and big dividends that were targeted by raiders. S&P 500 growth stocks rose about 290 percent between August 1982 and the end of 1989; the index's value stocks gained about 370 percent, according to Barra, a California company that analyzes market data. But after the raiders' demise, investors lost interest in cheap stocks and turned their attention to high-risk, high-growth companies. In the 1920s, electric and radio stocks were the speculative vehicles of choice; in the late 1950s and 1960s, conglomerates seized the market's attention.

Now telecommunications, technology, and biotechnology stocks became the market's focus. The Nasdaq, the home of the most promising young technology companies, rose 57 percent, its best year ever, more than twice the rise in the Standard & Poor's 500 and almost three times the gain in the Dow. And no company attracted more attention than a software maker called Microsoft.

Microsoft had gone public in March 1986, facing fierce competition from I.B.M., Apple Computer, and dozens of other deep-pocketed competitors. But over the next decade, as Microsoft's software became the industry standard, the company's sales rose fiftyfold. Profits increased even faster, hitting $2.2 billion in 1996. Microsoft's stock followed, doubling and splitting again and again. By the tenth anniversary of the company's offering, Microsoft's shares had risen almost one-hundredfold, adjusted for splits. An investor who had bought 500 shares of the offering and held them owned stock worth almost $1 million.

Microsoft's growth seemed to demonstrate the irrelevance of dividends in the new bull market. The company had never paid dividends, instead reinvesting its cash in its business. But without returning a dime to its shareholders, Microsoft had made them tens of billions of dollars. And even the most skeptical investor couldn't question whether Microsoft's profits were real; the company's cash hoard rose every year. Microsoft had almost no capital expenses, no expensive factories, and fantastic profit margins. It was the perfect growth stock. Its price-earnings ratio was always higher than the market's P/E, but it always justified the confidence that investors put in it. With Microsoft, the only mistake an investor could make was to sell.

Mesmerized by Microsoft (and its chip-making twin, Intel), investors began to seek out the next company that would dominate an important technology sector. Would it be Oracle? Dell? Sun? Cisco? In any case, the next Microsoft was likely to be found on the Nasdaq. After its 57 percent gain in 1991, the Nasdaq tacked on another 16 percent in 1992 and 15 percent in 1993.

———

Investors were not so sanguine about the overall market. The economy came out of the 1990–91 recession without much vigor, and after its strong 1991 performance, the S&P 500 limped through 1992 and 1993. The picture seemed to worsen in 1994. Fears of inflation and the intractable budget deficit drove interest rates sharply higher. The yield on the thirty-year Treasury bond hit 8 percent. Higher interest rates, in turn, dragged stocks lower. The S&P 500 fell about 2 percent. The long rally wasn't quite dead, but by all appearances it was ailing. "The rocky year in stocks was typical of a late-stage bull market," *The Wall Street Journal* wrote in its year-end review of 1994.[12]

But the market was set to surprise investors once again. In its pessimism over interest rates, Wall Street had ignored dramatic improvements in the economy. The decade-long restructuring of American business had paid off. U.S. manufacturers were finally competitive with their foreign counterparts. Consumer goods companies like Coke had strengthened their global dominance. American drug makers were on the verge of demolishing European competitors. And the United States had no peer in information technology. In 1994 the U.S. economy grew 4 percent, its fastest rate in six years. Inflation rose just 2.7 percent, the second smallest increase since 1965.

The corporate bottom line reflected those strengths. In 1994, earnings at the S&P 500 rose 40 percent, following a 16 percent rise in 1993. Profits were increasing so fast that analysts couldn't move their estimates up quickly enough. A *Business Week* article in November 1994 called profit growth the best in twenty years. "Institutions and the investing public are vastly underestimating the earnings power of corporate America," one mutual fund manager told the magazine, which forecast that "in a little less threatening interest-rate environment, they're more likely to appreciate it."[13]

In 1995 that prophecy came true. With inflation under control and the budget deficit finally shrinking, bond yields plunged and stocks exploded upward. Stocks weren't cheap at the end of 1994. The S&P's price-earnings ratio was about 15, and its dividend yield was 3 percent, in line with historical averages. But falling rates and rising profits proved an irresistible combination for investors. The Dow broke 4,000 in February 1995; nine months later it surged past 5,000. "The industrial average's swift race from 4,000 to 5,000 evoked memories of the great bull rushes of the 1920s and the middle 1980s," the *Journal* wrote. "Strategists, pointing to falling interest rates, rising productivity, and tame inflation, see no reason to call a halt to the stunning bull market."[14]

For once the conventional wisdom was right. In 1995 the frenzy had just begun.

Chapter 6

—

THE NUMBER
IS BORN

The frenzy. Five years of fun and excitement, of priggish pronouncements from Larry Ellison (are there any other kind?), of Napster and Kozmo.com and Tina Brown, all three now vanished without a trace, of two-by-fours (contracts that guaranteed investment bankers $2 million a year for four years) that turned into three-by-fives, of $60,000 dinners in London and million-dollar parties in New York. Robert Rubin was secretary of the Treasury. Osama bin Laden was just another fanatic with a beard and a grudge. The Internet was changing everything, if it hadn't already.

The frenzy. You remember, even if you wish you didn't. It was, to lift a phrase from the era, the perfect storm. If you can't wait to relive it, skip to Chapter 10. But to understand why the waves got so high, you'll need some history—starting with the two-decade-long breakdown in Wall Street research.

—

The quality and objectivity of research peaked in the 1960s and early 1970s, before the S.E.C. forced the Big Board to deregulate commissions on May Day.

Before May Day, unable to compete on price, securities firms depended on their research departments to differentiate themselves and win commissions from investors. Brokerage houses and institutional investors (a.k.a. the "sell side" and the "buy side," because brokers sell and investors buy) had an explicit quid pro quo. Firms that provided accurate, profitable research would be rewarded with trades—and commissions. By the late 1960s, research competition was fierce. At least eighty brokers offered research reports to big investors.[1] Institutional investors used commissions to support more than $100 million in research a year, and one author estimated that "more individuals and firms (are) involved directly and indirectly in the production of research than any other single function on Wall Street."[2]

Overall, trading commissions provided more than half of Wall Street's revenue. Investment banking work, such as underwriting new stock and bond offerings and helping companies negotiate mergers and acquisitions, accounted for less than one-quarter. (The rest came from profits from proprietary trading—stock trades that firms made on their own behalf—along with fees for managing money and interest on loans.) The investors who bought stock, not the companies that sold it, paid the industry's bills. As a result, firms had a strong financial incentive to make their research as good as possible. If they shaded their reports to win investment banking business from their corporate clients, they risked alienating the investors who provided the majority of their revenues. In fact, many firms didn't even have investment banking divisions. They survived solely on commissions and accurate research.

In the 1970s and early 1980s it was not unusual for analysts to pump out reports of twenty pages or more on a single company. Ann Knight, a top-ranked Paine Webber auto analyst, made her name in 1982 with a ninety-nine-page report about the car industry.[3] Analysts were expected to understand the internal dynamics of the companies and industries they covered. "When I started, we didn't even use computers," said Barbara Alexander, who worked as a Salomon

Brothers construction industry analyst from the 1960s through the mid-1980s. "You did spreadsheets by hand maybe once a year, and you had a very long-range strategic perspective. We used to forecast earnings, five, seven, even ten years out. And you really got to know a company. You might have an analyst, for example, following only one company."[4]

To be sure, it would be a mistake to over-romanticize the good old days. Then as now, analysts who wrote negative reports risked being ostracized and cut off by the companies they covered. Then as now, analysts had a natural tendency to like their companies and be overly optimistic about them. (An old Wall Street saying holds that "you start as an analyst, but you end as an ambassador.") And then as now, Wall Street preferred to hear good news. As Ray Dirks noted in 1979, "Investors want a positive story, one that tells them about a stock that might make them some money—and the major consequence of this condition is that very few analysts go after negative stories."[5]

But whatever the pressures that analysts faced, they could take comfort in the fact that research mattered in the way most important to Wall Street. It made money.

That began to change after May Day, as commission rates fell and other revenue streams became more important to firms. Still, in 1980, commissions accounted for about 35 percent of the industry's overall revenue, more than any other single source. Then the leveraged buyout boom began. With billions of dollars—and chief executives' jobs—at stake, companies gladly paid multimillion-dollar fees to investment banks for advice on how to defend themselves from (or make) takeover offers.

With stocks rising, trading boomed during the 1980s. Even so, commissions steadily fell in importance to Wall Street as the decade progressed. By 1990 commissions provided only 16 percent of Wall Street's revenues, while fees for mergers and acquisitions work made up 32 percent, up from 13 percent in 1980.* Merger work had become the single most important source of revenue and profits for the securities industry.[†]

By 1990 research no longer generated enough commission revenue to pay for itself. Firms subsidized their research departments with money from their investment banking divisions. At big firms, as much as 40 percent of the budget for research came from banking fees.[6] Wall Street's bills were now being paid by its corporate clients, not by investors.

The effects of that change did not take long to be felt. At pre–May Day commission rates of 28 cents per share, "you get total objectivity," Daniel Meade, research director for CS First Boston, said in 1990. "At 6, you get a little flavoring from the corporate finance side."[7]

As late as 1987, Knight, the Paine Webber auto analyst, could say publicly that she did not know if her firm was working on any underwriting or merger work at the companies she covered, a comment that would seem hopelessly naïve—or an outright lie—only a couple of years later.[8] Bankers did not necessarily overtly pressure analysts to put high ratings on stocks. Overt pressure usually wasn't required. Analysts knew that investment banking paid their salaries. In case they forgot, firms linked analysts' year-end bonuses, the bulk of their pay, to investment banking profits. Meanwhile, companies, aware of their new power, increasingly linked banking business to positive

---

*Interest on loans that securities firms made to hedge funds and corporate borrowers was also included. For some reason the Securities Industry Association, the source of these statistics, lumps interest and mergers and acquisitions fees together as "other securities-related revenues."

†Fees for underwriting stock and bond offerings were also becoming more important to the sell side. But initial public offerings were not yet creating perverse incentives for buy-side firms not just to ignore but to abet bad research, as they would during the peak of the late 1990s boom. More on this crucial topic in Chapter 10.

coverage. Inevitably, analysts became more and more positive, all the while insisting that their objectivity remained uncompromised.

If analysts showed too much independence, the pressure from investment bankers could become explicit. In a memo in September 1990, a senior executive at Morgan Stanley warned analysts not to make "negative or controversial comments about our clients." In another memo he proposed that analysts be graded for their "cooperation" with investment bankers. "We were held accountable to corporate finance (investment banking)—playing the game the way corporate finance dictated," Stacy Dutton, a Morgan analyst who had quit to join the buy side, said in 1992.[9] Morgan denied Dutton's allegations and said it had rejected the proposals in the memos, though Morgan's chairman acknowledged that "tension between investment bankers and research exists at every firm."

In reality, that tension had largely disappeared by the early 1990s. The war between investment banking and research was over; investment banking had won.[*]

---

[*]And yet it may be too simplistic to blame investment banking alone for the decline of research. Much of the research that was so carefully and expensively produced before May Day was never read. In a 1974 survey, institutional investors said they used only one-quarter of the reports that brokerages sent them, and they thought less than 10 percent were worth paying for. Investors bought research because they had to, not because they wanted to. Even research that was as close to objective and unbiased as Wall Street could make it had a difficult time finding an audience.

In fact, sell-side research has an inherent flaw, rarely discussed but impossible to fix. Investors use research reports for the same reason they use technical analysis or tea leaves: to make money. And on Wall Street, information is valuable largely to the extent that it is proprietary. But research, almost by definition, is public information. Even in the 1970s the Dow Jones wire service would publicize new research reports soon after they were released. Today, thanks to CNBC and the wires, any new information in a research report is available within minutes to everyone in the market, not just the clients of the firm that released the report. It is almost impossible for sell-side research to provide investors with a lasting informational edge. "It takes a lot of

—

By the mid-1980s, complaints about the quality of Wall Street research were endemic among professional investors. Sell-side analysts
talked too much to company managements and not enough to suppliers and customers. They spent too much time pitching recommendations and not enough considering trends in the industries they
covered. The burgeoning conflict between research and investment
banking only made matters worse. "I happen to think that very few
investors have made much money buying and selling stocks based on
recommendations from the Street," the chief investment officer of
Citicorp said in 1985.

But even as the criticism mounted, analysts' influence increased.
With newspapers publishing more business news and a small cable
channel called the Financial News Network building its audience,
analysts gained new outlets to reach investors. Those investors, espe-

---

time and work to just know what everybody else knows," one analyst told the *Times*
in an unintentionally revealing comment in 1985. "That's where an analyst spends
most of his time."

Of course, research reports aren't just about information. They're about analysis.
But an analyst who has genuine insight into the future of the industry he covers can
make more money on the buy side, as a hedge fund manager, than on the sell side. At
the peak of the 1990s bull market, top analysts made a few million dollars a year;
top hedge fund managers made tens of millions. Under those circumstances the best
analysts have an almost irresistible incentive to leave the profession and start to run
money for themselves. If you really know where the gold is buried, why sell maps?

Even into the late 1990s, Wall Street had a few genuinely superb analysts, men or
women who did not want to run their own funds and enjoyed the visibility that the
sell side offered. But they were the exceptions. The last firm of any size to provide
old-school, untainted, pre–May Day–style research is Sanford C. Bernstein, which
does not have an investment banking division. Bernstein's research is notably different from that of the rest of the Street. The firm's "black books," the staple of its
research efforts, are short on quick tips and long on proprietary surveys and in-
depth industry examinations. And unlike mainstream firms, which distribute their
research widely, Bernstein works to limit distribution of its books to the institutional
investors who pay its bills. In so doing, Bernstein fills a valuable niche, since even

cially individual investors, had very few good alternatives to sell-side research. Before 1994, when the S.E.C. began requiring companies to file their financial statements electronically, investors who wanted to see 10-Ks and 10-Qs either had to visit an S.E.C. office, pay a private research service to copy and send the documents to them, or request the filings directly from the companies, a process that could take weeks. And, of course, there were no Internet chat groups where individual investors could debate companies' financial statements and prospects.

Investors were almost forced to rely on brokerage reports. In addition, the flaws in Wall Street research might have been obvious to professional investors, but they weren't obvious to small investors, especially the more than 20 million Americans who bought stocks for the first time during the 1980s. Even skeptical stories about research, such as an October 1990 *Fortune* article that asked, "Can You Trust Analysts' Reports?" took as a given that "analysts' research

---

large mutual fund companies do not want to spend the time or money that Bernstein does for its surveys. Essentially, Bernstein works almost as a cooperative research service for the handful of big investors who are serious about understanding the stocks they own.

Demand for the high-quality research provided by Bernstein appears to be limited, however. As the 1990s progressed, the firm's influence slipped, and other efforts to launch major research-only firms sputtered. Despite their complaints about the weakness of Wall Street research, institutional investors apparently have little interest in working to improve it. Why should Fidelity Investments, the giant mutual fund company, demand better research from Merrill if Fidelity knows that Putnam Investments, its crosstown rival, will see the same reports it does? Fidelity is far better off trying to hire Merrill's best analysts to manage its funds. Economists have a catchy term for this problem: the tragedy of the commons.

So the demise of research was, in a way, inevitable. Standard sell-side research is not worthless because it is bad. It is bad because even at its best it has limited worth, at least for the sophisticated institutional investors who have the power to demand more. High commissions hid that fact for a while; when they disappeared, research had to stand on its own, with unfortunate consequences.

is still the best source of information about companies and how they're likely to do."[10]

The growing importance of what became known as "consensus estimates" further increased analysts' influence. The consensus was simply the average earnings forecast of all the analysts who followed a particular company. It had existed at least since 1970, when Lynch, Jones & Ryan, a mid-sized New York brokerage firm, began collecting information about the profit estimates made by analysts at other firms. Two years later Lynch began publishing the average, or consensus, estimate for six hundred companies in a monthly newsletter it called the Institutional Brokers Estimates System, or I/B/E/S. I/B/E/S quickly expanded, and two similar services followed; in 1978 a Chicago analyst named Leonard Zacks quit his job and founded Zacks Investment Research, and in 1984, nine major brokerage firms teamed to create First Call.

The initial impact of consensus estimates was limited by their narrow distribution and the fact that they were updated infrequently. Then, in the early 1980s, networked computers started to arrive on traders' desks, allowing them to see changes in consensus estimates in real time—and to compare instantly the actual earnings reports with the consensus. By 1985, I/B/E/S was providing reports on more than two thousand companies, and securities firms were examining how much stocks moved after "earnings surprises," either positive or negative.

The creation of consensus estimates undoubtedly increased analysts' importance. While estimates from any single analyst could be dismissed as unreasonable, the consensus rapidly became the benchmark for judging the success or failure of a company's quarter; General Motors had either met Wall Street's collective expectation, or it had missed. And once the consensus estimate became a de facto benchmark, both analysts and companies had strong incentives to make it as accurate as possible. Companies wanted to move the consensus to a point where they could match or beat it. Analysts wanted their estimates to be accurate, a difficult feat without the help of the companies they covered. If an analyst's estimate was not just wrong but also far from the consensus, he would look doubly foolish. A little company guidance could help every analyst look smart. As a Merrill, Lynch analyst whined in 1985 after one of his companies missed his estimates by 8 cents, "Management should have telegraphed the situation. I don't like surprises. Clients don't like surprises."[11]

A company whose sales or earnings fell short of the consensus could be badly punished; in late December 1984, shares of Toys "R" Us fell 15 percent the day after the toy store chain reported that its Christmas sales had risen less than analysts had predicted. Responding to the increased scrutiny, companies beefed up their investor relations departments and spent more time guiding analysts. "Obviously investors are more accepting of our performance when the forecast is somewhat accurate," a Nike executive told *Business Week* in a 1985 article headlined "Hell Hath No Fury Like a Surprised Stock Analyst."[12]

Slowly but steadily, consensus estimates grew in importance. *The Wall Street Journal* used the words "consensus" and "estimates" and "earnings" in articles nine times in 1985, 25 times in 1989, and 105 times in 1994. The trend was so gradual, and so natural, that its implications mostly went undiscussed. In retrospect, though, the new focus on consensus estimates proved insidious on at least three levels.

First, before the rise of the consensus, individual analysts often gave earnings estimates as a range, such as $1.90 to $2.00 a share, rather than a single to-the-penny figure. That convention had given companies a bit of leeway to meet estimates. It had also, probably unintentionally, helped to highlight accounting's natural imprecision. But consensus estimates were calculated to the penny, so companies began to face pressure not just to match the range of analysts' forecasts but to meet or beat estimates to the penny. A company whose earnings were expected by a couple of analysts to fall between $1.90 and $2.00 per share didn't need to worry much whether it earned $1.93 or $1.96. But when the same company faced an estimate—a *consensus* estimate—of $1.94, the difference between $1.93 and $1.96 became much more important. Even honest companies came under pressure to make sure they didn't fall a penny or two short of what slowly became known as "the number." In a 1994 column, Bill Barnhart, a reporter for the *Chicago Tribune,* warned that traders and investors were likely to focus on the headline earnings number and overreact to small deviations from the consensus:

> It's disheartening to think that the blood, sweat and tears of countless corporate employees come down to a single number—earnings per share, or, more precisely, the number of pennies by which the reported earnings-per-share figure is above or below the Wall Street consensus estimate . . .
>
> When you boil down the entirety of a corporate enterprise to a few pennies, the chances for error, misunderstanding and mischief are immense.[13]

Second, the earnings guidance that came as a necessary corollary to consensus estimates discouraged independent thinking or research by analysts. Why make time-consuming calls to customers and suppliers when its chief financial officer, with a wink and a nod, could steer you to the right estimate?

Finally, the rise of consensus estimates naturally encouraged Wall Street to focus on companies' short-term results rather than long-run trends. Even analysts who had little interest in making quarterly predictions found themselves judged almost solely on their ability to provide estimates that were a penny or two more accurate than their peers. They had little choice but to focus on getting those projections right.

So the number fed on itself. As it became more important, companies and analysts paid more attention to it, making it even more important, in an unceasing cycle.

Nonetheless, Wall Street's obsession with consensus estimates was only part of the reason that accounting chicanery erupted in the 1990s. Investors had paid attention to companies' earnings at least since the 1920s, when earnings replaced dividends as the core of stock valuation. They had compared earnings with analysts' estimates at least since the 1950s, when firms expanded and professionalized their research departments. The rise of the number sharpened Wall Street's focus on earnings and estimates; it didn't create that focus.

Besides, analysts did not pull their estimates out of thin air; companies guided them. *Companies* controlled the consensus; companies told analysts how fast they expected to grow. Sure, a company that found itself short of the consensus at the end of a quarter might be tempted to unearth a penny or two a share, a few million dollars in all, somewhere on its books. But the accounting frauds of the 1990s were about billions of dollars, not a few million. The companies and the executives who committed fraud at the end of the decade weren't trying to shade the truth; they were creating financial statements that had no basis in reality.

So why the sudden drop in executives' ethics? Why would the CEO of a Fortune 500 company, a man who controlled tens of thousands of workers and whose every need was met by a staff of loyal minions, risk losing his job by faking financial statements? Two words: stock options.

Chapter 7

—

OPTIONS

Wouldn't it be nice if companies could pay employees without actually having to pay them? Companies could report higher profits, because they wouldn't have to put salaries on their income statements. Employees could get more money, because who cares how much you make if nobody has to pay? It would be, as used-car salesmen and CEOs like to say, a win-win.

So God created options. And life was good, for a while. Then the bill came due.

An option gives its owner the right to buy a stock for a set price, called the strike price, anytime before the option expires. When the option is cashed in, or exercised, its holder receives the difference between the price of the stock and the strike price. For example, if Merck stock is trading at $50, a Merck option with a strike price of $30 would be worth $20 when it's exercised; if Merck is at $55, the option would be worth $25. If Merck is trading for $30 or less, the option cannot be exercised. In Wall Street parlance, it is "out of the money." But out of the money does not equal worthless. As long as the option has not expired, its potential value gives it value. Out of the money today; in the money tomorrow. Options are worth something even when they're not worth anything. They are as close as Wall Street comes to believing in an afterlife.

Options have been around almost as long as stocks; they were used as a form of executive compensation at least as early as the 1920s. But outside of Silicon Valley, where options culture took root in the 1960s and never withered, options had largely faded by the late 1970s. With the market skidding like a drunk in an ice storm, executives preferred the certainty of cash.

Then, in 1978, executives and store managers at Toys "R" Us, an obscure retailer, got a big chunk of options as an incentive to stay with the company as it emerged from the bankruptcy of Interstate Department Stores, its corporate parent. As Toys "R" Us took off and its stock soared, the grants produced a windfall for the company's management. Suddenly, the richest executives in America worked not for Exxon or AT&T but a toy store chain in Paramus, New Jersey. Charles Lazarus, the chairman of Toys "R" Us, made $156 million in the 1980s, almost twice as much as Steven Ross of Warner Communications, the nation's second highest paid executive. In 1987 alone Lazarus earned $60 million, almost entirely from options.[1]

To call this a watershed event in American business is to understate its impact. Lazarus had charted a path to wealth; hordes of CEOs would follow, beginning with Michael Eisner, the chief executive of Disney, who took home $40 million in 1988. Companies began giving out many more options to employees, especially those at the top. In the 1960s and 1970s, the chief executive of a New York Stock Exchange company might receive a few thousand options a year. By the late 1980s, grants had swelled to ten times that size.

The explosion in options was widely seen as a boon. In theory, options helped solve the corporate governance problem. They aligned the interests of executives and shareholders. Even lower-level employees might work harder if they knew they could benefit from a rise in their company's stock. And because options grants were doled out to employees over a period of several years, they allowed companies to lock up talented workers. (A typical employee option grant has a ten-year term and vests—or becomes the property of the employee—over a four-year period. Employees who quit in the first four years usually forfeit the portion of their grants that haven't vested yet.)

—

Companies had one more incentive to turn to options so enthusiastically. Thanks to a long-standing accounting loophole, they were free—in a manner of speaking.

Accountants have traditionally viewed options as costless for two reasons. First, companies can create them whenever they like, without having to pay anyone for the privilege, like corrupt dictatorships that balance their budgets by printing money instead of cutting spending or raising taxes. (In some cases, companies need shareholders' approval for new option plans, but those votes are basically a formality, the corporate governance equivalent of a vote in the old Soviet Union.) Second, valuing options precisely seems to be impossible. After all, when an option is issued, it is impossible to know how much it will be worth if and when it's exercised. If a company's stock stays flat or falls, the option may expire without ever being used.

Because options did not require a cash outlay and because their value was uncertain, companies had never been required to record a cost for issuing them, as long as their exercise price was set equal to the company's stock price on the day they were issued. Thus companies could give away as many options as they liked with no impact on their earnings. Options were free. And as their use increased, companies and accountants argued that they should stay that way.

The argument does not hold up under close scrutiny, or any scrutiny at all. Take the second part first. True, at the time an option is created, no one knows what it will eventually be worth. But that uncertainty does not mean the option cannot be valued. In 1973, two finance professors, Fischer Black and Myron Scholes, figured out how to determine the proper price for any option.* Thanks to the Black-Scholes equation, millions of options are now bought and sold every day on the Chicago Board Options Exchange and other fine institutions. You can even trade them yourself, though in the long run you'll probably wish you hadn't.

So companies can easily determine for themselves the fair market value of the options they are distributing. Their ultimate cost may be different, but that problem can be dealt with later when the options are actually exercised.†

The argument that options don't have a cash cost turns out to be equally bogus. Since options can be valued, they can be sold. For example, a company theoretically could raise money by selling options to outside investors. By transferring those options instead to its employees, the company is giving away something it could sell. And money not made is money lost. As Warren Buffett wrote sarcastically:

> Without blushing, almost all C.E.O.'s have told their shareholders that options are cost-free. For these C.E.O.'s I have a proposition: Berkshire Hathaway will sell you insurance, carpeting, or any of our other products in exchange for options identical to those you grant yourselves. It'll all be cash-free. But do you

---

*Basically, the more volatile the underlying stock and the longer the amount of time until the option expires, the more valuable the option. Interest rates and dividends also factor in; higher rates and lower dividends make options more valuable.

†The later adjustment is somewhat complicated; it should probably be made to the balance sheet, not as a gain or loss on the income statement. Otherwise all kinds of accounting madness are possible. But accounting for the adjustment is a technical problem; the initial cost of the option is the fundamental issue.

really think your corporation will not have incurred a cost when you hand over the options in exchange for the carpeting? Or do you really think that placing a value on the option is just too difficult to do, one of your other excuses for not expensing them? If these are the opinions you honestly hold, call me collect. We can do business. . . .

When a company gives something of value to its employees in return for their services, it is clearly a compensation expense. And if expenses don't belong in the earnings statement, where in the world do they belong?[2]

(Buffett's campaign against options follows a trail blazed by his teacher and mentor Ben Graham. In 1936, as usual several steps ahead of everyone else, Graham had satirically proposed that U.S. Steel pay its workers in options instead of cash.)[3]

In fact, options have a clear cost to a company's current shareholders. By creating new shares they reduce the value of the shares that already exist.* Sure, the cost is not obvious to the existing investors. The company's share base quietly creeps up, reducing the company's per-share earnings and making each share worth a little

---

*For example, suppose a company with 1 million shares outstanding grants its employees 1 million options (with a strike price of $10, the market price of the company's stock). Over the next year the company's stock jumps from $10 to $100, and its market value reaches $100 million. The employees then exercise all their options, paying the company $10 million. The company's new value is $110 million—the $100 million plus the $10 million the employees have paid the company. But instead of having 1 million shares, the company now has 2 million. Instead of owning the whole company, the old shareholders own only half of it. Employees own the other half.

Now, instead of being worth $100, each share is worth only $55. The company's existing shareholders are $45 million poorer—their million shares, which were worth $100 million, are now worth $55 million. That $45 million has gone to employees, who have paid $10 million for 1 million shares worth $55 million. The overall value of the company has not changed, but employees have taken part of it at the expense of shareholders.

less than it otherwise would be. But just because the cost is subtle does not mean that it is not real. Again: *The exercise of options transfers value from a company's investors to the employees who exercise them.* Like inflation, options are a hidden tax.

—

But accounting rules didn't recognize the cost of that tax, although as early as 1978 most major accounting firms had agreed that options should be expensed.[4] So companies could hand out as many options as they wanted,* and as the S&P 500 doubled between 1987 and 1994, it did not take long for the bigger grants to begin gushing cash. American executives had always been well paid compared to their workers and foreign executives; options put them in another universe.

In 1980, the highest paid executive in the United States was Robert A. Charpie, the president of Cabot Corp., an energy and chemicals company in Boston. Charpie made $3.3 million in total pay that year; the average chief executive made $625,000, about forty times the salary of the typical American worker.[5] A lot of money, sure, but not an unreasonable amount, given the responsibilities that come with running a publicly traded company. By the end of the decade the average salary of a chief executive had tripled, to $1.9 million. The average worker's salary had risen more slowly, so CEOs now made about eighty times as much as a typical worker.

The pay packages aroused grumbling among some Democrats, especially when the economy fell into recession in 1991. That year, Senator Carl Levin of Michigan introduced a bill urging the Financial Accounting Standards Board to come up with a more rational way to account for stock options. Two years later the board took the bravest action of its short happy life. It recommended that companies be required to expense the cost of options.

---

*Ironically, federal income tax rules did recognize that options had a cost—companies could deduct their expense from their tax bills. Thus options offered companies the best of both worlds, cutting taxes without affecting reported earnings.

Companies and accounting firms rose in revolt. If corporations could no longer pretend that options were free, they might have to cut back on grants, and smaller grants would mean . . . less money. There was only one solution. The FASB would have to be made to see reason. Before the new rule could take effect, executives and politicians from both parties not so gently suggested to the board that it might want to reconsider its decision. Opposition was especially fierce in Silicon Valley, where technology company employees had grown up believing that quick wealth was their birthright. On March 25, 1994, at the "Rally in the Valley," in San Jose, California, three thousand high-tech workers protested the board's decision. A few weeks later, the Senate passed, 88–9, a nonbinding resolution opposing the new requirement. Senator Joseph Lieberman, a Connecticut Democrat, proposed taking away FASB's control of accounting rules.[6] J. Carter Beese, a Republican S.E.C. commissioner, complained in a *Wall Street Journal* opinion piece that "the FASB is committed to rendering its final decision without regard to any of the social, economic, or public policy considerations involved."[7] Which was sort of the point. The board was called the Financial Accounting Standards Board, not the Financial Public Policy Considerations Board.

With brilliant illogic, Beese went on to argue in favor of a "compromise" proposal under which companies would be allowed to continue to pretend that options had no cost as long as they disclosed the actual cost in a once-a-year footnote to their annual reports:

Our financial markets, of course, value substance over form. Whether deducted from earnings or disclosed in a footnote, the estimated value accorded to the options will be quickly and efficiently analyzed, checked, re-estimated, and assigned its appropriate weight, as only our markets can do so well.

On the other hand, shareholders and the companies in which they invest care a great deal about form, and for good reason.

On the other hand? What other hand? Markets and shareholders are one and the same. Either markets couldn't be fooled into ignoring the hidden cost of options—in which case, why try?—or they could, in which case the cost, like all expenses, should be fully disclosed.

Meanwhile, the accounting industry was not exactly standing up on principle. The same firms that had agreed that options should be expensed in 1978 had somehow changed their views by 1994. On July 15, the Big Six*—the six major accounting firms that as a group audited almost every major publicly traded company— asked the FASB to back off. "We believe the best solution is to withdraw the proposal to change the accounting and, instead, expand disclosures . . . the proposal to record the fair value of employee stock options simply has not been accepted," the firms wrote the board.[8]

The members of the Financial Accounting Standards Board fought back, promising never to waver. But in the end they were only accountants, and all they had on their side was logic. They didn't stand a chance. On December 14, 1994, the board accepted the compromise proposal. It was unconditional surrender, disguised, barely, as peace with honor.

—

Not for the first time, accountants had crumbled in the face of political and corporate pressure. And not for the first time, investors would pay the price. Once the FASB wilted, the options floodgates opened wide. By the mid-1990s, many chief executives regularly received annual grants of 100,000 options or more, which would have been unthinkable only a few years before. Robert J. Ulrich, the chairman of the Minneapolis-based Dayton-Hudson (now Target) department store chain, took home 8,360 options in 1992, along with about $1.3 million in salary and bonus. In 1995, Ulrich's pay

*The successor to the Big Eight. More on this in Chapter 8.

was about the same, at $1.4 million, but his options haul had risen twentyfold, to 165,000. Funny money had arrived in the heartland.

The grants kept getting bigger. In 1996, Tony Ridder, the chief executive of the Knight-Ridder newspaper chain, received 70,000 options for his trouble, along with $1.4 million in salary and bonus. The late 1990s were not exactly good times for Knight-Ridder; the chain's profits fell from $277 million in 1996 to $184 million in 2001. Reflecting that sorry performance, Ridder's cash pay fell to $935,000 in 2001, yet his options grant rose to 150,000. Joseph Pichler, the chairman of Kroger, a grocery chain, received 20,000 options in 1992, and 360,000 in 2000. Even adjusting for stock splits, Pichler's grant rose almost fivefold in eight years.

But Pichler and Ridder were hardly at the top end of the scale. By the end of the 1990s, some chief executives received 1 million options for one year's work. Lee R. Raymond, the chairman of ExxonMobil, took home 1.05 million options in 2000 and 2001. Apparently the 850,000 share grant that Raymond received in 1999 didn't provide sufficient motivation. Alfred Lerner, the chairman of MBNA, received 2.25 million options in 2001, on top of 800,000 in 2000 and 1 million in 1999, a total of more than 4 million options in three years. In Lerner's defense, though, he had been an options hog even before mega-grants were fashionable. His 2001 grant merely matched the 2.25 million options he had received in 1994.

The biggest pig was Larry Ellison, the chairman of Oracle, the number two software maker. In 2000, Ellison—who already owned more than a billion shares of Oracle—took an option on 40 million more.

To be sure, top executives were not the only beneficiaries of options largesse. Many companies offered grants to mid-level managers, and a few gave at least a handful of options to every employee. In 1996, for example, Norwest Bank (now Wells Fargo) gave all its workers at least 100 options.[9] Grants were especially widespread in the technology industry, where young companies had a history of using options in place of salaries to conserve cash. As technology stocks boomed, secretaries made millions of dollars; software engineers tens of millions; a few executives literally made billions. "Enough Silicon Valley companies have delivered enough stock-option jackpots to enough employees to create an entirely new business culture . . . in which taking what in traditional business circles would be seen as foolhardy risks is considered the only rational way to behave," Justin Fox wrote in *Fortune* in July 1997.[10]

But for all the happy blather about the way options put fry cooks on an equal footing with CEOs, the vast majority of options have always gone to executives and senior managers, especially outside Silicon Valley. The National Center for Employee Ownership, a nonprofit group that supports options, estimated that no more than 3 million Americans received grants in 2001. A survey by the Department of Labor put the number at 2 million in 1999.[11] Most grants to nonexecutive employees are so small they are unlikely ever to be worth much. As Dick Kovacevich, the chief executive of Norwest, said of his 100-share grants, "The impact on people is far greater than I expected. They think there's more value in the options than there really is: It's free, and it's just sexy. You get these things only the fat cats got."[12]

Sometimes cynicism and smart management are indistinguishable. In truth, granting options to lower-level employees makes little sense, although it appeals to our sense of fair play. Companies that make grants to lower-level managers or hourly employees are doing so mainly to improve morale and hide salary costs.

In case you're wondering, Kovacevich received 294,353 options in 1996, along with $4 million in salary, bonus, and assorted other goodies. The next year, following a two-for-one stock split, he got 1.72 million options.

———

Paradoxically, the surge in mega-grants led to increases in other forms of executive pay. A whole new industry of pay consultants, who appeared to exist solely to find ways to make CEOs richer, sprung up. If a guy was getting a million options, keeping the rest of his comp to six figures or even low seven just seemed chintzy. So long-term incentive bonuses were added, as well as restricted stock grants (even better than options, because stock grants are valuable even if the stock doesn't go up). Then came split-dollar life insurance policies and souped-up pension plans, even as many lower-level workers had their pension plans cut.

The rush to find new ways to compensate executives defied logic. If the prospect of making tens of millions of dollars from options could not motivate executives to perform, then what possibly could? To bump up salaries and bonuses and "long-term incentive compensation" was to pay executives two or three or four times for the same job.

Nevertheless, compensation skyrocketed. At ExxonMobil, Raymond's pay went from $2.8 million in 1994 to $24 million in 1999, not including the value of his options. Ulrich's pay rose from $2.2 million in 1994 to $10 million in 1999, also not including options. Both men were above average, but not by much. The typical chief executive of a big public company made about $12 million in 1999, including options grants. (Even the $12 million figure is probably understated, because companies tend to lowball the value of the options grants they give executives.) Pay had risen sixfold in a decade and almost twentyfold since 1980.[13] The gap between executive pay and the typical worker's pay also burst open. By 1999 the average CEO made almost five hundred times as much as the average worker.[14]

With the market soaring and the U.S. economy growing strongly in the late 1990s, the vast pay increases generated little criticism. "Executive pay has managed to disappear as a political issue," *The New York Times* wrote in April 2000. "The American economy has been the envy of the world. . . . Executives, be they savvy bosses like General Electric's John F. Welch or Internet wunderkinds, are getting much of the credit."[15] The effect of high executive pay on society is a question for another book.* But the boom in pay, especially in options grants, unquestionably was bad for the stock market.

The explosion in options hurt investors on several levels. First, it allowed companies to overstate their profits by hiding compensation costs. When companies handed out only a few thousand options a year, their cost was basically a rounding error. But that changed when companies began to grant millions of options annually. Companies that used options heavily in place of salaries could boost their bottom line by 10 percent or more, sometimes much more. In 2001,

---

*It may be worth noting that companies and consultants routinely justify high pay for mediocre executives by arguing that they should make about as much as similar executives at their much more successful competitors. Wide pay gaps are unfair and can demoralize executives, they say. Take Bristol-Myers Squibb, an also-ran drug company in New York. (How also-ran? By the time you read this, Bristol may no longer be independent.)

In 2001, Bristol paid its outgoing chairman, Charles A. Heimbold, almost $5 million, a $1.7 million raise, and gave him 736,000 options—in a year when Bristol's stock fell almost 30 percent, far more than the average of other big drug companies. Why the pay hike? "Mr. Heimbold's cash compensation [should] remain competitive with the compensation of chief executive officers with similar experience at peer group companies," Bristol said in its proxy.

But that rationale apparently does not apply outside the executive suite. Executives have no problem with paying themselves hundreds of times as much as their bottom-rung employees make. Those gaps make sense because executives ultimately determine whether a company succeeds, the compensation experts say.

Well, which is it? If executives are truly vital to the success of their companies—and they probably are—then managers who make bad decisions should make far less than their winning counterparts. High pay for high performance; low pay for low performance. Over his nine years as chairman, William C. Steere Jr. built Pfizer into the world's largest and most profitable drug company. Perhaps he was worth the $17 million in pay and 800,000 stock options he received in 2000. But $17 million for Steere doesn't justify $5 million for Heimbold, who built Bristol into a takeover target.

As it is, though, executives have it both ways, getting the rewards of power without its responsibilities.

for example, Microsoft gave $3.3 billion in options to employees, one-quarter its pretax profit. Cisco Systems granted $2.6 billion in options. Overall, according to a study by Bear Stearns, S&P 500 companies gave executives and employees $47 billion in options in 2001 without recording any expense—more than one-tenth their pretax profits.[16] Price-earnings ratios are the most crucial measure of stock valuation; the increasing use of options significantly distorted that measure.

Second, the Financial Accounting Standards Board's independence was destroyed when the board was forced to reverse its initial 1993 ruling on options accounting. FASB was far from perfect; it was slow, understaffed, and prone to picayune industry battles. It was financially dependent on the firms and companies it was supposed to oversee, and its members came mostly from inside the industry. Even so, when it came to options, the board tried to be an impartial, honest judge. For its effort, it was pushed to the brink of extinction. It would not make the same mistake twice. For the rest of the 1990s, FASB would do little to stop the increasingly aggressive financial gimmicks being blessed by the industry it was supposed to regulate.

Third, the rise in executive pay actually blunted the link between pay and performance. Because grants got so large, and because they pushed up salaries and bonuses as well, by the late 1990s even mediocre executives took home millions of dollars a year. In June 2002 the financial writer Roger Lowenstein examined the pay of Edward E. Whitacre Jr., the chief executive of SBC Communications. In 2001, Whitacre was paid $82 million, including 3.6 million options, as his company's stock declined for the third straight year. Lowenstein noted that he had deliberately chosen an executive "well regarded in his industry." Yet, Lowenstein wrote:

Whitacre exemplifies how the system itself is shot through with hypocrisy. . . . Over his twelve years as C.E.O., while Whitacre reaped a fortune, his stockholders have done precisely average. Their return from appreciation and dividends is 11.5 percent a year—a notch below the S&P 500, at 12.8 percent, and a sliver higher than its peer companies.

Executive pay has been soaring for two decades, but over the last couple of years, as many big companies have seen their stock pummeled, the pay-for-performance rationale that was supposedly driving these packages has been exposed as a fraud. . . .

By turns, a system designed to motivate became one to simply enrich.[17]

Finally, and most important, mega-grants gave executives a perverse incentive to cheat their shareholders. Doctors like to say that the dose makes the poison. Too much of any drug, even aspirin, can be fatal, and so it is with options. Reasonably sized grants offer a powerful motive for executives to get their stocks higher. There's nothing wrong with that. That's their job. But executives who receive mega-grants can take home fortunes from a short-term boost in their stock. One good year can mean tens of millions of dollars; two or three can translate into a hundred-million-dollar payday. Making matters worse, the incentives that options provide are all one-way. While a falling stock leaves shareholders poorer, executives lose nothing if their options expire worthless. By offering the chance for reward without the threat of loss, options encourage executives to take risks, both business and financial, that might make their shareholders blanch. In fact, because executives generally get new options every year, they can actually benefit by making their stocks more volatile. If Cisco falls from $60 to $20 one year, then returns to $60 the next, its shareholders are no better off than they were to start. But thanks to the $20 options he received along the way, Cisco's chief executive has reaped a windfall.

Under those circumstances, executives have little reason to build companies with staying power, and every reason to do whatever they have to do to get their stocks up—until they cash out. And in the 1990s, as the bull market turned into a boom, managers knew all too well that the fastest and easiest way to get their stocks up was to show strong, steady increases in quarterly earnings. By the time the boom ended, the link between options windfalls and accounting chicanery would be hard to ignore. Nearly all the biggest frauds of the 1990s were run by executives who reaped $100 million or more from options along the way.

But options alone could not account for the massive breakdown in accounting standards of the late 1990s. Like any crime, financial scams are a product of motive and opportunity. Options provided the motive. The opportunity was arriving on a parallel track, thanks to changes in the accounting industry and weakness at the S.E.C. that combined to leave investors almost totally unprotected.

Chapter 8

—

ACCOUNTANTS
AT THE TROUGH

The Moss bill in 1978 (see Chapter 4) marked the peak of Washington's efforts to tighten oversight of accountants. After its failure, the industry settled back into the profitable obscurity it craved. But just as the S.E.C. and Congress turned their attention elsewhere, powerful forces began to change the economics and the culture of accounting, making major firms even more eager to please their corporate clients at the expense of investors.

Having beaten back government oversight, the Big Eight firms kept their worst instincts in check with a rigid ethos that prized conservatism over brilliance or innovation. The stereotype of accountants was that they were boring, middle-aged white men, country club Republicans, more diligent than talented. The stereotype was true. In his 1981 book, *The Big Eight,* Mark Stevens described the typical partners at major firms:

They are hardworking, sincere, intelligent devotees of the Protestant ethic. Most are intelligent but colorless, competent but unimaginative, honest but highly competitive. . . . A composite picture of the predominant group of partners shows a forty-five-year-old man, bespectacled, balding, and slightly paunch. A native of a rural Michigan town, he attended Michigan State, joined a fraternity, went directly to a Big Eight firm upon graduation, and married soon after. He has three children, looks rather pale, favors classic business suits in sober grays or dark browns. . . .

The rare partner with a penchant for fashion sticks out like a showgirl in a church. . . . There are unwritten laws at The Big Eight designed to keep everyone looking and acting like everyone else. The partnership exerts a collective pressure on those who stray from the norm, ostracizing the more adventurous souls or cutting back on their share of the profits.[1]

Like doctors and lawyers, the professionals with whom they hoped to be compared, accountants pretended that they did not particularly care about money. And, in fact, the Big Eight firms had a relatively flat salary structure, with partners paid mostly on the basis of seniority, not how much business they generated. At Price Waterhouse, the most prestigious of the major firms, chairman Joe Connor made about $250,000 in 1980, only about three times as much as the lowest-paid first-year partner.[2] Being promoted to partner was not unlike getting tenure, guaranteeing a job for life regardless of performance. During the first 115 years after its creation in 1865, Price Waterhouse fired only one partner.

The same aura of gentility surrounded the industry as a whole. The Big Eight frowned on competition, especially with each other. As the only firms big enough to audit multinational companies, the eight majors did not have to worry much about competition from below. For decades they had formed a comfortable oligopoly; by the mid-1970s their clients accounted for about 95 percent of the sales and profits of all the companies on the New York Stock Exchange. A partner at Coopers & Lybrand who heard that a client of Arthur Andersen was looking for new auditors was as likely to warn Andersen as bid for the business. "Price Waterhouse will compete for clients, yes," its chairman said. "But an audit is not a commodity. You cannot sell a professional service like a packaged good."[3] The vice chairman of Arthur Young, the stodgiest of the Big Eight, even complained about firms that offered dinners and theater tickets to partners or staffers who won new business. "It gives rise to questions such as what is now 'professional' or 'gentlemanly,'" he said. "Perhaps these concepts are old-fashioned, and some of us just haven't gotten the message."

The reluctance to compete was not merely custom. The American Institute of Certified Public Accountants, along with state CPA associations, prohibited members from advertising or actively soliciting each other's business.

Accountants could afford to be mannerly. Their business had boomed since the passage of the securities laws. In 1945 the AICPA had about 9,500 members. Thirty years later it had 95,000, and by 1980 well over 150,000.[4] Between 1920 and 1980 the number of accountants in America grew twice as fast as the number of lawyers and three times as fast as the number of doctors. The Big Eight grew even faster than the profession as a whole; revenues at Peat, Marwick, Mitchell (now KPMG) rose almost one-hundredfold between 1947 and 1981.[5]

Fat and happy, the Big Eight had leverage against clients who wanted to push the limits of accounting rules. With competition in check, the profession could theoretically worry about values other than the bottom line. Price Waterhouse and Arthur Andersen, the most highly regarded of the Big Eight, were also the most conservative. Based in Chicago, Andersen embodied midwestern levelheadedness and probity. Its motto was "Think straight, talk straight." Price Waterhouse, which was headquartered in New York, still carried the hauteur of its British roots.

On the other hand, a faint but distinct air of bottom-feeding surrounded Touche Ross, the smallest and most aggressive of the majors. "Old-timers—card-carrying members of The Big Eight

Club—consider Touche Ross to be a whorehouse of poor standards and low fees," Stevens wrote. Nasty language, but not surprising. Without external oversight, the Big Eight depended on internal censure to keep troublemakers in line, a judgmental sorority whose most effective punishment was gossip. Cultural reinforcement might be no substitute for real federal regulation, but it was better than nothing.

—

The Big Eight's cartel did not survive the 1970s. In 1977, the Federal Trade Commission and the Justice Department began to investigate whether the industry's self-imposed bans on advertising and marketing were anticompetitive. Facing the threat of an antitrust lawsuit, the AICPA quickly dropped many of its prohibitions.

Competition soon heated up. Firms promised quicker audits and discounted their posted hourly rates. (Like lawyers, accountants charge by the hour; unlike lawyers, they generally promise clients that an audit will take a set number of hours going in.) For the next several years auditing fees shrank in inflation-adjusted terms, squeezing profit margins. The industry's clubby atmosphere evaporated. Touche Ross aggressively chased and won new business, exasperating slower-moving firms such as Arthur Young, which complained in a report:

> No longer do accountants compete solely on the strength of their capabilities. Today, every accounting firm . . . competes with every other accounting firm in its market area for clients present and future, for attention, for exposure. Accounting firms compete with each other presentation for presentation, press release for press release, speech for speech, seminar for seminar, and increasingly, ad for ad.[6]

As the 1980s progressed, the fight for business grew fiercer. In 1985, J. Michael Cook, the chairman of Deloitte, Haskins & Sells, told *The Wall Street Journal*, "Five years ago if a client of another firm came to me and complained about the service, I'd immediately warn the other firm's chief executive. Today I try to take away his client."[7] In the front-page article, headlined "Total War: CPA Firms Diversify, Cut Fees, Steal Clients in Battle for Business—'the White Gloves Are Off' as Revenue Is Squeezed," the *Journal* noted that "many in the profession, government, and the academic world . . . worry that firms may get so cutthroat that they will fall down on what many see as their primary duty: independently auditing the books of publicly held companies. The biggest potential loser is the public, these critics argue."

The profession disagreed, arguing that lower fees and higher standards were not incompatible. But falling profits sparked a major cultural change at the firms, which became much less tolerant of partners who did not bring in new business. After taking over Deloitte in 1984, Cook overhauled the firm's compensation system. Partners were no longer paid in lockstep based on seniority; rainmaking and the status and profitability of a partner's clients accounted for as much as 90 percent of his pay. At about the same time, Peat, Marwick forced 10 percent of its partners to quit or retire. Being a good accountant was no longer enough.

———

At the same time, the Big Eight grew increasingly interested in selling services that had nothing to do with traditional auditing. During the 1970s, the firms had moved into management consulting, the lucrative business of helping executives make decisions that they are paid to make on their own, and information technology consulting, helping companies develop and run complex computer systems.

As they scrutinized the industry in the wake of the Equity Funding fiasco, regulators and Congress wondered whether to ban accountants from offering consulting services to companies they audited. With lucrative consulting contracts at stake, firms might not ask tough questions of their audit clients, and a firm that discovered a problem in its client's books might hide it long enough to get paid for its consulting work. Consulting "creates a professional and financial interest by the independent auditor in a client's affairs which is inconsistent with the auditor's responsibility to remain independent," the Senate found in its 1976 report on accounting. Two years later the Cohen commission recommended that accountants be banned from all nonaudit work for companies they audited.

Accountants disagreed, arguing that consulting made them more knowledgeable about their clients' businesses and thus better auditors. Besides, the Big Eight had integrity. They would never compromise their independence for a few million dollars in consulting fees.

In face of industry opposition, the Cohen commission's proposed ban, like its other recommendations, went nowhere. In 1979, the S.E.C. asked accountants to avoid certain consulting jobs, such as creating internal financial control systems that they might later have to audit. A firm that became too dependent on auditing revenues risked "impairment of its independence," the commission said. But, as usual, the S.E.C. confined itself to jawboning rather than taking real action. Accountants were still free to take on whatever jobs they liked as long as they gave the potential impact on their independence "thoughtful review." The reviews are not hard to imagine: *All partners in favor of turning down this $10 million consulting contract because it might create a conflict of interest, please raise your hands . . . and clean out your offices. It's been nice working with you.*

After the S.E.C. and Congress backed off, the Big Eight moved aggressively into consulting. At the beginning of the 1980s, consulting was a sideline for the industry, making up 10 percent of revenue at most firms and just over 20 percent at Arthur Andersen, which had been the first firm to recognize consulting's profit potential. Andersen had gotten its first technology consulting job in 1954, not long after computers were invented. The firm helped General Electric install a 30-ton, $1.2 million Univac computer capable of a princely six hundred calculations per second.[8] Leonard Spacek, who ran Andersen during the 1950s and 1960s and was legendary for his willingness to stand up to clients, worried from the beginning that consulting might present a conflict of interest for the firm. "Don't do anything that could possibly influence an audit," he told the head of Andersen's nascent consulting business even before the firm's first job was finished. But he never reined in the unit's growth, apparently calculating that he could keep it in line.

By 1986 consulting had grown to 20 percent of the revenue at most of the Big Eight, and more than 30 percent at Andersen. Its importance increased into the 1990s. In 1994, almost half of Andersen's U.S. revenue came from consulting, and another 20 percent from tax advisory services; just one-third of the firm's business was traditional accounting. Price Waterhouse also received more than half its revenue from tax and consulting services.

As consulting exploded, concerns about the potential for conflicts of interest increased. Even *Forbes,* which as a rule reflexively opposed regulation, wondered in 1987 about the impact of consulting fees:

When a company lavishes huge consulting and advisory fees on its accountants for services unrelated to the actual auditing of financial statements, the accounting firm may be less likely to ask tough questions about a client's financial health.

Accountants pooh-poohed those worries. But somewhere between the mid-1980s and the mid-1990s the worst fears of the profession's critics came true. With accounting profits declining while consulting took off, the Big Eight shredded the last of their self-imposed ethical restraints. Consultants—and accountants who understood the importance of cross-selling consulting services—seized power from the old-school accounting partners who viewed themselves as the moral equivalents of doctors and lawyers.

In 1989, facing the threat of open revolt from its consultants, who felt they didn't get a fair share of the firm's profits, Andersen agreed to allow its consulting division to operate essentially as a separate company within the firm. Almost immediately, Andersen's accounting partners went into the consulting business for themselves, *competing* with their supposed colleagues in Andersen Consulting. At an October 1989 meeting in Dallas, accounting partners were treated to a display of salesmanship better suited to a hyperactive college football team. A trainer held a tiger on stage while the head of Andersen's U.S. auditing business told the partners in the audience that they needed "the eyes of a tiger, eyes that seize opportunities, eyes that are focused on the kill."[9] So much for thinking straight and talking straight.

The same dynamic that played out within Andersen took place in the industry as a whole. Firms that aggressively sold themselves stole business from those that didn't. In 1989, Touche rose for the first time out of eighth place. Touche still had a reputation for cutting corners, but that no longer hurt its growth.[10] While Touche grew, Arthur Young, the firm that had complained at the start of the 1980s that accountants were not being judged "solely on the strength of their capabilities," lagged in revenues and salaries. In 1989 it sold itself to Ernst & Whinney in a deal that gave partners at Ernst most of the profits from the combined firm.[11] (At about the same time, Deloitte, Haskins & Sells and Touche Ross merged, and the Big Eight became the Big Six.)

Outside the Big Eight, firms proved even more willing to kowtow to clients to win business. The ninth largest accounting firm, Laventhol & Horvath, quadrupled its revenues, from $70 million in 1980 to $275 million in 1986, thanks largely to explosive growth in its consulting practice. "We don't have the highest God-almighty standards, but we don't have the lowest. I like to say that we're practical," a top partner at Laventhol said in 1987.[12]

In 1991, Mark Stevens returned for another survey of the industry.

In *The Big Six,* his follow-up to *The Big Eight,* he wrote that firms "have sought to transform their partners from archetypal Caspar Milquetoasts, who entered the profession specifically because it offered them a safe harbor from the selling required in other fields, into an army of Ed (publisher's sweepstakes) McMahons."[13] (Parentheses in original.) By the beginning of the 1990s, the Big Six were no longer accounting firms that happened to have consulting units; they were professional services organizations, using audits as a way to sell consulting and tax advice. The firms had once been genuine partnerships with a few hundred partners, nearly all accountants, who considered themselves—and were paid as—equals. Now they had thousands of partners, including many who had never been accountants, and huge salary discrepancies. They were partnerships in name only. In reality they were multinational companies, run from the top down by partners who called themselves chief executives and chairmen, not managing partners.

The change was profound. Accountants had never lived up to their lofty rhetoric, but before the 1980s they at least had *seen* themselves as public servants. No longer.

—

Discovering a direct link between the growth in consulting and the decline of accounting standards is impossible. Firms never explicitly told partners to sacrifice their objectivity to win business. But inside the firms, the cultural change was clear, and it accelerated as the 1990s progressed. In 1992, for the first time ever, Andersen's senior partners overruled its Professional Standards Group, which decided what accounting treatments were proper. The disagreement, not surprisingly, was over options. The accounting gurus felt that options should be counted as an expense; Andersen's management disagreed. Over the next decade, as high standards became an obstacle to winning business rather than a source of pride, the standard-setters steadily lost influence at Andersen. In the 1960s, George Catlett, the group's head, worked only a few feet from Spacek,

Andersen's managing partner. By 2001, seven layers of management separated the group from Joseph Berardino, the firm's chairman and chief executive.[14]

Just how badly corrupted the big firms had become would not be fully evident until the bull market ended, but by the second half of the 1990s, signs of serious trouble surfaced. For more than two decades after the collapse of Equity Funding in 1973, accounting restatements or charges of fraud at major publicly traded companies were rare. Between 1977 and 1989, only thirteen companies a year, on average, restated their earnings. And most of the companies that restated were small. Through the 1990s, restatements steadily increased, to almost ninety by 1997. Still, most restatements were relatively minor.

Then, in April 1998, Cendant, a big franchising company, said that it had overstated its profits by $640 million from 1995 through 1997. Worse, the fraud was not discovered by Ernst & Young, Cendant's auditors. Cendant was the product of the 1997 merger between CUC International, which specialized in promoting "membership clubs" that offered overpriced credit insurance and dubious travel discounts, and HFS, which franchised also-ran hotel chains like Days Inn. When they examined CUC's books after the merger closed in 1998, HFS executives quickly unearthed serious problems. CUC had booked revenue it shouldn't have, inflating its 1997 earnings by more than $100 million. The fraud was "simple," Cendant later told the *Journal*. "People just made things up."[15] But what HFS unearthed in a matter of weeks had gone unnoticed by Ernst & Young for years.*

---

*One of the most entertaining ironies of the CUC fraud is that no single individual lost more money because of it than Henry Silverman, the chairman of HFS. Before the merger, HFS was a second-rate company with third-rate brands whose most important skill was accounting gimmickry; Silverman, a former investment

The losses from the CUC fraud were enormous. The day after Cendant disclosed the first irregularities, its stock fell 46 percent, from $35.62 to $19.06. The drop cost shareholders $14 billion, more than the value of Nike and at the time almost certainly the largest loss caused by an accounting fraud.* But anyone who expected that Ernst & Young would admit responsibility for its shoddy audits was mistaken. "Nothing has been brought to our attention to suggest that our work was not in accordance with professional

---

banker, was—and remains—a top-rank pay pig. In February 1998, just before Cendant crashed, he sold $55 million in stock. (There is no evidence that he knew of the fraud at the time he sold.) After the crash, Silverman convinced his board of directors to allow him to trade twenty-five options that were far out of the money and unlikely ever to be valuable for 17 million options with much lower exercise prices. Even if Cendant stock regained only half its losses, Silverman would make more than $100 million on his new options—while his shareholders remained under water.

Still, Silverman lost $800 million in paper wealth when Cendant's stock collapsed after the fraud was revealed. For years afterward he never missed an opportunity to whine about how CUC had deceived him. "This is very painful, personally, professionally, and financially," he said in June 2000. "We need closure." Perhaps the $8.3 million in pay and 3 million options Silverman received in 2000—a year when Cendant's stock fell 60 percent—provided him with some relief.

*An important note on estimated losses: When numbers like $14 billion for Cendant or $80 billion for Enron or $150 billion for WorldCom are tossed around, take them with more than a grain of salt. In one way they are real. Cendant had 900 million shares outstanding, and each of those shares lost more than $15 in value on April 16, 1998. It's therefore true that Cendant's shareholders suffered a paper loss of $14 billion as the company's stock fell, but the key phrase is *paper loss*. Cendant's investors, as a group, could never have cashed out all their shares for $30 billion even before the fraud was admitted. If they had tried, Cendant's stock would have fallen sharply, and they would not have received $30 billion.

From another point of view: It is not as if Cendant raised $30 billion from investors and then wasted that money, or as if the company's executives sold $30 billion worth of stock they received from options. In the years prior to the fraud, most Cendant investors were buying and selling shares from each other. Many of those investors bought at a price lower than the $35 a share at which Cendant traded

standards," a spokeswoman for E&Y said the day after Cendant disclosed the fraud, raising the question—not for the first time or the last—of what exactly those standards were.[16]

Eighteen months later, in December 1999, Ernst & Young paid $335 million to resolve shareholder lawsuits for its shoddy work. At the time, the payment was by far the largest ever from an accounting firm to shareholders of a public company. Still, Ernst & Young remained defiant, as if it, not the shareholders it was supposed to protect, had been wronged. The settlement is not "an admission of wrongdoing," the firm said. "In the litigious environment in which we operate today, settlements are an unfortunate reality." (The legal fallout from CUC continues; Cosmo Corigliano, CUC's former chief financial officer, and two other CUC managers, pled guilty to fraud in 2000. Walter Forbes, its former chairman, and E. Kirk Shelton, its former vice-chairman, are scheduled to stand trial in 2003. Meanwhile, Cendant's stock has never recovered from its 1998 collapse; in late 2002 it traded around $15 a share.)[17]

Accounting problems sprang up at other big companies at about the same time as Cendant. In November 1997, Oxford Health Plans, a major health maintenance organization, admitted that its billing

---

before it disclosed the fraud. Yes, they suffered paper losses when the stock fell, but those were offset in part by their previous paper gains.

So how much money—how much *cash*—is really lost when a company's stock falls after a fraud? The answer depends on how many shares it and its executives, have sold in the previous months and years, and at what price they were sold. The $55 million Silverman raised by selling Cendant stock in February 1998 was money that came out of unsuspecting investors' pockets, no two ways about it. But $55 million is a long way from $14 billion.

I don't mean to say that paper loss figures are totally irrelevant. They are the simplest way to compare the scope of losses at different companies. But be aware that comparing, say, the $150 billion loss suffered by WorldCom's shareholders to the $150 billion federal budget deficit is misleading. The deficit must be paid off dollar for dollar; WorldCom's investors never really had $150 billion in cash to begin with.

and payment systems were so overwhelmed that it had no idea if it was making or losing money. The company's shares fell 62 percent the day of the announcement. Oxford's problems had been invisible to Wall Street and to KPMG, its auditor—although not to doctors, who had protested for months that Oxford was not paying them. Three months later, Oxford forced out its chief executive and reported a loss for 1997 that wiped out all the profits it had ever made. From its all-time high of $89 in July 1997, Oxford fell below $10 by the end of 1998. (It has since recovered about half its losses.)

Oxford's crisis apparently resulted from incompetence rather than fraud. That was not the case at Sunbeam, the appliance maker run by "Chainsaw" Al Dunlap, who reveled in his reputation as a heartless CEO who liked firing workers.[18] In a series of disclosures that began in March 1998, Sunbeam admitted that it had inflated its sales for the quarter ending December 1997. Sunbeam said it had encouraged retailers to buy barbecue grills, not normally a big seller in cold weather, by offering steep discounts and promising not to bill them for several months. By June, Sunbeam had fired Dunlap, whom it had hired less than two years earlier, and admitted that its problems ran much deeper than one misguided promotion. Sunbeam's stock, which had reached $53 in March, fell to $15 the day the company ousted Dunlap. In November, Sunbeam restated its profits downward for the entire period that Dunlap had been its chief executive and fired its auditor, Arthur Andersen.

An S.E.C. investigation later found that Dunlap had used a grab bag of accounting tricks to inflate Sunbeam's earnings. He hid the company's operating expenses inside a big one-time "restructuring charge" and booked a profit on spare parts that the company had supposedly sold to one of its distributors. The spare parts gimmick was too much even for Andersen, which demanded that Sunbeam reverse the profits it had booked from the "sale." Sunbeam agreed to shrink its "profit" from the sale to $5 million from $8 million. At that point Andersen decided the profit from the fake sale was too small to argue about—even though it equaled 12 percent of Sunbeam's fourth-quarter profits in 1997 and was part of a larger pattern of gimmicks. Andersen's decision illustrated perfectly the level to which auditors had sunk. Andersen had permitted all sorts of accounting chicanery; then, after trying to draw a line against one particularly indefensible trick, the firm had allowed Sunbeam to use it anyway.

(The aftermath of Dunlap's reign at Sunbeam showed the damage that accounting gimmicks can cause even at healthy companies. Before Dunlap took over, Sunbeam had been a solid, if mediocre, appliance maker. But he overloaded the company with debt, and his willy-nilly job cuts ruined employee morale and product quality. It filed for bankruptcy in February 2001, and its stock now trades at 4 cents. Meanwhile, Dunlap took home tens of millions of dollars for his two years at the company, even after paying $15 million in 2002 to settle civil suits against him and $500,000 in September 2002 to settle fraud allegations by the S.E.C., without admitting wrongdoing in either case.)*

Taken together, Oxford, Sunbeam, and Cendant were serious warning signs. Accountants seemed to have lost their ability to detect even the crudest frauds.

Yet accountants insisted that they were as committed to investor protection as ever and continued to slough off scattered efforts by the S.E.C. to rein in consulting work and return their focus to accounting. The industry's arguments were always the same: No one had ever proved a connection between consulting fees and shoddy audits, and firms would never sully their reputations by compromising on

---

*In September 2002, the Justice Department opened a new criminal investigation into Sunbeam's activities during the time of Dunlap's tenure at the company. Better late than never.

their work. "The reputational capital of a firm is one of its prime assets," Barry Melancon, president of the American Institute of Certified Public Accountants, said in 1997.[19] "You have a built-in check and balance system."

Meanwhile, accountants grew even closer to their auditing clients. By 1998, consultants for Ernst & Young were working essentially as employees of software companies that the firm audited. Nearly one thousand Ernst & Young consultants installed human resources management software from Peoplesoft at big companies around the world. Other accounting firms had similar relationships.[20] In every case, the firms denied that their dual roles presented a conflict. "We very much separate the work we do in consulting and the work we do in auditing," said Philip A. Laskawy, the chairman of E&Y. "We just do not believe that this is an issue." Laskawy never explained how E&Y could be independent and objective when it might have to audit sales made by its own consultants.

By 2000, consulting provided the U.S. revenues at two of the five remaining major firms—PricewaterhouseCoopers and Deloitte & Touche—as well as 40 percent at KPMG. (The 1999 merger of Price Waterhouse and Coopers & Lybrand had turned the Big Six into the Big Five.) Traditional audit and accounting services made up only about one-third, with tax advice the remainder. Even Andersen, which had spun off its $5 billion consulting unit in August 2000 after a decade of internal warfare, received about 26 percent of its revenues from the *new* consulting unit it had created only in 1989. Powered by consulting, the firms grow huge; PricewaterhouseCoopers had U.S. revenues of $8.3 billion and worldwide revenues of $20 billion in 2000. The total worldwide revenues of the Big Five topped $55 billion, and they had thirty-two thousand partners. Two decades earlier, not one of the Big Eight had even $1 billion in revenues. Individual partners shared in the largesse. Between 1990 and 2000, Andersen raised its average per-partner salary from $200,000 to

$450,000, far ahead of the rate of inflation. Salaries were similar at the other firms in the Big Five.

———

So when Arthur Levitt, the chairman of the Securities and Exchange Commission, belatedly tried to rein in consulting, the Big Five were displeased, to put it mildly.* In 1997, dipping its toe into the consulting/accounting morass, the S.E.C. created an Independence Standards Board to study whether accountants should face stricter rules. Never mind that the issues had first been studied by the Cohen commission *more than twenty years earlier.* Making matters worse, the board had eight members: four nominated by the S.E.C. and four from the industry. Not surprisingly, the board did not exactly leap into action.

Three years later, with the board a distant memory, Levitt decided to face the Big Five head-on. In June 2000 he proposed that accountants be barred from technology consulting at companies they audited, or setting up internal audit systems at companies where they were also the external auditor, on the principle that accountants should not audit their own work.

At a nasty meeting between Levitt and KPMG, Deloitte & Touche, and Andersen, the three firms most opposed to the proposal, Andersen's chief executive told Levitt, "If you go ahead with this, it will be war."[21]

The firms meant what they said. With a presidential election coming up, they hoped to outlast Levitt, knowing he would probably resign if George W. Bush was elected. The Big Five were among the largest corporate political donors, having given $39 million in political contributions between 1989 and 2001, and they skewed their contributions heavily toward the G.O.P.[22] PricewaterhouseCoopers was the fourth-largest donor to the Bush campaign in 2000; Andersen was fifth.

---

*More on Levitt and the S.E.C. in Chapter 9.

Faced with the threat of delay, Levitt tried to rally public opinion to his side. At a speech to state accounting boards in September, he complained of "a stonewall by some of the profession's leadership to prevent truly independent oversight" and suggested that smaller firms take control of the industry. In turn, the Big Five pushed their Republican allies in Congress to slash the commission's budget—an aggressive move for private companies to take against a federal agency. W. J. "Billy" Tauzin, a Republican congressman who ran the Energy and Commerce Committee and had received $280,000 in contributions from accounting firms during the 1990s, demanded that Levitt prove that consulting damaged auditors' independence before moving ahead with his proposal. Tauzin also asked barbed questions about Levitt's personal stock holdings. "It was a shot across the bow from the industry," Levitt recalled later. "They were saying, 'If you go forward, expect a lot of pain.' "[23]

In a prescient column in July 2000, *New York Times* reporter Floyd Norris, who had covered Wall Street for a generation, warned the Big Five that they might one day regret their arrogance:

> They are very confident that the public has confidence in them, and point to high stock prices as evidence that investors trust the financial statements they certify. To the extent there is a perception that they lack independence, they blame the S.E.C. for raising the issue. You get the impression everything would be fine if Mr. Levitt would just shut up or go away. . . .
>
> They are lining up allies in Congress and preparing to go to court. They hope to delay action until a new president can appoint a new S.E.C. chairman.
>
> They may win that fight. But such a victory would be Pyrrhic. Highly publicized resistance to rules that are described as seeking to promote auditor independence will be remembered when—as will surely happen—there is another case of an audit gone awry, particularly if the auditing firm got far more

money from consulting relationships than it did for doing the audit.

The industry should seek a compromise.[24]

The industry did not. And the fight's resolution, when it came, was much to the Big Five's liking. Facing strong opposition from Congress, and unable to generate public interest in what appeared to be technical rules changes, Levitt backed off his June proposal. In November, following negotiations with the industry, he announced that except for some minor restrictions on technology consulting, the firms could continue consulting as much as they wanted as long as the fees they received were disclosed to investors in corporate proxies. "I knew it wasn't enough," Levitt would later say.[25]

The firms had won their Pyrrhic victory. Consulting fees would continue to flow. Even as the market plunged over the next eighteen months, the drawbridge for accounting chicanery would stay down, as it had throughout the boom. Only in 2002, after not one but dozens of cases of "audits gone awry," would Andersen and the rest of the Big Five pay the price for their myopia and hubris.

—

Chapter 9

ARCHAEOLOGISTS
AND DETECTIVES

Levitt's effort to take on the Big Five represented his gutsiest performance as S.E.C. chairman. He deserves kudos for his serious, if belated, attempt to rein in an out-of-control industry. But in other important ways, both Levitt and the agency he ran from 1993 until 2001 failed to live up to the motto that the S.E.C.'s third chairman, William O. Douglas, had coined: "We are the investor's advocate."

One episode more than any other sums up the strengths and weaknesses of Levitt's reign as S.E.C. chairman. On September 28, 1998, with the bull market about to begin its final, manic phase, Levitt, one year into his second term as chairman, sounded an urgent alarm over earnings gimmicks. In a speech in New York called "The Numbers Game," he said:

Increasingly, I have become concerned that the motivation to meet Wall Street earnings expectations may be overriding common sense business practices. Too many corporate managers, auditors, and analysts are participants in a game of nods and winks. In the zeal to satisfy consensus earnings estimates and project a smooth earnings path, wishful thinking may be winning the day over faithful representation. . . .

While the problem of earnings management is not new, it has swelled in a market that is unforgiving of companies that miss their estimates. I recently read of one major U.S. company that failed to meet its so-called "numbers" by one penny and lost more than six percent of its stock value in one day. . . .

This is the pattern earnings management creates: companies try to meet or beat Wall Street earnings projections in order to grow market capitalization and increase the value of stock options. Their ability to do this depends on achieving the earnings expectations of analysts. And analysts seek constant guidance from companies to frame those expectations. Auditors, who want to retain their clients, are under pressure not to stand in the way. . . .

Today, American markets enjoy the confidence of the world. How many half-truths, and how much accounting sleight-of-hand, will it take to tarnish that faith?[1]

Levitt had bluntly diagnosed the cancer that threatened the markets' integrity. Then, scalpel in hand, he marched out of the operating room. "This is a financial community problem," he said. "It can't be solved by a government mandate: It demands a financial community response."

But the S.E.C. had the duty of ensuring that response, if auditors and analysts and investment bankers failed. The agency was the last line of defense, the shotgun behind the door. If the S.E.C. believed a company's financial statements were flawed or untrue, it could demand an explanation—and halt trading in the company's stock if it found the explanation unsatisfactory. If the S.E.C. suspected fraud, it could open a civil investigation or even work with federal prosecutors on a criminal case. The S.E.C. was far from powerless. It only seemed to be.

—

From the beginning, the S.E.C.'s reach had exceeded its grasp, as Joel Seligman noted in *The Transformation of Wall Street,* his 1982 history of the commission. But the two-decade-long bull market had not merely strained the agency's resources; it had taxed them beyond the breaking point.

Between 1980 and 2000, trading volume grew thirtyfold; money raised in new initial public offerings rose from $1.4 billion to $61 billion. The mutual fund industry, also under the jurisdiction of the commission, exploded from $46 billion to $5.1 trillion. Accounting became significantly more complex. The Nasdaq stock market and other electronic networks grew into important trading venues. By 2001, the S.E.C. was responsible for "700,000 registered representatives [brokers], over 5,000 investment companies, and 7,400 registered investment advisers . . . [and] 14,000 companies that have issued securities," the General Accounting Office, the investigative arm of Congress, said in a 2002 report.[2]

Yet the commission's staff had not grown much since 1980—or 1939. That year, when 260 million shares traded on the New York Stock Exchange, the agency had seventeen hundred employees. In 2001, when 2 billion shares *a day* changed hands on the Big Board and the Nasdaq, the agency had the equivalent of 2,936 full-time workers. Making matters worse, the commission's staff had become increasingly green as the 1990s progressed. More than 30 percent of the commission's employees quit between 1998 and 2000. Among professionals, turnover was even higher. By 1999, lawyers worked at the agency for an average of only 2.5 years before quitting, down from 3.4 in 1992. One-third of the branch chiefs in the Division of Enforcement, which brought fraud cases, had been in their jobs for less than a year.[3]

It wasn't hard to figure out why the commission could not hold on to workers. Eighty-seven percent of all employees said they were dissatisfied with their pay compared to the private sector. No other issue came close. Of course, government employees had always made less money than their business counterparts, in return for better job security and shorter hours. But by the 1990s the gap between private and public salaries had become almost untenable, especially for the lawyers and accountants the commission needed to prosecute complex securities frauds. In 2000, first-year associates at major law firms in New York and Washington earned well over $100,000, more than senior S.E.C. lawyers. A third-year attorney at the agency could easily double or even triple his pay by jumping to the private sector. To cover the gap, the commission tried to use retention grants and special bonuses, but the meager size of those awards showed just how little money the agency had. In 1999, the commission's average performance bonus was $1,600, compared to the Christmas bonuses of $20,000 or more that top law firms offered their first-year associates.[4]

As the agency's employees were acutely aware, their salaries even lagged those of other government financial regulators. Bank regulators such as the Office of the Comptroller of the Currency were allowed to exceed the standard government salary scale to get qualified workers. The Federal Reserve, as a quasi-independent agency, could also set its own salaries. But the commission was stuck with the standard pay scale.

In the General Accounting Office survey, the commission's staffers sounded almost desperate: "The S.E.C. simply does not pay enough to allow a professional with a family to make ends meet in New York. I had no choice but to leave," one commented. Another said: "I love my job here. The only reason I am going to have to leave one day is because I can only forbear [postpone repayment] on my law school student loans for so long. Once I have to begin repayment, I will need more money."[5]

—

Inexperienced and understaffed, the S.E.C. found itself barely able to do its job.

Besides the Division of Enforcement, the commission's most important unit is its Division of Corporate Finance, which reviews financial statements and other corporate filings for potential problems. The division is the S.E.C.'s first line of defense, checking annual reports, prospectuses for IPOs, and proxy statements before they are released to the public. But as the number of new offerings soared from 171 in 1990 to 856 by 1996, the division spent more and more of its time reviewing prospectuses. As triage, the focus on IPOs made sense, since new companies posed the biggest risks for investors, at least in theory. But the division had almost no time to review other filings, even annual reports, the cornerstone of the disclosure laws. By the late 1990s the S.E.C. had given up hope of reviewing every company's annual reports every year. Instead, it set a goal of reviewing annual filings once every third year. What would happen the other two years was out of its hands.

The S.E.C. found itself unable to meet even that modest target. In 2001 the division reviewed only 2,280 of the 14,000 annual reports it received. In other words, more than 80 percent of all annual reports were released to investors without any review. Overall, the commission reviewed only 8,500 of the 99,000 filings it received in 2000, not quite 9 percent.[6] So much for catching aggressive accounting before it went public.

The Division of Enforcement was similarly overwhelmed. Between 1991 and 2000 the number of pending cases nearly doubled, to 2,240, while the division's staff of investigators and attorneys increased only 16 percent, to 482. Rampant turnover made the backlog worse. Turnover "has resulted in old cases not being closed or ongoing cases being delayed until other staff can take over," the S.E.C. told the General Accounting Office.[7]

Although it tried to keep up by opening more cases, the commission acknowledged to the G.A.O. that it had no hope of investigating every alleged fraud. "S.E.C. officials said that they cannot prosecute every case and, therefore, must prioritize the cases they will pursue," the G.A.O. said. Then came an astonishing admission: "According to S.E.C. officials, [the] S.E.C. generally prioritizes cases in terms of (1) the message delivered to the industry and public about the reach of [the] S.E.C.'s enforcement actions, (2) the amount of investor harm done. . . ."

In other words, the agency was so strapped for resources that it did not prosecute the largest and most important cases. It prosecuted the cases the public would *think* were the largest and most important. The agency had become the law enforcement equivalent of a Potemkin village, counting on press coverage to do for it what it could not do for itself. Unfortunately, its weaknesses were all too evident. A front-page 1999 article in *The Wall Street Journal* was headlined "Beat Cop: As Huge Changes Roil the Market, Some Ask: Where Is the SEC?" It began:

> On the eighth floor of the Securities and Exchange Commission headquarters in Washington, a group of 10 lawyers leads the government's effort to fight securities fraud on the Internet. . . . Investors may not be reassured to know, though, how primitive the S.E.C.'s armament is: One of the few technological tools it relies on is Yahoo!, the free Internet search engine.
>
> Strapped for funds, the agency hasn't been able to buy the more sophisticated software it says it needs to monitor the Web. As a result, says Michael Bartell, the S.E.C.'s chief technology officer, lawyers spend hours typing in phrases such as "risk-free returns" and "ground-floor opportunities" that might hint at fraud. . . .
>
> There are artificial-intelligence programs available that would do more in a few hours than the S.E.C. lawyers can do in weeks of such searches. But though the cost would be relatively modest—about $1 million—Congress is only just now likely to approve such funds.[8]

And Internet fraud, because of its high visibility, was one of the commission's priorities. No wonder that by the late 1990s short-sellers joked that S.E.C. investigators were archaeologists, not detectives.

———

In 1998, as a reporter for *TheStreet.com,* an online financial news service, I saw firsthand just how weak the S.E.C. had become. I was investigating Tel-Save, a Pennsylvania long-distance company whose stock had soared after it signed a deal in 1997 to sell its service through America Online. At its peak, Tel-Save was worth about $2 billion; its biggest cheerleader was a smarmy analyst at Salomon Smith Barney named Jack Grubman who would soon become the living symbol of the decline of Wall Street research.

Tel-Save's business model was flawed; it was losing hundreds of millions of dollars annually, and its accounting was extremely aggressive. Public documents and a letter from Daniel Borislow, Tel-Save's CEO, showed that Tel-Save had used another public company, Group Long Distance, to shift expenses off Tel-Save's books. (The letter also revealed that Borislow had a bit of a temper. "Shove it up your ass," he wrote the Group Long Distance shareholders who had complained about his maneuver. "You are not worthy of being in business, maybe life.")

Through the summer of 1998 the battle between Tel-Save and short-sellers intensified. In August and September, Tel-Save bought back millions of shares of its own stock. Considering that Tel-Save's losses were rising and that it needed to conserve cash, the share repurchase made no business sense. Borislow said publicly that he had begun the buyback mainly to cause a short squeeze that would force short-sellers to cover their positions and drive Tel-Save stock higher—a form of stock manipulation banned by the 1933 Securities Act.

In addition, in August someone had hired the Kroll Associates private detective agency to follow me—just after I'd written yet another negative article about Tel-Save. (This article revealed that the chief executive of a California telecom company that Tel-Save planned to buy for $600 million was a convicted cocaine dealer. Before his 1982 conviction, the CEO, Roger Abbott, drove a red Porsche with a license plate that read CRACK.)

It is still not clear who put Kroll on me. Borislow and Abbott denied any involvement, and Kroll never revealed who had hired it. But in November 1998, after *Brill's Content,* the now-defunct media magazine, wrote about the harassment, Borislow quit. The announcement sent Tel-Save's stock up 20 percent.

But Borislow laughed last. He had sold almost 20 million shares of Tel-Save stock between March 1997 and January 1999, including 10 million shares in the fall of 1998, just as Tel-Save was buying back its stock. In fact, a cynic might wonder if the buyback was engineered simply to pour Tel-Save's cash into Borislow's pockets. (Tel-Save now trades around $2 a share, down almost 95 percent from its 1998 high.)

The case should have been a natural for the S.E.C. Tel-Save had engaged in very aggressive accounting. The company had tried to manipulate its stock. Its chief executive had made hundreds of millions of dollars selling his shares while its stock plunged. And it—or someone connected to it—had probably hired a private detective agency to intimidate a reporter.

Yet the S.E.C. never took any action against Borislow and Tel-Save. In fact, as far as I can tell, the S.E.C. never even opened an investigation into the company. Borislow walked off without a scrape, moving to a $12.5 million mansion in Palm Beach (where, like O. J. Simpson, he was protected by Florida's bankruptcy laws) and spending millions of dollars on Thoroughbred horses. By December 2000 he was feeling cocky enough to brag about "the $250 million I profited on by selling my Talk.com (Tel-Save) securities. I guess that makes me somewhat more intelligent than my counterparts in telecom and Internet stocks who decided to hold their stock."[9]

It made him somewhat more intelligent than the S.E.C. as well.

—

The S.E.C.'s budget crunch did not happen overnight, or by accident.

Libertarians and conservative Republicans had never really accepted the agency's existence, even though Wall Street had. To the hard right, the commission was a relic of the New Deal that served no useful purpose. Markets could and should regulate themselves. End of story. Libertarian economists had played variations on this theme for a generation. In 1973, for example, George Benston of the University of Rochester argued that disclosure requirements were pointless. If investors demanded more information, companies would provide it or lose access to capital. Fraud was unlikely, because in the long run executives and corporations needed the trust of share-holders to survive. In fact, stock markets had actually been quite honest before the S.E.C. was created, Benston argued. "A search of the available literature . . . fails to reveal much evidence of fraud in the preparation or dissemination of financial statements prior to 1934."

The libertarian argument did not hold much weight with main-stream economists and lawyers. "Benston's suggestion that there was little securities fraud before 1934 was ludicrous," Joel Seligman wrote. "In the year 1932, the State of New York alone secured injunctions against 1,522 persons and firms and instituted 146 crimi-nal prosecutions."[10] Seligman, by no means an apologist for the com-mission, concluded his book by arguing that "although the wisdom of specific policies of the SEC reasonably could be doubted, the over-all value of the agency reasonably could not be. In reducing securities fraud and unfairness through its corporate disclosure and enforce-ment programs . . . the S.E.C. had made signal contributions to the nation's financial system."[11]

To be sure, the S.E.C. had hardly eliminated securities fraud. Until Levitt's fight in 2000 over consulting, it had ducked the systemic problems in the accounting industry. During the 1980s and 1990s the commission did not hold even one public hearing on accounting.[12]

Its record on encouraging better corporate governance, or forcing mutual funds to disclose their risks, was equally spotty. But whatever its flaws, the mere fact of the commission's existence had encouraged honesty in the markets. The S.E.C. might not catch a questionable accounting change. It might not put a fraudulent penny stock brokerage out of business. It might not discover an executive engaging in insider trading. But then again it might. Examining the agency in 1978, two Wharton professors summed up the case for the commission:

> Vast amounts of money were lost in the pre-S.E.C. period as a result of activities that have been greatly reduced by securities legislation. These amounts would appear to exceed greatly any reasonable estimate of the costs of the legislation. Stock-market pools, bucket-shop operation, misuse of insider information, and other types of manipulation and fraud, which frequently relied on the deliberate use of manipulation and the absence of full disclosure, were widespread in the pre-S.E.C. period . . . and seem less prevalent today.[13]

But conservatives did not agree. When the G.O.P. took control of Congress in 1994, it put the commission high on its list of targets. The commission "has become an expensive regulatory burden for investors as well as a significant tax on capital," New York Republican Daniel Frisa, a first-term congressman appointed by G.O.P. leaders to review the commission, said in a 1995 press release. "The S.E.C. should not put companies into a regulatory straitjacket. That hurts competition and makes companies waste money on complying with unnecessary rules."[14] The fact that the U.S. markets were the deepest and most liquid in the world seemed to have escaped Republicans, who appeared to live in a parallel universe where an all-powerful commission, just for the hell of it, frequently denied deserving companies the chance to sell stock. "It's frighteningly expensive to raise capital," Stephen Blumenthal, a lobbyist and the former Republican counsel for the House Commerce Committee, told the *Journal*.[15] That pronouncement probably came as news to the 622 companies that had gone public in 1994, raising $31 billion.

The attack on the commission was not merely rhetorical. In July 1995, House Republicans introduced legislation that would have fundamentally altered the S.E.C.'s mission. Instead of being focused on investor protection, the commission would have had to show that any new rule it imposed would benefit investors more than it would cost businesses.[16] The legislation would have tied the commission in knots. Even if the S.E.C. could prove that a new rule would have a positive effect, companies or brokerage firms would inevitably challenge the commission's methodology, preventing the regulation from taking effect for years or decades.

The proposal to change the agency's mission landed with a thud. Even Wall Street thought the S.E.C. played an important role in keeping investors confident that the market was fair. So the G.O.P. tried to starve the agency instead. In September 1995, Phil Gramm, a Republican senator from Texas, proposed cutting 20 percent of the S.E.C.'s $300 million budget, a move that would have forced the commission to lay off almost one thousand workers. Levitt fought off Gramm's proposed cuts, but the G.O.P. had made its position clear. The question was not whether the commission's budget would be increased but whether it would avoid cuts. Between 1995 and 1998 the S.E.C.'s budget did not keep pace with inflation. As late as 1999, when the strains on the commission were obvious, Republican congressman Thomas Bliley, who ran the House Commerce Committee, proposed cutting the S.E.C.'s budget by 5 percent.[17] "The SEC has grown pretty much already," Bliley told *The Wall Street Journal*. "When you look at trading volume in the markets, obviously the public has confidence in them, or they wouldn't be putting their money in the markets." Under that logic, the Federal Aviation Administration's budget should have been cut whenever a new airline started up.

Of course, President Bill Clinton could have stood up for the commission. But the S.E.C. had no natural constituency in the Democratic Party. It had no pork to dole out, and what did unions, environmentalists, or trial lawyers care about the stock market? Nor did the agency's weakness resonate with the general public. With the S&P 500 rising 20 percent a year, securities fraud was not exactly a hot-button issue in the late 1990s. Besides, the president had plenty of problems with Congress already. Why make more trouble? So the commission withered.

—

With friends like Bill Clinton and enemies like Phil Gramm, Arthur Levitt was in a bind. By 1999, Levitt was stretched as thin as the commission he ran. He was simultaneously:

- trying to protect the S.E.C.'s turf as Congress prepared to allow commercial and investment banks to merge for the first time in sixty-five years;
- hoping to cadge more money for his employees;
- prodding the New York Stock Exchange (still!) to change its rules so other exchanges could compete more fairly;
- publicly lambasting the get-rich-quick ads being run by online brokerage firms;
- monitoring the growing number of semiprofessional day traders who traded with extremely high margin.

In addition, Levitt was about to take on the accounting industry over consulting. It was not an easy job.

Still, Levitt should not entirely escape criticism for the agency's inability to stop, or even slow, the 1990s fraud epidemic. After he retired from the commission in 2001, he cultivated an image as an outsider who had stood up to the accounting industry and other

entrenched interests. And he had, to a point. But Levitt was a nego-
tiator and conciliator first and foremost. Although his personal ethics
were beyond question, he had run the American Stock Exchange, the
bane of regulators, from 1977 to 1989. In 1994, in his first major
decision at the commission, he supported the options junkies who
overturned the FASB's ruling on expensing grants. He would later
call that decision his "biggest mistake," but he never seriously tried
to overturn it.[18] Levitt even made nice to Phil Gramm, telling inter-
viewers that he liked Gramm and their shared passion for Labrador
retrievers. Perhaps Levitt felt he had no other choice, that the forces
arrayed against him were too strong and that he would never triumph in a confrontation with Congress. In any case, he never publicly laid his job on the line to win a battle, whether the issue was pay
raises for employees or consulting by auditors. Instead, he fought the
Republicans to a draw and tried, with limited success, to use the
power of his pulpit to convince accountants and Wall Street to work
for investors. He was a good chairman who loved his job; he might
have been better if he had loved it less.

Moreover, Levitt made one serious tactical error. In the late 1990s
the commission was strapped for cash, but it was not exactly broke;
it had more than one thousand lawyers and five hundred accountants
and financial analysts. Levitt and Richard Walker, the director of
enforcement, could have focused their resources on rooting out
fraud and gimmickry at the biggest companies. Some major S.E.C.-
mandated restatements or, even better, a fraud case or two might
have sent a message to the rest of the market that companies that
broke accounting rules would face more than speeches from Levitt.
Instead, as it admitted to the G.A.O., the commission was addicted
to easy publicity. The S.E.C. spent inordinate amounts of time chasing Internet scams run by college students and teenagers, cases that
cable news networks lapped up but that did not exactly strike fear
into the hearts of chief executives.

In doing so, the S.E.C. played into the hands of its critics. The losers in penny stock schemes are often only a half-step removed from their perpetrators; despite the commission's heavy breathing about innocent victims, almost nobody buys a 25-cent-per-share bulletin board stock expecting it to be legitimate. So the commission's conservative foes could argue, with some justification, that the S.E.C. was wasting its time looking for victims where none existed. Then they extended that argument to the rest of the market. In a nasty *New York Times Magazine* article in 2001, writer Michael Lewis did his best to make Levitt look like a fool for prosecuting Jonathan Lebed, a fifteen-year-old from New Jersey who had made $800,000 hyping bulletin board stocks. Lewis might best be described as an utterly cynical libertarian: The market is a game, and everybody knows it, so why should the government spoil the fun? Using the Lebed case for a broad attack on the S.E.C., Lewis argued that individual investors no longer needed the commission's protection:

> To anyone who wandered into the money culture after, say, January 1996, it would have seemed absurd to take anything said by putative financial experts at face value. There was no reason to get worked up about it. The stock market was not an abstraction whose integrity needed to be preserved for the sake of democracy. It was a game people played to make money. Who cared if anything anyone said or believed was "real"? Capitalism could now afford for money to be viewed as no different from anything else you might buy or sell.[19]

The notion that the market might actually play an important role in allocating capital to growing businesses, or that many investors—not all, to be sure, but many—trusted the accuracy of financial statements and made life-changing investment decisions based on them? *Forget that. It's all just a game.* Lewis had the luxury of cynicism, of course. He was, after all, a Princeton-educated millionaire. That a

forty-five-year-old nurse or a fifty-year-old engineer saving for retirement might actually trust the numbers put out by WorldCom or
Enron—how banal. How utterly unimaginative.

———

The S.E.C.'s weakness echoed through the justice system. Without
the commission to help them, prosecutors largely avoided fraud
cases, which are harder to explain to juries than drug or other criminal charges. A study by a Syracuse University professor found that
the S.E.C.'s enforcement division referred only 609 cases to prosecutors between 1992 and 2001, and that prosecutors decided to bring
charges in only 200 of them. The grand total of prison sentences that
resulted from *a decade* of S.E.C. referrals was 87. Overall, federal
prosecutors brought only 226 securities fraud cases in 2000, and
most of those were low-end Ponzi scheme and boiler room cases,
according to an internal Justice Department study. By 2002 only
about one thousand white-collar criminals were in federal prison,
less than 1 percent of the total federal prison population.[20]

It is impossible to know what might have happened if the S.E.C.
and Justice Department had uncovered the fraud at Enron—and
gone after its executives—in 1998 instead of 2001. Would the games
have stopped? Almost certainly not. Forces far beyond the commission's control drove the explosion of gimmickry. But maybe a few
other CEOs would have decided that honesty was the best way to
stay off the commission's radar screen. Maybe a few companies
would have stayed inside the lines.

The commission's focus on small-scale fraud had the opposite
effect. The S.E.C. seemed intimidated by large, complex cases. Executives thinking about stretching accounting rules knew that the commission was unlikely to catch them. "Though securities officials like
to brag about their enforcement records, few in America's top-floor
suites fear the local sheriff," *Fortune* wrote in a 2002 cover story.
"They know the odds of getting caught."[21]

In fact, by the late 1990s it seemed as though the S.E.C. had conceded its responsibility for stopping financial fraud to a small group of short-sellers.

—

Let me admit my bias up front: I like short-sellers. Not the thirty-one-year-old hedge fund managers who bought Internet stocks in 1999 and called themselves shorts in 2002. Those aren't short-sellers; they think shorting means playing telephone tag, trading (sometimes starting) rumors about a company that is already in trouble, calling reporters in the hope of finding out what will be in the next day's *Times* or *Journal*. They short for a day or a week, and cover as soon as the market turns higher.

Real short-sellers are very different. They have the souls of detectives, not investors. They spend their days poring over financial statements, looking for clues to fraud: numbers that don't add up, footnotes that don't make sense, mysterious changes in accounting principles. They research companies more thoroughly than most longs, since unlike longs they don't have the advantage of having their questions answered by management. They don't just talk to suppliers or competitors, they hire private detectives to scour the Belgian docks to find container ships supposedly filled with used cars. They get obsessed. In fact, sometimes they get too obsessed for their own good, falling into pitched battles with companies, forgetting that the point of the exercise is to find stocks that will go down, not to discover the truth at any cost.

Shorts look for the negative in every announcement and financial statement. Were sales up? Maybe margins were down. When they try to go long, they often fail. They are too smart, too cynical, too focused on the reasons a business won't work instead of the reasons it will. Forget Starbucks; people will never pay $4 for a cup of coffee. The clash between longs and shorts is about more than money; it is the eternal battle of hope and realism. Executives by nature are righteous optimists, certain of their own goodness. They believe their own hype. They have to. Capitalism does not reward introspection or uncertainty. Short-sellers are the little voice in the middle of the night, the voice a CEO cannot allow himself to hear: *Your numbers are crap. Your new product is way behind schedule. You're booking sales for which you'll never get paid. You're burning cash. The competition is ruinous. You don't have a chance. That $200 million you raised last year, it's gone. What now?* To executives, that voice is death, so the shorts are killers. But the shorts view themselves as nothing more than messengers; they don't cause companies to fail or succeed. They are simply telling the market hard truths it doesn't want to hear. To the shorts, hype is the real sin, especially when it comes out of the mouths of executives who are simultaneously selling their stock.

But by the late 1990s, in the face of the biggest wave of hype ever to hit the markets, the shorts were almost extinct.

Since the 1930s, when they took the rap for the crash, short-sellers have been considered disreputable, their craft little different from outright manipulation. Real Americans bought stocks; they didn't try to profit from failure. The S.E.C. imposed a rule that a stock could be shorted only as it was rising, in an effort to prevent short-sellers from ganging up on a stock and driving it to zero. Shorting did not quite disappear, but for fifty years it was confined to the fringes of Wall Street. Finally, in the 1980s, shorting enjoyed a brief renaissance. Uncertain of how long the new bull market would last, pension funds and other institutional investors tried to protect themselves by giving at least some of their assets to a new group of professional shorts.

"Both the ranks of short-sellers and the market impact of short-selling have increased in recent years," *The Wall Street Journal* reported in a front-page 1985 article, noting that short interest, the number of shares sold short and not yet bought back, had reached a record. The article, which was headlined "Market Hardball: Aggressive Methods of Some Short-Sellers Stir Critics to Cry Foul," vividly illustrated the distrust with which mainstream Wall Street still viewed short-sellers. "They specialize in sinking vulnerable stocks with barrages of bad-mouthing," the *Journal* wrote. "They use facts when available, but some of them aren't above innuendo, fabrications, and deceit to batter down a stock."[22]

The article focused on a young short-seller named James S. Chanos, only twenty-seven but already well known thanks to his accurate prediction that Baldwin-United, a piano maker turned insurance company, would collapse. "People think I have two horns and spread syphilis," said Chanos, who at the time worked for Deutsche Bank. At least two companies had hired private investigators to look for dirt on Chanos. They found nothing more damning than that he was a "yuppy." In fact, *Journal* readers would have been well served to follow the advice Chanos offered in the article. He suggested shorting Coleco, a toymaker that collapsed in 1989, and Integrated Resources, a Michael Milken–backed financial company that filed for bankruptcy in 1990.

Shortly after the article ran, Chanos left Deutsche and founded his own firm, Kynikos Associates. (The name was based on the Greek word for *cynic*.) By 1990, Chanos managed $500 million. He was not the only short-seller who was prospering. Shorting's popularity rose through the late 1980s, helped by the 1987 crash and the short bear market in the fall of 1990. By 1991 about twenty-five short-only funds controlled perhaps $3 billion in assets. Hedge fund managers such as Michael Steinhardt, who went both long and short, ran billions more. The legendary Feshbach brothers alone managed $1 billion. Short-selling appeared to be on its way to respectability at last.

But as a new bull market began in 1991, and especially after the boom accelerated in 1995, the shorts faded away. The Feshbachs lost 56 percent in 1991[23]; by the mid-1990s they had switched to the long side. Chanos dropped 40 percent in 1993, gained 46 percent in 1994, then fell 49 percent during the first nine months of 1995; his fund shrank below $200 million.[24]

Like many shorts, Chanos lost badly in the mid-1990s betting against technology stocks. The shorts simply did not understand how long or powerful the Internet boom would be. America Online was the ultimate example. Throughout 1995 and 1996 short-sellers complained that AOL had used an accounting gimmick to hide its marketing expenses and overstate its profits. In November 1996, the company essentially acknowledged that the shorts had been correct. It took a one-time charge to write off $385 million in marketing costs from its books. The charge wiped away all the profits AOL had ever earned.

But in their fury over the accounting, and the busy signals that plagued the service in 1996, the shorts were blind to the franchise that AOL was building. "We got the numbers right, but we got the business wrong—the growth in their market was so spectacular, it overrode the accounting issues," Chanos later said. Between 1996 and 1999, America Online's sales rose from $1.1 billion to $7.7 billion and its profits from $30 million to $1.2 billion. Its stock soared even faster, from $1.70 in November 1996 (adjusted for splits) to $95 in December 1999. The shorts seemed out of step with the Internet and the telecom revolution, Cassandras whose dire predictions had the misfortune of being wrong. As the market's rise accelerated from 1997 through 1999, even investors who had considered shorting in the past jumped to the long side.

By 1999 fewer than a dozen full-time short funds remained, scattered around the country in Dallas, San Francisco, Seattle, and New York. While the market's value had quadrupled since 1991, to $15 trillion, the total assets controlled by short-sellers had shrunk to $1 billion, less than a single medium-sized mutual fund. "We're an ant on the ass of an elephant compared to the other capital that's out there," one would later say.

Though few in number, the shorts were a diverse group. The largest and most successful were (and are) Kynikos and Rocker Partners, which was managed by Marc Cohodes, M. W. "Monty" Montgomery, and David Rocker. Other well-known shorts included David Tice of the Prudent Bear Fund and Bill Fleckenstein of Fleckenstein Capital. Though they traded tips and advice, and gathered once a year at a conference hosted by Chanos in Miami, they operated independently and had distinct styles.

Chanos, a buttoned-down Yale graduate, was probably the best *investor* of all the major shorts, because he never allowed himself to get too obsessed with his picks. He found companies that were overvalued and had dubious accounting, made his case to Wall Street and the media, and moved on, win or lose. On the other hand, the partners at Rocker took their battles personally and weren't afraid to publicly call executives liars or crooks. Cohodes once bet an analyst a car that a company Rocker had shorted was cooking its books. (The company *was* a fraud, although Cohodes never collected.) The shorts' preferred targets also varied: Fleckenstein focused on technology and Internet companies, while Montgomery specialized in looking at the complicated balance sheets of financial companies. Cohodes generally targeted companies whose market value was no more than $5 billion, while Chanos often took aim at very large companies. Then there were several silent shorts, West Coast investors who preferred to avoid the press but who were brilliant at unearthing fraud at smaller public companies.

In terms of the assets they controlled, the shorts were almost laughably small. But they refused to fold. In fact, as the bull market accelerated and the accounting games became more blatant, the shorts took their self-appointed mission even more seriously. If the S.E.C. and the rest of Wall Street wouldn't do their jobs, the shorts would blow the whistle for them.

And as the boom became a bust, the shorts would be vindicated.

By 2002, Chanos, Cohodes, and the rest of the gang could claim credit for unearthing many of the most important frauds, including Enron. In fact, the shorts probably discovered more bad accounting between 1995 and 2002 than the entire S.E.C. The shorts' success proves that the commission, despite the constraints imposed on it by Congress, could have done more to stop the numbers game.

Chapter 10

—

FRENZY

Sometimes history is hard to figure. What really triggered the Depression? Why couldn't Palestinians and Israelis come to terms on a peace plan in 2000 when many experts thought agreement was inevitable? How could anyone have thought that O. J. Simpson was innocent?

But sometimes history gives up its secrets without a fight. Sometimes its tipping points are so obvious that they can be recognized even as they happen. August 9, 1995, was one of those days, the moment when Wall Street began in earnest to blow a bubble that wouldn't pop for almost five years. (Yep, August again.) On August 9, 1995, Netscape Communications Corporation went public.

Netscape had created the first widely used browser software, enabling computer users to see "Web sites" on the Internet. Investors figured that as the Internet became more important, Netscape's power would inevitably grow. The company might turn Navigator into a sort of Internet-wide operating system, becoming the first real challenger to Microsoft in years. Netscape might even become the next Microsoft.

This cheery analysis ignored the fact that Netscape was only fifteen months old and had never made a profit—and that Microsoft, which had won every battle it had ever fought, was about to unveil a browser of its own. Nevertheless, driven by the three magic words, every investor who had missed the original Microsoft in 1986 resolved not to make the same mistake with Netscape.

———

Initial public offerings are as good a reason as any for Wall Street to exist. Companies get cash they can use for expansion. Investors share in the growth of young, dynamic businesses. IPOs are good for investment banks as well; securities firms typically keep seven cents out of every dollar that they raise. An offering that raises $150 million leaves your friendly neighborhood investment banker $10 million richer. But before the Netscape IPO, offerings could sometimes put investment banks in a touchy spot.

In an IPO, the bank underwriting the offering serves as a middleman between the companies that sell stock and the investors who buy it. It is supposed to set a price fair to both sides. To figure out the right price, banks check a company's price-earnings (assuming it has earnings) ratio and other valuation measures against its competitors. In the weeks leading up to the offering, they also hold "roadshows" for institutional investors to answer questions and gauge demand for the stock.

Still, setting an offering price is as much art as science.* Before the Netscape offering, banks generally tried to set IPO prices so that companies rose 8 to 10 percent on their first day of trading. Ideally, a company that sold shares to investors at $17 ended its first day around $19. In 1992, examining several IPOs that had risen 20 percent or more on their first day, the *Journal* questioned whether investment bankers were underpricing offerings. "Fast-money investment

———

*In fact, some states once banned small investors from buying offerings that were "too expensive." In 1980, for example, Massachusetts kept Apple Computer from selling shares to its residents. Apple was trading at ninety times earnings; no company trading at more than twenty times earnings could be offered in the Bay State.[1]

funds and other stock buyers seem to be getting rich at the expense of young companies entering the stock market," the newspaper wrote. Glenda Flanagan, the chief financial officer of Whole Foods, a Texas-based supermarket chain, complained that her company had "left money on the table" during the offering. Defending the process, a Credit Suisse First Boston investment banker said, "You know you've done your job when neither the issuer nor the investor is entirely happy."[2]

The Netscape offering changed that equation.

Originally, Netscape planned to sell 3.5 million shares to the public at $14 each, a price that valued the company at about $500 million. Given that Netscape had posted only $17 million in sales—sales, not profits—during the previous six months, a half-billion-dollar valuation seemed highly optimistic. But not to investors looking for the next you-know-what. Netscape's roadshows were mobbed; tech geeks who had never before bought a stock wanted to own the Navigator. One technology stock analyst said getting a session with Netscape's management before the offering "was like getting a one-on-one with God."[3]

With demand overwhelming, Netscape and Morgan Stanley, its underwriter, increased both the size and price of the offering, eventually selling 5 million shares at $28. Still, demand far outstripped supply; investors placed orders for 100 million shares, and Morgan Stanley had to decide which clients to favor with the limited number of shares it had available. "They don't get any hotter than this," the *Journal* reported the morning that Netscape opened for trading.

With so much unmet demand, it was obvious that Netscape would begin trading far above the $28 offering. After struggling for hours to set a price, the Nasdaq's market makers finally opened Netscape at $71 per share. It rose as high as $75 before settling back to end the day at $58.25. At that price the company was valued at more than $2 billion—one hundred times its trailing sales.

Compared to the IPOs that followed, the Netscape offering would seem small potatoes. But at the time the company's valuation shocked many investors. The offering "was the height of lunacy," a skeptical analyst said.[4] Even Netscape's fans couldn't really explain how the company should be valued. "You pick a price you're willing to pay, and you find a way to rationalize it," one said.[5] Over the next four months investors would rationalize higher and higher prices; by December the company's stock reached $171, six times its IPO price. Investors were no longer demanding that a young company be successful before they bought it; the mere possibility of profits now supported multibillion-dollar valuations.*

The success of its offering ended the tug-of-war between issuer and shareholder. Investors had no complaints, of course; they had doubled their money the very first day. But the company didn't mind, either. Netscape's rocketing share price made news far outside Wall Street, winning priceless publicity for the company, and Netscape didn't have to worry about the money it had left on the table. Traditionally, companies wanted to raise as much capital as possible in offerings because they had immediate needs for the cash. But Netscape, like the Internet and technology companies that went public after it, had no pressing need for capital at the time of its IPO. By the late 1990s, private technology companies could get all the cash they wanted from venture capitalists. In addition, if a company's stock stayed strong after its IPO, it—and its executives—could easily

---

*In the long run, Netscape would lose its battle with Microsoft; in 1997, its last full year as an independent company, it would lose $115 million. In November 1998, Netscape agreed to be taken over by America Online for about $82 a share, adjusted for splits; an investor who bought on the first trade after the IPO and held until the takeover earned about 15 percent over three and a third years, an annual return of barely 4 percent a year. An investor who bought at the company's December 1995 high would have lost more than half his investment. But by then investors would have turned their attention from Netscape to newer and shinier tech stocks.

raise more cash in a secondary offering a few months later. Finally, a big IPO made employees happy, since options grants were an important part of their pay. The higher the company's stock went, the more those grants were worth. Suddenly, a company with a hot offering wasn't leaving money on the table; it was printing it.

—

Within a few months of Netscape's IPO, the printing press was running full steam. With the Internet exploding in popularity, investors had an almost insatiable demand for technology and telecommunications stocks.

In 1996, 850 companies sold shares for the first time, the most ever, raising $52 billion. And the size of first-day run-ups continued to grow. Three months after Netscape went public, a software company called Secure Computing tripled on its first day of trading; in April 1996, Yahoo rose from $13 to $33. The success of one offering fed the next; if investors were willing to value Netscape at $5 billion, then Yahoo's $1 billion market capitalization made perfect sense.

As they had in the 1960s and 1920s, IPOs helped fuel the market's frenzy, feeding the myth that stocks could, and should, double or triple in a day. Not every investor could get shares of Yahoo at $13, but there were surely other stocks around ready to soar, if not in a day then in a month or year. Investors' expectations ratcheted upward; an annual gain of 20 percent for the S&P 500 hardly seemed outlandish compared to the 100 percent overnight return offered by Netscape.

At the same time, the boom stripped Wall Street research of whatever remnants of objectivity it still possessed.

After 1990, only two factors prevented analysts from totally prostituting themselves in the service of investment banking. The first was professional pride, always a thin reed. The second was that an analyst who recommended too many losing stocks could lose the respect of institutional investors. They might punish his firm by sending trades to other banks or, worse, by refusing to buy its stock and bond offerings.* Securities firms made more money from investment banking than commissions, but they still needed big investors to buy stock to make the system work. With the IPO boom, the easiest way for institutional investors to make money was by getting shares in hot offerings. What happened to the offerings in the long run made little difference; big investors often sold most of their IPO shares in the first few days after a company opened for trading. The old quid pro quo of good research for commissions had turned into a new quid pro quo: hot IPOs for commissions. Institutional investors no longer even pretended to care about research.

So analysts' most important job became traveling with investment bankers to "bake-offs"—the contests that companies held to pick underwriters—and begging that their firms be chosen. Instead of rating companies, analysts were being rated by them.

Even if they had been free to write objective reports, analysts hardly had time to put them together, between bake-offs and trading tips with brokers and institutional investors. "There is an inverse relationship between career success and the time spent on fundamental research," Michelle Clayman, a onetime Salomon Brothers analyst who had become a hedge fund manager, said in 1996.[6]

By the late 1990s the pressures on analysts had become so serious that almost no one who understood Wall Street took research seriously. Big investors judged analysts mainly by their ability to offer trading tips and provide access to a company's management. "Research analysts have become either touts for their firm's corporate finance departments or the distribution system for the party line of the companies they follow," Stefan D. Abrams, chief investment

---

*To be sure, before the late 1990s big funds might not have cared about improving sell-side research (see Chapter 6), but that didn't mean they wanted to pay for research that was patently useless.

officer at the Trust Company of the West, said in 2000. "Not only are they not doing the research, they have totally lost track of equity values."[7]

Some sophisticated individual investors also realized how badly analysts had been compromised. But others still trusted and depended on sell-side research. The Internet had made financial information more widely available, but average investors still didn't have the expertise to build detailed earnings models—or figure out the impact of accounting changes on a company's quarterly profits. And sell-side reports certainly *looked* respectable, with spreadsheets projecting sales and earnings out to eternity and explanations of a company's "discounted cash flow" and "net present value." At the same time, the continuing growth in business news made analysts even more visible to investors. They appeared on CNBC, the business news channel, and in newspapers or financial magazines like *Red Herring*, in articles that gave only the faintest nod, if any, to the pressures that analysts faced to write positive reports. And reporters didn't hold analysts accountable for making bad recommendations. An analyst could make a bad pick on CNBC one month and return the next, his mistake forgotten, free to pump his firm's newest hot offering.

With so much pressure to be bullish, analysts became ludicrously positive as the decade progressed. By 1999 about two-thirds of all analysts' recommendations were buys or strong buys. Nearly all of the rest were holds, which sometime during the decade had become Wall Street's euphemism for sell. Less than 1 percent were outright sell recommendations.

———

Not that convincing investors to buy was difficult.

The IPO boom was only the most visible manifestation of the market's giddiness. With the economy and corporate profits soaring and inflation under control, the Standard & Poor's 500 index rose

34 percent in 1995, its biggest gain in four decades. The Nasdaq composite index soared 40 percent. A new world was unfolding, and anyone who picked the right companies would prosper. Microsoft had begat Cisco, and Cisco had begat America Online. *Everybody ought to be rich.*

In 1996, with profits rising 14 percent, the S&P 500 rose 20 percent; the Nasdaq gained 23 percent. The total two-year gain was the biggest in four decades. Some market watchers, including the most powerful of all, wondered whether the rally had gone too far. On December 5, 1996, at a speech in Washington, Alan Greenspan, the chairman of the Federal Reserve, asked, "How do we know when irrational exuberance has unduly escalated asset values? . . . And how do we factor that assessment into monetary policy?" Translation: *Are we in a bubble? And if I think we are, should I raise interest rates to pop it even if that means putting the economy in recession?*

Investors paid attention to Greenspan's comments . . . for about two hours. In trading the next morning, the Dow Jones industrial average fell more than 2 percent. But stocks quickly rallied, ending the day down less than 1 percent. Even the head of the Fed couldn't dent Wall Street's optimism. Since the beginning of the bull market in 1982, stocks had had their best fifteen years in history. But instead of asking themselves if equities were fully valued, investors became even more bullish. In a poll in 1996, 90 percent of mutual fund shareholders said they thought that prices would rise as quickly or more quickly between 1996 and 2006 as they had over the previous decade.[8] At that rate the Dow Jones average would top 20,000 by 2006. "Investor expectations, it would appear, are high," Floyd Norris wrote dryly in the *Times* at the beginning of 1997.

High, but not high enough, for 1997 was another spectacular year. The U.S. economy expanded 4.4 percent while inflation dropped to 1.7 percent, a combination not seen since the 1950s. The federal budget deficit shrank to its lowest level since 1972. And stocks responded. The S&P 500 gained 31 percent, ending within a few points of the 1,000 mark. The Dow rose 23 percent, the first time ever that the index had gained more than 20 percent three years in a row.

By the end of 1997, stocks were extremely expensive by any measure. The price-earnings rates of the S&P 500 topped 24, the highest P/E in at least sixty years, and its dividend yield fell below 2 percent, the lowest ever. And more investors were buying with borrowed money. Margin loans had doubled, from $61 billion in 1994 to $126 billion in 1997, the highest level ever.[9] As it had in the 1920s, the increased use of margin added to the market's upward momentum and the risk of a sudden downward break. "Stock Market 'Best Since 1928,' Say Investors," *The Onion,* a satirical weekly newspaper, joked in July 1997.

But with the economy apparently in perfect shape, few serious analysts were willing to call the market overvalued. Most of those who did, like Barton Biggs of Morgan Stanley, had been bearish, and wrong, for years. Bulls branded the skeptics as irrelevant "permabears" who didn't understand the revolutionary effects of the Internet. The market's heroes were optimistic strategists like Abby Joseph Cohen of Goldman, Sachs, who had been bullish since the rally began and argued that stocks still had room to run. Even Greenspan appeared to have put aside his doubts. No further complaints about irrational exuberance came from the mouth of the Fed chairman, and the Fed kept short-term interest rates relatively low, allowing the rally to roar along.

———

While Wall Street fell in love with the Internet, the Internet fell in love with Wall Street. A new industry of online brokerages sprang up, making it easy and cheap for investors to trade stocks via their computers. Commissions, which had been falling for two decades, plunged further. Between early 1996 and late 1997, the average on-line commission fell from $53 to $16.[10] By 1998 some online brokers were offering $8 commissions. With commissions so low, more than 3 million investors opened online accounts by the end of 1997, and the words "day trading" entered Wall Street's lexicon.

Day traders tried to do what professional traders at firms like Goldman, Sachs had always done: profit from the market's intra-day moves and sell out their positions by day's end. Falling commissions made day trading possible; an investor hoping to make $100 on a 1-point move in Cisco can't afford to pay $50 to buy it and $50 more to sell. He can, at least in theory, pay $8.

With the market rising, day trading seemed to many small investors like an easy way to make a little—or a lot—of extra money. The industry's growth was abetted by hyperactive market commentators like James J. Cramer, a hedge fund manager who had founded TheStreet.com, an online financial news service, in 1996. (I worked at TheStreet.com between 1996 and 1999 and have occasionally appeared on a CNBC television show hosted by Cramer and Lawrence Kudlow. I like Cramer personally and think he is extremely smart, but there's no escaping the fact that he was caught in the late 1990s mania and gave small investors reams of bad advice.) Cramer and other gurus promised individual investors that with quick thinking, low commissions, and fast Internet connections, they could compete with Wall Street's professionals.

This counsel was at best misleading and at worst outright dangerous. True, the information gap between professional traders and amateurs had closed dramatically between the 1960s and the 1990s. But the big trading desks still had an edge. They heard about downgrades *before* they became official instead of on CNBC. In addition, they could see the orders that small investors had placed and position themselves against those orders, selling when buying pressure was strongest and buying when it lightened. An individual trader, especially one trading from home without real-time information about the bids and offers posted by the Nasdaq's market makers, could hardly hope to compete.

But with stocks soaring, many amateur investors decided to try. For the first time since the 1920s, Americans quit their jobs en masse to seek their fortunes trading stocks. "Many of those now crowding Wall Street have burned their bridges . . . [and] look forward to lives of leisure and affluence spent at this easy and entertaining game," John Brooks had written in *Once in Golconda.* Now a new generation of investors, far too young to remember the crash of the 1920s or even the bear market of the 1970s, joined the game. This time they didn't even need to go to Wall Street to play. The market came to them, to trading rooms in Miami and Atlanta and Dallas where sallow-faced men sat in front of brightly lit computer screens, surveying charts and graphs, trying to divine the intentions of the big boys and get in front. Was Goldman buying Cisco? Then they would, too, hoping to ride the stock higher for a point or two before getting out. Hundreds of thousands more investors played the game part-time in basement offices or converted dens at home.

The growth of online trading, and especially of day trading, fed the market's madness. As anyone who has ever bought or sold stock over the Internet knows, trading online is almost addictively easy. With a couple of keystrokes and a couple of mouse clicks, you too can become the proud owner of 500 shares of Sun Microsystems. And if you change your mind, you can reverse field with just a few more clicks. There's no pesky broker to offer advice or warn you that trying to compete with professional traders is a mistake.

Day trading, in fact, has more than a little in common with video poker, the most addictive form of gambling. It is screen-based, interactive, and promises immediate rewards. It pulls its users into a realm of fantasy unconnected to the outside world. "To say it is a superficial life exaggerates its depth," Gregory Millman wrote in *The*

Day Traders, a 1999 book that was half how-to guide, half twelve-step pamphlet.[11] In a *New York Times Magazine* article in November 1999, the author Matthew Klam profiled a day trader named Dave Goehl, who traded stocks in his Washington, D.C., apartment with a shelf full of books like *The Complete Idiot's Guide to Making Money on Wall Street.* "Since the beginning of time there have probably been ways that you could take your money and make it into a lot more money without having to work very hard," Goehl told Klam. "Day trading is like that. Except it's on steroids."

Still, Klam complained that he didn't understand the appeal of day trading. Then, with Goehl's encouragement, he made his first trade, buying 100 shares of Drugstore.com—an Internet company that had just gone public—at 52. He watched breathlessly as it rose to 56 and fell back to 53 in a matter of minutes, sold out for a $100 profit, and wrote:

> I was wrong about day trading. . . .
>
> It's not boring. I now understand what Dave means when he says it's the ultimate. Gambling with big money is fun; just imagine leveraging everything you own. Add this to the arsenal of American addictions. Of course I want to go another round. . . . I hate to admit it, but over the next week, I think very seriously about taking money out of my savings account and following a few of Dave's tips.[12]

Of course, not every online investor was a day trader, and not every day trader a plunger gambling with borrowed money. But the explosion in trading was another ominous sign that Wall Street was sliding into a speculative frenzy. Following dozens of companies, placing scores of orders each day, day traders could hardly consider the fundamentals of the stocks they bought. They didn't care about price-earnings ratios or dividend yields or interest rates. They focused on technical analysis: a stock's fifty-day and two-hundred-day moving average, its "trend line," prices that signified "support" or "resistance." To the extent they were aware of fundamentals at all, day traders paid attention to just one number: earnings per share, because Microsoft and Cisco and Dell had proven that investors could never pay too much for a stock with rising earnings.

—

In offices in Boston and New York and San Francisco, mutual fund managers were reaching a similar conclusion.

Money gushed into mutual funds in the 1990s, driven by the rise of 401(k) plans and small investors' search for diversification. In 1990, investors bought $12 billion in stock funds. Five years later the funds received $124 billion in new cash. And in 2000, investors put $310 billion into funds, more than $1,000 for every person in the United States.[13] Overall, stock funds grew from $240 billion in 1990 to $4 trillion in 2000. More than 50 million households, 90 million individual shareholders, owned funds, and funds owned almost one-quarter of all U.S. stocks.

But this flood of money didn't lessen the pressure on mutual fund managers. To the contrary: The industry grew more competitive than ever as thousands of new funds opened during the decade. And with the market rising, as it had been during the previous Age of Performance in the 1960s, investors didn't care about safety. They wanted upside.

The downfall of Jeffrey Vinik illustrated what happened to mutual fund managers who didn't perform. In 1992, Fidelity Investments, the giant mutual fund company, picked Vinik, who had a stellar record at its Growth and Income fund, to run its Magellan fund, the largest and highest-profile mutual fund in the world. (The previous manager, boy genius Morris Smith, had tired of the pressure after two years and retired at thirty-four to move to Israel. Smith said he'd had a spiritual reawakening while grocery shopping.) For three years Vinik out-gained the S&P; in 1995, thanks to a successful bet on technology stocks, Magellan rose 37 percent, in line with the index and better than the average stock fund. But in late 1995, Vinik decided that stocks, especially tech stocks, were too expensive. He blew out his technology holdings and loaded up on bonds. As stocks rose in 1996, Magellan began to lag. By May the S&P 500 had risen 10 percent for the year; Magellan was up only 4 percent. And on May 23, Fidelity announced that Vinik had resigned to start a hedge fund. His replacement would be Robert Stansky, whose Growth Company fund had risen 13 percent for the year and whose biggest holdings were blue-chip growth stocks like General Electric. Fund managers had been taught a lesson: If Vinik could be pushed out after few bad months, no one was safe.*

Vinik's departure also spelled the death of any attempt by fund managers to judge whether the overall market was fairly priced. Before the 1990s, fund managers routinely held cash if they couldn't find stocks they liked or if they felt the market as a whole was too expensive. In 1990 the average fund held about 12 percent of its assets in cash.[14] But the market's mid-1990s rise meant managers who held a big cash position were almost certain to trail the S&P 500, the benchmark index for most funds.† In addition, to hold cash as stocks were rising was to be not just wrong but very publicly out of sync with the market, as Vinik had learned. So fund managers adopted the mantra that they were not "market timers." Their shareholders had

---

*Magellan's subpar returns were not the only reason Fidelity was disenchanted with Vinik; six months earlier he had publicly touted the merits of a couple of the technology companies in his portfolio as he was selling them. But Magellan's weak performance unquestionably played a part in Vinik's downfall.

†The more the S&P gains, the wider the gap between its returns and cash, and the better a fund's stock picks have to do to keep the fund's overall returns even with the index. For example, if the S&P 500 rises 10 percent in a year and Treasury bills pay 3 percent, a manager who holds 80 percent of his assets in stocks and 20 percent in cash had to pick stocks that rose 11.75 percent to produce a 10 percent return on his overall portfolio and match the S&P. If the S&P rises 20 percent, the manager needs a 24.25 percent return on his stock picks just to match the S&P.

paid them to be fully invested—in stocks, not bonds or pork bellies. Fully invested they would be.

"If someone buys a stock fund, what they want is a stock fund, not something that's making a market-timing call and owning cash instead of stocks," the chief investment officer of Putnam Investments in Boston said in 1998.[15] By the end of 1997 the average stock fund had cut its cash position to 6 percent. The idea that professional managers should stay out of the market if they couldn't find reasonably priced stocks had disappeared.

Instead, the industry focused more than ever on the short-term performance that made for gaudy ad copy and won stories in personal finance magazines. Fund managers had always been aware how they stood relative to their benchmark indexes, but by the mid-1990s their focus on immediate gratification verged on the ridiculous. In 1996, Michael DiCarlo, the manager of the $2 billion John Hancock Special Equity fund, would be profiled in *The New York Times Magazine* checking the Nasdaq "two or three times an hour." At 10:00 A.M., when the markets had been open for thirty minutes, DiCarlo would tell his co-manager, "We're up sixteen basis points and the world is down sixteen basis points." A basis point is one-one-hundredth of a percentage point. The manager of an important mutual fund was celebrating—or at least noting—the fact that his fund had outperformed the market by one-third of a percentage point *for half an hour.*[16]

In the long run, the most certain way to beat the indexes is to find cheap stocks and wait for the market to see their value. But in the short run, the way to beat the indexes is to buy what's rising and hope it keeps going up. Besides, Wall Street had a natural bias toward technology stocks. Mutual fund managers were young, smart, and rich, classic early adopters of technology. They had no objection to paying premium prices for the fastest computers and Internet connections; why would anyone else?

And so, as they had in the 1960s and the 1920s, professional managers piled into the stocks that were rising, especially technology companies and "mega-cap" stocks like General Electric that seemed able to deliver consistent earnings growth. Historically, value stocks had slightly outperformed growth stocks. But beginning in 1997, growth beat value by increasingly large margins.[17]

"The investment process consisted merely of finding prominent companies with a rising trend of earnings, and then buying their shares regardless of price. Hence the sound policy was to buy only what everyone else was buying," Ben Graham had written of investment trusts in 1934. Not much had changed. Looking back on the 1990s from 2002, one fund manager would write that "what has taken the place of detailed fundamental analysis over the years is the wholesale adoption of earnings per share as the sole basis for securities analysis."[18]

—

And so the number became Wall Street's unblinking focus, bringing with it the strange quarterly ritual of "earnings season."

Under S.E.C. rules, public companies had forty-five days after the end of their quarters to file 10-Qs (quarterly financial reports) and ninety days after the end of their fiscal years to file 10-Ks (annual reports).* Companies generally announced their profits within a month after their quarters ended even if they had not yet filed their Qs and Ks.† January, April, July, and October became Wall Street's most anxious months as analysts and investors tracked thousands of

*In 2002, the S.E.C. tightened the rules. By 2006, companies will be required to file their 10-Ks no later than sixty days after the end of their fiscal year, and 10-Qs within thirty-five days of the end of a quarter.

†Shareholders should be wary of any company that routinely scrapes against the S.E.C.'s deadlines for filing reports, especially if it has announced its earnings months earlier. Companies may file slowly in the hope of burying a telltale footnote or balance sheet item—or if they're fighting their auditors for every penny of earnings. A company that requests an extension is probably in serious trouble. Since the S.E.C. or Nasdaq often suspends trading in the stocks of companies that didn't file on time, companies generally ask for extra time only if their books are in serious disarray.

earnings reports, any of which could cause a company's stock to soar or plunge, and perhaps even roil the broader market.

About ten days into each of the four months, earnings season began. Companies lined up to announce their quarterly sales and profits on press releases delivered over PR Newswire. Some reports offered a full gamut of financial information, including balance sheets and detailed sales breakdowns. Others presented little more than a bare-bones income statement; investors who wanted more data had to wait for S.E.C. filings. The reports came in no particular order, though some technology companies prided themselves on reporting especially quickly, to show Wall Street that they could close their books almost immediately. Industries tended to report in clumps so that analysts could quickly compare the results from different companies.

To keep trading smooth, the reports were usually released before 9:30 A.M. or after 4:00 P.M. Eastern time, after the Nasdaq and the Big Board had closed. But after the markets had shut, investors could trade directly with each other over electronic networks in "after-hours" sessions. Even a slight head start on the data could prove profitable, so Dow Jones and other financial wires raced to pull the most valuable information from the releases and flash it to traders' terminals. The anchors at CNBC did the same on air. The most precious nugget of all, of course, was earnings per share: How did it compare to the previous quarter and the previous year? What about the consensus?

After putting out their releases, companies hosted conference calls to discuss their results and their outlook for the future. Before the mid-1990s, the calls had been confined mainly to analysts and a few institutional investors, but in the face of complaints that they were discriminating against small shareholders, many companies opened their calls, first to the press, and then via Webcasts to the public. The world now had the chance to hear analysts sucking up to the company managements. *Great quarter, guys! You really hit the ball out of the park!* Occasionally, short-sellers were able to sneak in a tough question—*we hear your lab tests show that the X2000 has a little, uh, flammability problem; can you talk about that?*—but most companies carefully managed their calls, favoring friendly analysts and giving shorts little time to ask questions.

Although companies could control their calls, they couldn't control investors' reaction to their earnings, which grew more violent as the 1990s progressed. It is impossible to pinpoint exactly when the market became obsessed with the number. Late 1996, when CNBC and day trading and the Internet reached critical mass, seems to have been the turning point. After tripling between 1989 and 1994, the number of articles in the *Journal* that used the words "consensus" and "estimates" and "earnings" rose nearly tenfold from 1994 to 1999, from fewer than one hundred articles to almost one thousand.

Further proof of the number's increasing importance came from a University of Arizona study that showed that between 1992 and 1995, companies whose earnings were 2 cents behind the consensus fell an average of 1 percent in the three days around their earnings releases. But over the next three years the market's reaction doubled, according to the study. A company that fell 2 cents short lost an average of 2 percent of its value.[19] And those averages masked enormous swings at technology companies, which routinely moved 5 percent or more after earnings releases. The market's focus on the consensus bordered on the nonsensical. In May 1996, for example, Hewlett-Packard reported that its earnings for its April quarter had risen from $1.10 a share in 1995 to $1.37 a share in 1996. Revenue had soared by one-third. It was by any standard a blowout quarter, but H-P's stock promptly dropped 8 percent; the consensus had been $1.45, and H-P was 8 pennies short.[20]

By 1996, Wall Street's fixation on the number no longer stopped with the published consensus forecast. Analysts rarely changed their written forecasts after a quarter had ended, even when they had reason to believe—sometimes thanks to a tip from a friendly CEO—that a company had beaten their estimates. Instead, they told their biggest clients what to expect, giving institutional investors a chance to buy before the rest of the world heard the good news. Inevitably, the rumors made their way to the broader market. CNBC began to report on "whisper numbers," the unpublished earnings forecasts. Whispers were sometimes taken more seriously than the published forecast. In January 1997, for example, Intel reported earnings of $2.13 a share for its December quarter, far ahead of the First Call estimate of $1.84 a share. But Intel fell $5.13, or 3.5 percent, the day after the announcement. As good as Intel's earnings were, they didn't match its whisper number of $2.20. Recounting the incident, *The Wall Street Journal* warned investors to "take those official earnings estimates with a grain of salt, and listen for the whisper. In a market obsessed with the earnings momentum of technology stocks, many traders and analysts are ignoring published earnings estimates and trading stocks based on whether they meet or beat the 'whisper' earnings."[21]

The whisper number was yet another sign, not that any was needed, that Wall Street's obsession with quarterly earnings had gone too far. A published earnings forecast, however shoddy, at least bears some relationship to a company's real business. It predicts sales, margins, and expenses. But a whisper number is a figure plucked seemingly out of thin air, unconnected to reality and unsupported by analysis. Was Intel going to make $2.20 a share instead of $1.84 because its margins had improved or because it had shipped more chips? In relying on whispers, investors were saying implicitly, and not so implicitly, that the answer wasn't important. All that mattered was that Intel make $2.20 a share, no matter what.

—

By 1998, in the wake of the debacles at Sunbeam, Cendant, and Oxford Health, a small but persistent chorus of critics had begun to warn that the pressure to meet earnings estimates was causing more companies to resort to accounting gimmickry. The loudest protests, of course, came from short-sellers, but independent experts such as Jack Ciesielski, the publisher of the *Analyst's Accounting Observer* newsletter, also had concerns. In an August 1998 piece in *Barron's,* the financial weekly newspaper, Ciesielski wrote:

> Expectations have been set in the market—with generous assistance from companies—and managements scramble to meet those expectations. Sometimes delivery of goods or services is accelerated or decelerated, depending on what's needed to "make the numbers." They don't teach "earnings management" in business school, but every manager quickly learns how to do it. Managers also learn that, however controversial the practice, it's usually defensible—merely planning to achieve stated goals. Such a lesson, however, sets a bad precedent, for there's a far worse kind of earnings management that's often tolerated as well. This is the kind of earnings management produced by the deliberate tweaking of accounting assumptions, or the penning of a misleading journal entry.[22]

The worries weren't confined to professional cynics like Ciesielski and the shorts. Arthur Levitt's "Numbers Game" speech in September revealed the S.E.C.'s nervousness about the state of financial reporting. Even some corporate executives and accountants admitted that standards were slipping. "The penalties for missing your earnings are intense," T. J. Rodgers, the CEO of Cypress Semiconductor Corp., said in October. "If you miss one or two quarters, you can see your net worth and market cap cut in half. It's harder to retain people if their stock options aren't worth anything. Lots of CEOs have succumbed to that pressure."[23] A few months earlier, J. Terry Strange, the head of auditing at KPMG, had said, "There's probably more pressure to achieve results than at any time that I've seen."[24]

But during the next few months, the drumbeat faded, in part because of the media's lack of interest in accounting issues. Given the choice, most business reporters would prefer to write about anything but accounting. Financial gimmickry can be difficult to explain, and companies almost always counterattack when they're accused of misleading their investors. Most reporters quickly decide that their time would be better spent elsewhere. And despite Levitt's speech, the S.E.C. did not come up with cases that galvanized the press to make fraud a priority.

There were exceptions. My old employer, TheStreet.com, ran more than a dozen articles about accounting gimmickry in a September 1998 series called "Cracking the Books." We looked at in-process research and development write-offs, at whether options should be expensed, at companies that repeatedly took "one-time" restructuring charges. In the introduction to the series, Jesse Eisinger, a TSC reporter who now works for the *Journal,* wrote prophetically:

> More than any single detail of any of our stories, what we hope you'll take from this series is the understanding that accounting is no idle academic exercise. Accounting counts, figuratively as well as literally. Without the real numbers, there's no way to determine if a brilliant-sounding business plan is gold—or just gold-plated. And without true accounting, there are no real numbers.[25]

But TheStreet.com was read mainly by a small coterie of professional investors and day traders; we lacked the reach to matter. The series came and went without much trace. Even if the *Journal* had managed a similar effort—and it didn't—its effect probably would have been limited. Without proof of a systemic crisis, Wall Street simply refused to believe that accountants and the S.E.C. would let companies manufacture profits out of thin air. Sure, companies might fudge around the edges, but their numbers were basically accurate. The market's steady rise only reinforced that attitude. "It takes two to create a deception—deceiver and deceived," *Forbes* wrote in March 1998. "Plenty of the latter are around these days. Fifteen years of nearly unbroken bull markets have made people willing [and] eager to believe in financial miracles."[26]

—

By the summer of 1998, investors had plenty of miracles to believe in. The S&P 500 was trading at 1,150, more than twenty-five times earnings. The Nasdaq had broken 2,000; it was up more than 25 percent for the year. The market's speculative fires were burning hotter than they had since the 1920s. And then the fire chief showed up— with a blowtorch, a bucket of gasoline, and a cigarette dangling from his lips.

The collapse of Long-Term Capital Management has mostly been forgotten, but in September 1998, LTCM's pains made front-page news. Long-Term Capital, a huge hedge fund, had made an enormous bet that interest rates around the world were likely to converge. Long-Term Capital had been wrong. A debt crisis in Russia caused investors to pull their money out of dangerous Third World economies and into well-regulated (*heh-heh*) markets in the United States and Europe. Long-Term Capital, which had borrowed $120 billion on an equity base of $5 billion, couldn't handle the swing. It lost hundreds of millions of dollars a day. By the middle of September it was effectively broke. And Wall Street suddenly got very nervous. The worldwide debt market simply could not absorb all of LTCM's bonds at once; a forced sale of its assets might push its lenders, including some big investment banks, to the brink of insolvency. The risk of a systemic crisis in the banking system appeared higher than it had been since the crash of 1987. Through September, stocks and bonds plunged.

So Alan Greenspan and the Federal Reserve did two things. One was smart; the other would prove in retrospect to be very, very stupid. First, the Fed organized a rescue of Long-Term Capital. The Fed's action has been called a bailout, but it wasn't; no public money was involved. Instead, on September 23, William McDonough, the president of the New York branch of the Fed, persuaded a consortium of banks to put up $4 billion in new capital and take over the fund. The new money bought the traders at LTCM the breathing room they needed to sell the fund's bonds slowly, effectively ending the risk that problems at Long-Term Capital would set off a wider crisis.

But Wall Street didn't immediately recognize that the crunch was over. Although economic indicators, such as unemployment claims, showed that the U.S. economy was fundamentally healthy, stocks and bonds kept falling. The "spreads" between the interest rates paid by risky borrowers and those paid by blue-chip companies widened, a sign that the bond market feared more turmoil. Instead of waiting for the markets to settle, Greenspan panicked. On September 29, the Fed cut short-term interest rates by a quarter percentage point. Then, to show he was serious about supporting the markets, Greenspan pushed through a second, surprise rate cut on October 15, a week after stocks had already bottomed and begun to recover.

Greenspan's medicine was only too effective. The Dow Jones industrial average rose 330 points after the Fed announced the surprise cut, the third-highest point gain ever. By the end of October, the markets had risen more than 20 percent from their lows earlier in the month. By late November, stocks set new highs, and the IPO frenzy reached new heights.

The run-up continued until the year's closing bell on December 31. The Nasdaq closed 1998 at an all-time high of 2,192, up 40 percent for the year. Many technology stocks had far bigger gains: Amazon.com rose tenfold. The S&P 500 gained 27 percent. The Dow jumped 16 percent to finish the year at 9,181. Suddenly the bulls' outlandish predictions of "10 in 2"—that the Dow would reach the glorious 10,000 mark by the year 2000—didn't seem so outlandish after all. Alan Greenspan had once again waved his magic wand and saved Wall Street.

And that was precisely the problem. By the end of 1998, investors believed more than ever that they could buy stocks without risk, that Greenspan would never let markets fall for too long. Another "dip" had turned out to be yet another painless three-month bear market, another buying opportunity. Greenspan would have been wiser to let credit stay tight and recognize that growth needed to slow to take the froth off the markets. With the United States expanding at better than 4 percent, he had plenty of room to let the economy slow without falling into recession. William McChesney Martin, a former chairman of the Federal Reserve, once said his job was to "take away the punchbowl just when the party really gets going." In the fall of 1998, Greenspan had the perfect opportunity to do just that. Instead, he found the vodka and started pouring.

To be sure, this critique has all the benefits of hindsight. In September and October, Greenspan was under intense pressure to cut rates. Alan Blinder, a former Fed vice-chairman, proclaimed in mid-October that "we're in the midst of a financial panic worldwide." But Alan Blinder wasn't running the Fed.[27] Alan Greenspan, the most respected chairman of the Federal Reserve in history, was. *A financial panic?* If there were bank runs or big corporate bankruptcies anywhere in Japan or Europe or the United States, they somehow went unreported. Credit spreads widened; money-losing companies had trouble getting funded. That's no panic; that's the beginning of the end of a bubble. On September 25, during the worst of the "panic," the Internet auction site eBay went public, and its shares more than doubled on their first day of trading. Hot IPOs are not usually a sign of a financial meltdown.

Even at the time, some observers warned that the Fed might be feeding a bubble. In a November 24 opinion piece in the *Journal* called "Market's Silver Lining Hides Some Clouds," *Journal* deputy editor George Melloan wrote:

> From Wall Street's point of view, Mr. Greenspan looks like a bloomin' genius.
>
> But what about an economy . . . where corporate profits are losing steam even though credit-financed consumption is running flat out; where economists are revising their economic growth forecasts downward? . . . Is there anything anomalous about a stock market heading toward a 10,000 Dow when such conditions exist in the real world?
>
> If Wall Street is chasing a chimera, it wouldn't be the first time. And if bubbling stock prices are being financed with the Fed's magic money, it wouldn't be the first time for that either.[28]

Had Greenspan let the economy and Wall Street slow in 1998, the 1990s might have been a replay of the 1960s, a medium-sized bubble followed by an unpleasant but not awful bear market. (After the end of the 1960s bull market, stocks didn't really go into a tailspin until 1973, and then mainly as a result of the oil shock, not because of problems intrinsic to Wall Street.) Instead, thanks at least in part to the Fed's too-quick rate cuts, the greatest wave of speculation in history swamped the market.

———

1999 was at once inevitable and impossible. It was by any standard the biggest bubble ever—the South Sea Bubble and 1929 and the Gold Rush in one. Even in retrospect, the market's insanity defies belief.

The Nasdaq soared 86 percent, the biggest ever one-year gain for a major market index. The S&P 500 rose 20 percent; the Dow jumped 25 percent, breaking not just 10,000 but 11,000. A book called *Dow*

36,000 came out and was taken seriously. It was a Wile E. Coyote market: *Just don't look down and everything will be fine.* CNBC played in bars and airports and restaurants. In the fall, for the first time, its ratings surpassed those of CNN.[29] The market's moves seemed to dominate every conversation, and not just in New York. In early 2000, the *Journal* traveled to a Cape Cod barbershop and found:

> Neither sports nor politics—even in this election year—are the topics of choice at Bill's Barber Shop. Just about any time of day, stocks are the subject. . . . And not just any stocks, but in particular, tech stocks. . . .
>
> Most of the people who gather at Bill's hold jobs in the old economy, but none are buying blue-chip industrial stocks. "You get three or four times in your life to make serious bucks," says Ron Danforth, owner of a local direct-mail business and a regular at Bill's Barber Shop. "If you miss this one, you're crazy."[30]

The barber, William Flynn, had turned $100,000 into $600,000 by loading up on technology and biotechnology stocks, especially EMC, a Massachusetts data storage company that had risen from $7 to $130 in three years. He confidently expected EMC—which made up about half of his portfolio—would triple again by 2003, giving him enough money to retire. "Somebody else can cut hair then," he said. Flynn was not alone in his hopes. Almost 80 million individual Americans owned stocks or mutual funds, up from 50 million a decade earlier. Nearly 10 million investors had online trading accounts, and online traders made more than a million trades a day.[31]

The madness worsened as the millennium neared. On December 29, Walter Piecky, an analyst for PaineWebber (now UBS Warburg) earned his place in history by projecting that Qualcomm, then trading at about $500 a share, would double to $1,000. At that price, Qualcomm, a cell phone equipment company with $4 billion in sales and $300 million in profits, would have had a market value of about $175 billion. Piecky's absurd price target marked a fitting end to a decade when sell-side research went from merely bad to flat-out deceptive.

But investors were all too willing to play along. Qualcomm gained $156 a share, more than 30 percent, the day that Piecky released his report. It ended 1999 at $717, up 2,619 percent for the year, by far the largest annual gain for a big company in the history of the Nasdaq.[32]

Valuation no longer mattered; winners rose at any price, while stocks with solid earnings and assets languished if they didn't show the growth that investors wanted. Although the indexes posted strong gains, the market was exceptionally narrow. Investors bought technology and a few "mega-cap" companies, such as General Electric, that posted predictable and rising earnings. They avoided everything else. Despite the S&P's 20 percent gain, more than half of the stocks in the index fell for the year, and the index's growth stocks rose almost three times as fast as value stocks. "Technology is the only thing that's working," one fund manager said. "I can give you a lot of cheap growth stocks outside technology, but to be honest, the market doesn't care."[33]

With investors seeking the most speculative companies, the IPO market reached a new peak. Offerings raised more than $63 billion in 1999, the most ever. On December 9, VA Linux, a computer company, went public at $30 a share and ended the day at $242.38, a price that valued the company at $11 billion, almost one thousand times its 1999 sales.

Ben Graham had once advised investors to buy stocks where they could "get the future for free." Now an old bull market chestnut was more true than ever: Investors were discounting profits not just in the present and the future but in the afterlife as well. And they were doing so with borrowed money: Margin loans rose to $229 billion in

1999, nearly double their level two years earlier and eight times their level in 1990.

———

The madness didn't end with 1999.

Hoping to undo the damage caused by his 1998 easing, Greenspan had repeatedly raised short-term rates during the fall of 1999 in an effort to slow the economy and cool the market. Long-term interest rates had also risen, above 6 percent by early 2000. A quick comparison of the S&P 500's price-earnings ratio to long-term rates showed that stocks were at least 20 percent overvalued.

But the rate hikes made no difference to investors. Wall Street broke one of its own cardinal rules and fought the Fed. During the first three months of 2000, the Nasdaq jumped through 4,000, then 5,000. Investors desperately sold "Old Economy" stocks to buy Internet and technology companies; the Dow Jones industrial average fell 1,400 points, 12 percent, in January and February. Sober-headed skeptics were now certain—*certain*—that the market was in the midst of a terrible bubble. "This market is stark, raving overvalued, and it will not last," *Fortune* wrote in January.[34]

But the sober-headed skeptics had been certain before, and wrong before. They had lost all credibility. Even Jim Grant, the most permanent of the permabears, beat his breast and tried to make peace with the market. "I happen to have been profoundly wrong, negative on this greatest of all bull markets," Grant said in December 1999.[35]

The opinions that mattered came from the bulls: strategists such as Abby Joseph Cohen of Goldman, Internet analysts such as Mary Meeker of Morgan, Stanley, and fund managers such as Kevin Landis of Firsthand Funds, a technology-oriented mutual fund company whose biggest fund had risen 181 percent in 1999. And the bulls grew more enthusiastic with every point the market rose. Questions about valuation or the quality of earnings were irrelevant. Buying the winners was all that mattered.

Cohen expected the S&P 500 to gain 10 percent in 2000. Ralph

Acampora, a strategist at Prudential Securities, was less restrained. He predicted the Nasdaq would gain another 33 percent and the S&P 27 percent, with big technology companies leading the way. "Intel and Microsoft and Dell are about to explode," he said.[36]

No one preached the new gospel more fervently than James J. Cramer. At the Sixth Annual Internet and Electronic Commerce Conference and Exposition in New York, Cramer named ten "Winners of the New World," ten stocks that investors should buy at any price, in a speech that will forever stand as a monument to the moment:

> You have to throw out all of the matrices and formulas and texts that existed before the Web. You have to throw them away because they can't make money for you anymore, and that is all that matters. We don't use price-to-earnings multiples anymore at Cramer Berkowitz. If we talk about price-to-book, we have already gone astray. If we use any of what Graham and Dodd teach us, we wouldn't have a dime under management. . . .
>
> We have a phrase on Wall Street. It's called raising the bar. If you can raise the bar, or brighten the outlook for your company, if you can see your growth accelerating, your stock will go higher and you will be given the currency to expand, acquire, and do whatever you want.[37]

Cramer then argued that the Internet would fundamentally change the economics of every industry. "It eliminates any bricks-and-mortar company that doesn't embrace the Net. . . . It just destroys retail as we know it. . . . How can Bank of America compete with Nokia as a way to bank?" He finished by saying:

> So, if you can't own the retailers, and you can't own transports, and you can't own banks and brokers and financials, and you can't own commodity makers and you can't own the newspapers, and you can't own the machinery stocks, what can you own?

A-ha, that just leaves us with tech. . . . That's why, despite the 80 percent increase in the Nasdaq last year, we are looking at another record year now. . . . Only those companies are worth owning. The rest?

You can have them.

It was February 29, ten days before the Nasdaq topped out at 5,048.62. The S&P 500 peaked two weeks later at 1,527.46, with a price-earnings ratio of 29 and a dividend yield of 1 percent. Seventy-five percent of analysts' recommendations were buys or strong buys, the highest percentage ever. Just seven out of every one thousand recommendations were sells or strong sells.[38] The same month, the amount of cash held by stock funds fell to 4 percent, the lowest level ever. Surveys showed that investors were as bullish as they had ever been. "Everyone is sold on the idea of the New Economy and everyone wants in," one strategist said on March 10, the day after the Nasdaq topped out.[39]

It was the worst moment to buy stocks in seventy years.

Chapter 11

—

TRUTH

Bubbles are fun. Bubbles are great. But the days when the market truly grips the imagination are the days when it is crashing, when every six seconds brings another tick down, when the Dow seems to be (and sometimes *is*) dropping 10 points a minute, when Bloomberg screens are filled with red and the anchors on CNBC speak slowly and don't try to hide their distress. *We're all in this together,* their faces say. *We'll get through it.* During the worst panics, the market does not make even a halfhearted attempt to rally. It closes at the day's lows, and one has the sense that if not for the 4 P.M. bell, prices would fall until the Dow and the S&P 500 and every stock in them all hit zero, and even then traders would try to sell short. The very concept of a bottom is laughable. Only a night's rest can bring sanity back to the world.

But the worst crashes do not last just one day. The margin calls go out, investors decide they must sell at any price, and the downward spiral resumes at the opening bell. And so the night becomes a time for watching and waiting: What are S&P futures doing in Japan? Where have the European exchanges opened? Are there any government reports due out that might end the turmoil, or make it worse? All this even though the market's behavior in the midst of a crash is utterly unpredictable. Investors can take a weak economic number as proof that the Federal Reserve will cut interest rates and boost stocks—or as proof that the economy is falling into a bottomless depression. After the first day of a crash, no one can know where it will end. It is a force of nature as much as any hurricane or earthquake.

The earthquake hit in April 2000.

Technology stocks had lost air for a couple of weeks, falling about 10 percent from their highs. Then, on Monday, April 10, the Nasdaq fell 6 percent, the beginning of a week when it would lose more than one-quarter of its value. At first confined to technology stocks, the rout spread by Friday to the rest of the market; the Dow dropped 617 points that day, its biggest point loss ever, while the Nasdaq dropped almost 10 percent. As in 1929, no single profit report or piece of economic data caused the sell-off; investors simply decided en masse they could no longer justify owning stocks that traded at two hundred or three hundred or five hundred times earnings, or had no earnings at all and no prospect of making any.

In midtown Manhattan, dazed investors wandered into brokerage offices to watch the losses mount; in windowless rooms upstairs, brokers made margin calls. By the time the market closed on Friday, April 14, the Nasdaq had fallen to 3,321, down 1,700 points in a month, and it was immediately obvious that the index would not be setting more new records anytime soon. "There was a sense of shock among many investors on Friday, a suggestion that the game had run its course," the *Times* wrote on April 16.[1]

———

The April plunge punctured the Nasdaq's bubble, but it didn't immediately end the broader bull market. Stocks tried to recover during the summer; the S&P 500 rose as high as 1,500 in September, and the Nasdaq returned to 4,000. Some soothsayers even argued that the crash had put the market on sounder footing, deflating the speculative excesses of the 1990s and setting the stage for yet another multi-year rally. The fact that the S&P 500 was trading at thirty times earnings, with the economy slowing, didn't seem to bother them.

This time it was the bulls who would seem naïve. As summer turned into fall, investors learned that their expectations for profits were much too high. The bubble had stoked growth more than Wall Street wanted to admit; Internet and telecom companies had raised more than $1 trillion in stock and bond offerings since 1995, money that had been spent on everything from airline tickets to television ads to computers. Now the United States had too many money-losing fiber-optic companies, too many money-losing Internet retailers, too many money-losing Web commerce software makers. The IPO boom, and the economic stimulus it had provided, ended almost overnight. New stock offerings, which had totaled $56 billion in the first nine months of 2000, fell to $5 billion in the fall.

The market's rise had also led investors to splurge on luxury cars and other baubles, further fueling growth. The Nasdaq's plunge constricted that "wealth effect." Through the fall, the economy slowed and stocks skidded. And for the first time, a blue-chip, mega-cap company—Lucent Technologies—was brought low by its focus on the number.

Lucent, the world's largest manufacturer of communications equipment, had used a variety of aggressive accounting gimmicks to boost its earnings during the late 1990s. The company hid some of its operating costs in a "restructuring reserve" and changed the way it accounted for its pension fund. The tricks, disclosed deep in Lucent's filings with the S.E.C., had increased its reported profits by at least $300 million in 1999. To further increase sales, Lucent had fallen into the trap of giving its customers loans, encouraging them to buy more gear than they needed or could afford. Even so, Lucent couldn't sell all the equipment it was making; its balance sheet showed that inventories of unsold goods had piled up in its warehouses.

"The fundamental issue is that the company, in my estimation, is trying to grow too fast," Steve Levy, an analyst at Lehman, said in

1999.[2] Driven by demand for the Internet and cell phones, the communications equipment industry had skyrocketed during the late 1990s. Cisco had grown tenfold in five years. To keep up, Lucent had promised investors it would add $6 billion in sales a year and grow profits by 20 percent.

The company needed to admit that growth rate was unrealistic, Levy said. But Lucent insisted it could meet its goals, and most analysts agreed. In December 1999, the company's stock topped $80. Lucent had a price-earnings ratio of 70 and was valued at $250 billion, as much as General Motors, Disney, Philip Morris, and McDonald's combined. Its top executives sold hundreds of millions of dollars in stock in 1999; in a display of corporate arrogance impressive even by late 1990s standards, it was spending $45 million to build a private golf club for its executives. The five-thousand-acre Hamilton Farm Golf Club included a twenty-thousand-square-foot guesthouse, two eighteen-hole courses, and a helicopter landing pad for busy CEOs.[3]

In January 2000, even before the bubble burst, Lucent admitted that its sales for fall 1999 had fallen short of expectations. Still, Wall Street continued to believe in Lucent; its stock stood at $65 in July 2000. Then the company disappointed investors again, saying that its earnings for 2000 would fall far short of the consensus, and the rout began.

In its rush to make its numbers, Lucent had overestimated demand for its equipment, which was losing market share. In response, Lucent had ratcheted up sales pressure, encouraging companies to buy months or years before they needed its gear with the promise of discounts and easy credit. "Customers behave the way you train them to behave," said Levy, the Lehman analyst. "The customer might not be ready to buy a certain product, so you go to them and say: 'O.K., I need to make my number so I'll give you better terms, or I'll finance it, or I'll discount it.'"[4]

"I take this personally. I'm accountable for what happened," said

Richard McGinn, Lucent's CEO. By October, McGinn was out of a job; a month after that, Lucent announced it had booked sales that it shouldn't have. The company "became intoxicated with Wall Street's expectations," chairman Henry Schacht said. "The gamble of pulling business forward betting that the new business would fill in the gap didn't work."[5] By the end of the year, Lucent's stock had fallen to $15. (The company is now struggling to avoid bankruptcy; its shares fell below $1 a share in 2002. It sold the golf club in July 2001 to a Maryland developer, making about $5 million, which made Hamilton Farm a much more successful investment than the billions of dollars Lucent had wasted on financing its customers.)

Lucent's collapse should have been a wake-up call for investors and analysts who thought they could ignore accounting. Previous accounting debacles had hit second- and third-tier companies. Lucent was a blue-chip giant, with 155,000 employees. It was one of the most widely followed and owned companies on Wall Street, covered by dozens of analysts. Yet while the shorts warned that Lucent was using accounting and sales gimmicks to paper over fundamental problems, Wall Street analysts—aside from Levy and a few others—remained bullish on Lucent and largely ignored the company's gimmickry. That cavalier attitude turned out to be very costly. Despite its size and status, Lucent had fallen far and fast.

—

Though not as far or as fast as Lernout & Hauspie Speech Products, the other big accounting disaster in 2000. Lernout, a Belgian company that made speech recognition software, had been the target of short-sellers for years. Marc Cohodes of Rocker Partners had first come upon Lernout's software while he was looking for a speech recognition program for his son Max, who has cerebral palsy. Cohodes quickly decided that Lernout's software didn't work as promised and became an implacable foe of the company, alleging that it had inflated its sales. But Cohodes and Rocker seemed to be fighting another losing battle. Lernout had attracted investments from Microsoft, Intel, and Michael Dell. Its sales had jumped from $100 million in 1997 to $344 million two years later, and its stock had risen twenty-fivefold between 1996 and March 2000, giving it a market value of about $10 billion. As late as August 2000, Lernout traded above $35 a share.

But even a cursory examination of Lernout's sales revealed a strange trend. All of the company's 1999 growth had come from Singapore and South Korea, where sales had risen from almost nothing in 1998 to $150 million in 1999. Considering that Lernout's most important products were English-based, the explosion in Asian revenue seemed unusual. Cohodes and several other shorts began to investigate.

Before long they had found enough to pique *The Wall Street Journal*'s attention. In a series of articles that began in August 2000, the *Journal* revealed the secret of Lernout's success. Many of the company's Korean "clients" said they had never bought software from Lernout. Meanwhile, Lernout's Singapore customers turned out to be a group of companies that had supposedly paid Lernout for the right to convert its software into languages like Armenian. Oddly enough, most of these companies were headquartered at the same office, and none had any employees. Either Singaporean businesses were looking to get a head start on the market for speech recognition software in Third World nations, or Lernout and its founders had invented fake companies and contracts to inflate its sales.[6]

The answer didn't take long to come out. In late November, barely three months after the *Journal*'s first exposé, Lernout filed for bankruptcy. (A few days earlier, John Duerden, an American whom Lernout had named its chief executive in an effort to quell the scandal, flew to South Korea to get $100 million that the company supposedly had in its bank accounts there. As he began to ask Joo Seo, the president of Lernout's Korean subsidiary, what had happened to the cash, three men ran into Seo's office and dragged Seo into another office nearby, where Duerden heard them beating—or pretending to beat—Seo. Duerden quickly left South Korea and readied Lernout for bankruptcy. "The only thing I know for certain," he said, "is that the money is not in the bank.")[7] The company would later be liquidated; Belgian and U.S. prosecutors continue to investigate Jo Lernout and Pol Hauspie, its founders.

The fraud at Lernout was relatively small compared to the problems at Lucent, or even Cendant two years earlier. Still, like Lucent, Lernout represented a striking victory for short-sellers and new evidence of the dangers that investors faced. During the 1990s, many of the biggest short-long battles, such as America Online, had ended with the shorts defeated even when they won. Analysts and investors had forgotten the very basics of stock valuation; why would they worry about pension plan accounting or inventory buildup? As long as a company's accountants signed off on its numbers, they were good enough for Wall Street.

But the audacity and scope of Lernout's fraud offered more proof that accountants were failing in their most basic responsibilities. The terms of Lernout's licensing deals weren't credible; KPMG, Lernout's auditors, should have made Lernout prove that its sales to its Singapore customers were real, arm's-length transactions, if necessary by forcing those Singapore companies to disclose their investors and any connections they had with Lernout. The speed at which Lernout's Korean business grew, from $1 million in the first half of 1999 to $127 million in the same period in 2000, was even more far-fetched; the *Journal* demolished the Korean sales with a handful of telephone calls.

Lernout hadn't just tweaked its numbers on the margins; it had committed wholesale fraud under the noses of Microsoft, Intel, and a Big Five accounting firm. And it would have kept doing so if not for the shorts. Thanks to Lernout and Lucent, the next time the shorts alleged that a company—even a big, well-respected company—was playing games with its books, their voices would be heard a bit more clearly.

—

But only a bit. Wall Street's overconfidence had taken decades to build; it would not disappear overnight.

The last gasp of the new era came in February 2001 when Cisco—after fourteen straight quarters of meeting or beating the consensus—said it had missed its number.[8] By March 2001, the S&P 500 had fallen to 1,120, a year-over-year decline of 27 percent. The Nasdaq had plunged more than 60 percent.

Yet many small investors still believed in stocks. The *Journal* revisited Bill's Barber Shop in March 2001 and found that even though Bill's portfolio had shrunk from $600,000 to $250,000, he and his friends remained optimistic. "I still think long term the market is where you want to be," said Joe O'Keefe, who owned a painting and wallpapering business. "Six months from now we'll look back and say there were some real buying opportunities."*[9] Professional investors shared that confidence, figuring that with the Federal Reserve cutting rates to support the economy, earnings would soon resume their upward track. Through the spring and summer of 2001, stocks mainly moved sideways, as economic concerns, not accounting issues, dominated the financial headlines.

Meanwhile, the accountants and analysts and executives who had fueled and profited from the great fantasy of the 1990s were pretending that nothing had changed. Having shown Arthur Levitt who was boss, the Big Five happily sucked down consulting fees while they waited for George W. Bush to loosen the few feeble regulations that

---

*I'll plead guilty here, too. In March 2001, I wrote a column for the *Times* advising investors that it was "time to be greedy," because prices had fallen so far in just a year. Bull market habits are hard to break.

bound them. Analysts remained almost as bullish as they had at the peak; 70 percent of recommendations were buys or strong buys. Not only did executive pay not follow the market lower in 2000, it actually rose. And CEOs remained as arrogant as ever; on a conference call with investors in the spring of 2001, Jeffrey K. Skilling, the chief executive of a Houston energy company called Enron, called a Boston hedge fund manager an "asshole" after the manager asked a question about Enron's accounting that Skilling didn't like.[10]

No company showed more contempt for investors than Computer Associates, the world's fourth largest software company, which dominates the market for the "mainframe utility" programs that help big computers run smoothly. Based on Long Island, Computer Associates had eighteen thousand employees and $6 billion in sales in 2000, up fivefold from a decade earlier. In early 2001, its market value topped $20 billion.

Computer Associates' strong results had always been something of a mystery in the software industry. The company wasn't known for the quality of its programs, and it had a reputation for bullying customers and providing minimal technical support. Yet it had regularly reported strong growth. (In at least one area, Computer Associates led the competition: In May 1998, the company gave its three top executives a stock grant worth $1.1 billion, one of the largest management paydays in history. Graef Crystal, an expert on executive compensation, said the awards were so excessive that the company shouldn't be allowed to deduct them from its taxes as a reasonable business expense.[11] Shareholders' anger over the payout worsened two months later when Computer Associates announced that its sales would fall far short of expectations and its stock plunged. The company shrugged off the criticism. The pay package was "a good plan," said Charles Wang, its chairman.[12] It was certainly good for Wang, who took home $660 million. Wang soon put some of his windfall to use, buying the New York Islanders hockey team and raising concerns in Oyster Bay Hamlet, a Long Island town, by buying up more than sixty-five buildings for $50 million. Mr. Wang "says he doesn't have a plan," one resident complained. "It's hard to believe that someone who is so invested here, with so much property on his hands, wouldn't have an actual plan."[13])

After the flap over the payout, Computer Associates stayed quiet for a couple of years. Then, in October 2000, the company announced that it would change the way it sold software. Instead of forcing clients to sign multi-year contracts, it would offer more flexible terms, such as month-to-month software licenses. The "new business model" would give the company a competitive advantage, chief executive Sanjay Kumar promised. "C.A.'s strength has always been in the diversity and excellence of our software products," Kumar said in a statement. "Our new business model empowers clients to take full advantage of that diversity."[14]

Oh, and one more thing: Along with its new business model, Computer Associates would use a new accounting method to figure out its profits and losses. The company would continue to report its sales and profits under standard GAAP accounting rules, but it would also publish a second, "pro forma" set of results. And as Computer Associates primly noted in its October press release, "This information will be the basis upon which C.A. will offer its guidance and estimates." In other words, the company expected investors to judge it on its pro forma numbers, not the regular figures.

Computer Associates was not the first company to adopt "pro forma" results, which had become popular during the 1990s. The trend had begun in the media industry, which had somehow convinced Wall Street that it should be valued on the basis of "EBITDA"—earnings before interest, taxes, depreciation, and amortization. Many analysts sloppily referred to EBITDA as cash flow, as if interest payments and taxes didn't really count as cash expenses. So what if companies could generate billions of dollars in EBITDA without ever making a bottom-line penny for their shareholders? It was the thought that counted.

Gradually, other forms of pro forma accounting spread. Internet and technology companies added back various "noncash" charges to their earnings.* Amazon.com briefly reported its results on an EBIT-DAM—earnings before interest, taxes, depreciation, amortization, and marketing costs—basis. Other companies began to factor out the impact of currency swings or other supposedly one-time events, especially if those events had cost them money. Disney disregarded the costs of its Go.com Internet startup; for fifteen straight quarters, Motorola offered results that ignored "one-time" restructuring changes.[15] Lynn Turner, the S.E.C.'s chief accountant, derisively referred to pro forma profits as "EBBS"—earnings before bad stuff.[16] But the commission didn't ban companies from reporting results pro forma as long as they also reported their regular GAAP earnings. By 2000, hundreds of companies were reporting their results pro forma. Analysts generally played along, judging companies on the basis of pro forma numbers. The smiley-face figures became the standard, while lower GAAP earnings faded into oblivion.

Pro forma numbers could be seen as less dangerous than other kinds of accounting gimmickry. After all, they didn't directly compromise the integrity of financial statements; investors could always ignore the pro forma numbers and judge a company under its regular results. And pro forma numbers generally had at least some relationship to standard earnings. Shareholders could calculate EBITDA for any company based on the information in its S.E.C. filings. Ditto for pro forma results that excluded restructuring charges or other one-time events.

---

*For decades analysts had added back noncash amortization charges to a company's net income to figure out its true earnings. Goodwill is an asset that doesn't really exist but is kept on a company's balance sheet for accounting purposes. Before 2002, companies had to "amortize" goodwill, or write it off over a period of years. The amortization lowered reported earnings but had no effect on companies' cash flow.

But Computer Associates took pro forma to an extreme. The company's pro forma results had no connection to its standard GAAP results, and Computer Associates didn't reconcile them for investors. A reconciliation would have been nice, since the results were very different. Just how different became clear on January 22, 2001, when Computer Associates reported its pro forma numbers for the first time. On a pro forma basis, the company said it had earned $247 million on sales of $1.3 billion for its December quarter, up from earnings of $193 million on sales of $1.1 billion the previous year.

"The new business model was very strong," Kumar told analysts on the conference call that followed the earnings release. "I can tell you reception was better than what we expected. At the end of the day"—one of Kumar's favorite expressions; he was a bottom-line, end-of-the-day sort of guy—"our clients are signing up and doing business with us." Kumar was "audibly jubiliant" about the company's "better than expected" earnings, Newsday, a Long Island newspaper, reported the next day in an article headlined "Upbeat Report for CA."[17]

But under standard accounting rules, the company's report didn't look so upbeat. On a GAAP basis, Computer Associates had lost $342 million on sales of just $783 million, compared to a profit of $401 million on sales of $1.7 billion the previous year. And the company's employees didn't think its results had been "very strong." In the winter of 2001, Computer Associates had fired hundreds of workers worldwide. The company had tried to avoid paying severance to the employees it laid off, claiming that the firings were for "nonperformance," though many of the fired workers had just received positive job reviews. Business was bad, and Computer Associates was anxious to cut costs, the fired workers insisted.

Meanwhile, despite the company's talk about its new business model, software industry consultants said Computer Associates was selling software exactly as it always had. In fact, the new model appeared to be nothing more than a couple of sentences that Computer Associates had put in its contracts promising free software upgrades to customers. Neither the business model nor the accounting made sense. What was going on?

——

The answer—according to employees, industry consultants, and evidence from the company's own financial statements—was rooted in accounting gimmickry by Computer Associates that had played a big part in the growth the company had supposedly shown during the 1990s.

Software companies with big corporate clients, such as Computer Associates, almost never sell their programs outright. Instead, they rent them, charging a large up-front license fee for the right to use a program for a year, followed by annual maintenance fees to keep using it and get technical support. They also offer long-term contracts that allow customers to spread the up-front fee, plus the annual fees, over the term of the contract.

Accounting rules allowed Computer Associates or any software company to book revenue immediately, even if it would not be paid for many years, if it classified the fees it would receive as related to the initial license instead of ongoing maintenance. By calling fees licenses instead of maintenance, Computer Associates could inflate its current reported sales and profits—at the expense of the future, when it would actually be paid. And subject to outside auditors' approval, the company had considerable discretion over how to classify the fees.

Throughout the 1990s, the company had taken full advantage of that flexibility. When Computer Associates bought smaller software companies, it encouraged their clients to "reroll," or extend, their contracts for ten years or more. The company then classified most of the future fees as new license revenue and booked them immediately, as if it had made a new sale instead of simply extending a contract on software that was already installed and running. "A lot of what's being booked as new revenue is taking an existing contract that's expiring and adding years on to it," a former Computer Associates executive told me in April 2001. "It's rerolling a contract."

The effect of the rerolls could be seen in the company's financial statements. By the end of fiscal 2000, Computer Associates' accounts receivable—sales it had already booked but for which it hadn't yet been paid—had mushroomed to $6 billion. And the company wouldn't receive $4 billion of that money for at least a year.

Rerolls made Computer Associates seem much more profitable and faster growing than it was. Unfortunately, Computer Associates couldn't use the trick forever. Once the company had rolled over a contract, it could not roll it again for several years. To keep reporting growth, Computer Associates needed a steady supply of contracts to turn over. To find them, the company spent more than $10 billion on takeovers between 1995 and 2000. By then it had a near-monopoly in many kinds of mainframe software and had practically run out of competitors to buy.

Suddenly Computer Associates was in a very bad spot. No acquisitions meant no rerolls. No rerolls meant no "new" license revenue to book. The fact that Computer Associates was being paid on its earlier contracts didn't help the company; it had booked those sales and profits years before. The full dimensions of the squeeze Computer Associates faced became clear in July 2000 when it said that its results for the June quarter had fallen far short of expectations. Its stock plunged 42 percent.

Three months later, Computer Associates announced its new business model—and its pro forma accounting. The secret to both could be found in one line of the company's October 2000 press release: "Under this model, C.A. will account for contracted revenue over the life of the license term." In English, that sentence meant Computer Associates planned to report profits and sales under pro forma that *it had already booked under standard accounting rules.* Since it couldn't find new customers, Computer Associates would double-count previous sales. The three sentences that formed the company's "new business model" gave its auditors at KPMG the cover to sign off on the change.*

Computer Associates' pro forma move was the most audacious accounting gimmick yet by a big company. The company had made its standard results irrelevant and replaced them with numbers of its own choosing, numbers that enabled it to report sales and profits twice. It had attacked head-on the core of the securities laws, the principle that public companies should report their results under a consistent set of rules. And it was doing so without protest from its auditors, the Wall Street analysts who covered it, and the institutional investors who owned its stock. The S.E.C., of course, was nowhere in sight.

On Sunday, April 29, 2001, I wrote an article for the *Times* explaining the company's tricks. Computer Associates stock had closed Friday at $35.25. On Monday it fell about 8 percent, to $32.50.

But investors' reaction ended there. So what if the company had inflated its sales and earnings for a decade and its new numbers were pure fiction? Computer Associates was profitable and growing, or so it said. Pro forma, GAAP, whatever. The company ended 2001 at $34.39. Fidelity Investments, the largest mutual fund company, was an especially big fan. In 2001, Fidelity spent at least $1 billion to buy 38 million shares; by year end it owned 70 million shares, 12 percent of the company.

Wall Street and corporate America were *still* in denial.

---

*Technically, by promising customers that it would give them software upgrades for free if it ever wrote new code, Computer Associates had created a potential liability whose cost couldn't be measured until the contract had expired. As a result, under accounting rules, it had to book revenues under a "pro rata" basis, a little at a time over the life of the contract. The fact that Computer Associates had no intention of ever spending a dime on software upgrades was irrelevant.

———

September 11, 2001, was the most awful day in Wall Street's history, and no one really knew in the days that followed what would happen when the markets reopened—or even when they'd reopen. But after six days of nonstop work by the New York Stock Exchange and the rest of the securities industry, the opening bell rang at the Big Board on September 17, with the smell of smoke still lingering over lower Manhattan. And investors, especially small investors, refused to panic. On September 10 the Standard & Poor's 500 index closed at 1,092.54. Three months later it stood above 1,100. As New York and Washington shivered, families and companies in Sacramento and Charlotte and Dallas went about their business. The nation slowed but did not stall; once again the American economy displayed its astonishing resilience. After shrinking during the spring and summer of 2001, the United States actually grew in the fall, and many economists figured 2002 would be a year of recovery for the economy and stocks.

But as the nation focused on Afghanistan and the hunt for Osama bin Laden, the collapse of Enron revealed that the deepest threat to that resilience came not from foreign terrorism but the corruption inside the nation's executive suites.

During the 1990s, Enron had grown from its roots in the natural gas pipeline business into the world's largest trader of gas and electricity. The company appeared fabulously successful; its earnings (before various one-time charges, naturally) soared from $500 million in 1997 to $1.2 billion in 2000; by early 2001 its stock topped $80. Its arrogance grew even more quickly. Enron didn't just tell analysts that its stock was a buy; at a January 2001 conference it told them exactly how much it was worth: $126 a share, a price that valued the company at more than $100 billion. Wall Street lapped up Enron's attitude; the company's fast growth made it a favorite of analysts and aggressive mutual fund groups such as Janus Capital, the

Denver fund family that during the late 1990s had made huge profits on America Online and other technology companies.

Neither the fund managers nor the analysts seemed to mind that Enron's financial statements were indecipherable. The company's 10-K for 2000 listed billions of dollars of "price risk management assets" and footnotes about huge "derivative transactions" and "forward contracts" with related parties—companies it or its executives owned. In a March 2001 article called "Is Enron Overpriced?" Bethany McLean, a writer for *Fortune,* raised the first serious questions:

> But for all the attention that's lavished on Enron, the company remains largely impenetrable to outsiders, as even some of its admirers are quick to admit. Start with a pretty straightforward question: How exactly does Enron make its money? Details are hard to come by because Enron keeps many of the specifics confidential for what it terms "competitive reasons." And the numbers that Enron does present are often extremely complicated. Even quantitatively minded Wall Streeters who scrutinize the company for a living think so. "If you figure it out, let me know," laughs credit analyst Todd Shipman at S&P.[18]

A few months later, investors wouldn't be so amused. Enron's stock slid slowly through the summer of 2001. Then, in August, Skilling quit, citing unspecified personal problems. Enron's press reps hinted that one of his kids needed some extra attention, an explanation that if true would have made Skilling the first CEO ever to put family life ahead of business.

Skilling's resignation was the beginning of the end for Enron. In October the company reported "operating earnings" of $393 million, excluding $1 billion in one-time charges. Wall Street accepted the report at face value; Enron rose slightly after it was released.

"The underlying earnings . . . were solid," said Andre Meade, an analyst at Commerzbank Securities.[19] Of seventeen analysts, fifteen rated the company a buy.[20]

But what was good enough for analysts was no longer good enough for the press or the S.E.C. With help from short-seller Jim Chanos, who also contributed to *Fortune*'s March story, the *Journal* questioned Enron's relationship with a mysterious partnership run by Andrew Fastow, its chief financial officer.* By the end of October, Enron's stock plunged and its trading operations shriveled. The complexity of Enron's financials, which hadn't mattered when times were good, became a curse; how could lenders, suppliers, or trading partners trust Enron if they couldn't understand it?

In early November, Enron appeared to find a savior. Dynegy, another Houston energy company, offered to buy it for $9 a share, including an immediate $1.5 billion cash infusion. But two weeks later Enron revealed that it had overstated its profits for the previous three years by at least $600 million and possibly much more. Even more disturbing, the new $1.5 billion had vanished. "We went back to Enron and we asked, 'Where did the cash go?'" Dynegy chief executive Chuck Watson said.[21] When Enron couldn't answer, Dynegy walked away. (Cash seemed to be disappearing everywhere; Dynegy would soon face similar questions.)

On Sunday, December 2, Enron laid off thousands of employees and filed for bankruptcy. It was the worst-case scenario, the one that the system of securities laws and audits had been designed seventy years before to prevent, the one that was never supposed to happen in the United States. In less than two months, financial fraud had caused a major American corporation to implode.

---

*It may seem that I am quick to say that other reporters rely on short-sellers but don't mention the help they give me. In fact, I talk regularly to the shorts, including Chanos, and they have helped me many times. But none of them was involved with the Computer Associates article; I stumbled across that story on my own.

Short-sellers throw around words like "fraud" and "fake" and "bankruptcy" all the time, but even they never imagined that Enron would collapse as quickly as it did. Enron wasn't some obscure Belgian software company. It had twenty thousand employees. Kenneth Lay, its chairman, had been on the short list to become President Bush's energy secretary. Millions of investors owned its shares directly or through mutual funds.

Enron proved beyond all doubt that the system had come undone.

—

A year afterward, the reasons for Enron's quick collapse are still being unraveled. The company's accounting was monstrously complicated, and the details of the schemes that it used are mind-numbing.

In essence, though, Enron's sins fell into two main categories. First, the company had made all manner of money-losing investments: in power plants in Brazil and India plagued by cost overruns, in failing telecom companies, in fiber-optic networks that didn't have traffic. Enron wanted to hide those losses and the debt associated with them, so it pretended to sell the projects to partnerships of outside investors at a profit. In fact, though, the partnerships were funded and backed by Enron. The company was really selling the assets to itself. Had Enron kept those losses on its books, as it should have, the profits it reported in the late 1990s would have been much smaller.

Meanwhile, as Enron hid real losses, it was reporting fake profits, thanks to a gimmick called "mark-to-market" accounting. Essentially, mark-to-market accounting enabled Enron to estimate what its future profits would be every time it signed a deal or made a trade— and then book those profits right away, without having to see whether its estimates were right. It was as if McDonald's reported ten years of profits up front every time it signed a lease for a new restaurant.

Enron's bankruptcy finally brought home to the public how bad corporate accounting had become. Investors might not fully understand the details of the Fastow partnerships or the vagaries of mark-to-market accounting. But they saw that Enron's financial statements were filled with sawdust and that a few dozen executives at the top of the company had reaped enormous profits from what looked a lot like a Ponzi scheme. In the three years before Enron collapsed, twenty-nine executives had sold more than $1 billion in stock.[22] Skilling took home $67 million; Fastow sold $30 million. The biggest winner of all was Lou Pai, the head of Enron Energy Services, which used an especially egregious version of mark-to-market accounting. Pai sold $354 million in stock, then quit the company to hole up in a ranch in Colorado.

Then there was Lay. After Skilling quit in August, Lay encouraged Enron employees to buy its stock. In late September, during an online discussion with workers, Lay said that he had recently bought Enron stock.[23] That comment turned out to be . . . misleading. In February 2002, Enron disclosed that Lay had taken advantage of a loophole in S.E.C. regulations to sell $70 million in stock in 2001 without telling investors. The sales were disclosed in a once-a-year report to the S.E.C. called a "Form 5," which was so obscure that few investors had ever heard of it—and it could not be found in the S.E.C.'s electronic database.

The Form 5 sales made up only a fraction of the money Lay had taken out of Enron. Overall, including pay, bonuses, and stock sales, Lay had made about $275 million in the three years leading up to the company's bankruptcy filing. Still, Lay's wife, Linda, insisted on a nationally televised interview that the family's money was "gone." Gone, that is, except for the Lays' $8 million home in Houston and a couple of houses in Aspen. Somehow Linda's comments didn't elicit the sympathy that the Lays had expected; the family did not plead poverty again, at least in public.

———

With Enron's collapse the spotlight turned on Andersen (formerly Arthur Andersen), the company's auditor. The firm quickly deflected any responsibility for the failure of its second largest U.S. client. Two days after Enron filed for bankruptcy, Joseph Berardino, Andersen's

CEO, wrote an opinion piece in the *Journal* promising that "if we have made mistakes, we will acknowledge them."[24] In the meantime, Berardino acknowledged that lots of other people had made mistakes, blaming investment bankers, analysts, and money managers for not doing their jobs. "We need to consider the responsibilities and accountability of all players in the system," Berardino wrote. Michael Rapoport, a Dow Jones columnist, quickly dissected Berardino's excuses:

> But nowhere in his piece does Berardino address the central questions: Why didn't Andersen, in its capacity as Enron's auditor, prevent the apparently misleading accounting that helped lead to this collapse? Why didn't someone at Andersen put his or her foot down and say, "No, this misleads investors about the true state of Enron's finances, and we will not sign off on this?" One number suggests a possible answer: $52 million. That's how much Enron paid Andersen in fees in 2000 for auditing and consulting services.[25]

For a month it seemed as though Andersen might bluster its way through Enron's collapse, the way Ernst & Young and KPMG had escaped responsibility for the failures of Cendant and Lernout. Then, on January 10, an announcement from Andersen put the firm's future in doubt and gave the public vivid proof of how badly the culture of the Big Five had decayed. In a brief statement, Andersen admitted that it had shredded Enron-related documents in October, *after* Enron had received a subpoena for information about its financial statements from the S.E.C. It was not immediately clear if what Andersen had done was illegal. What was clear was that Andersen, like its client, regarded regulators and accounting rules as obstacles to be cleared.

Andersen tried to blame the shredding on David Duncan, the partner in charge of the Enron account. But that argument rang hollow. In 2001 the S.E.C. had fined Andersen $7 million for its role in a massive fraud at Waste Management, the garbage hauling company, that lasted most of the 1990s. Reexamining that case after Enron's collapse, prosecutors found that Andersen had promoted instead of punished several partners who had signed off on the Waste Management audits. At the same time, Andersen began encouraging employees to destroy their audit-related working papers so that regulators would have a harder time tracing the compromises it made with clients. The Enron shredding was no isolated incident; it was part of Andersen's culture.

Meanwhile, congressional investigators released internal Andersen emails that showed that senior Andersen partners had overruled lower-level accountants concerned about Enron's accounting gimmicks. In 2001, Andersen had removed one of its accountants from day-to-day work with Enron after he argued that one of the Fastow partnerships had "no substance." At about the same time, Andersen called the mark-to-market accounting used by Enron "intelligent gambling."[26] Of course, Andersen had never shared its concerns with investors.

With every new revelation, Andersen's position grew more precarious. In March, federal prosecutors indicted the company on obstruction of justice charges related to the shredding. "The question finally came down to 'How many times do investors have to lose millions of dollars because they relied on Andersen before somebody finally charges them with a crime?" said one person on the case.[27] Three months later a jury in Houston found Andersen guilty, effectively putting the firm out of business because S.E.C. rules bar accountants convicted of a felony from auditing public companies. Andersen, with a ninety-year history and eighty-five thousand employees worldwide, had gone down almost as quickly as Enron. The rot crippling the accounting industry had claimed its biggest victim.

—

The collapse of Enron and the revelation of Andersen's misdeeds showed the public just how dishonest the system had become. A poll in January found that 40 percent of Americans believed Enron's failure was of great importance, and 70 percent feared that many other large companies were similarly corrupt.[28] For the first time since the 1960s, the word "plutocrat" crept into the lexicon. But the outrage didn't translate into panic in the markets, which stayed solid through the winter. Executives, accountants, Wall Street, and the White House insisted that the system needed only a bit of tweaking.

The Bush administration had had little to say when Enron filed for bankruptcy, perhaps hoping that if it stayed quiet the public would forget that the company had been the biggest single financial backer of George W. through his political career and that Bush had offered handwritten birthday greetings to his good friend "Kenny Boy" Lay. Even if Bush hadn't known Lay, Enron would have been tricky for the White House; a decade earlier, Bush had sold $848,000 in stock in Harken Energy, a floundering oil company where he was a director, a few weeks before Harken announced an earnings shortfall and its stock plunged. The S.E.C. investigated but took no action against Bush, whose father was president at the time.[29] Meanwhile, Vice President Dick Cheney had his own accounting bugaboo; in May, Lowell Bergman and I would reveal that in 1998, Halliburton—an oil services company that at the time was run by Cheney—had changed its accounting rules so that it could report as revenue about $89 million in disputed cost overruns on its projects. Accounting experts said the change might have been improper; Halliburton said it had been routine, but the S.E.C. opened an inquiry into it after our story ran.

Finally, in late January, Bush claimed that he was "outraged" by Enron's collapse. "My own mother-in-law bought stock last summer, and it's not worth anything now," he said, offering the Republican version of *I feel your pain.*[30]

Nor did the S.E.C. jump into the breach. To replace Arthur Levitt as S.E.C. chairman, Bush had in August 2001 appointed Harvey Pitt, who had represented the accounting industry in its battles with the commission during most of the 1990s. While Enron crashed, Pitt spent most of his time talking about the need for the commission to have a less adversarial relationship with the Big Five. The S.E.C. needs to be "a kinder and gentler place for accountants," he said in October 2001.[31]

After Enron collapsed, Pitt stopped talking about how accountants needed more freedom, but he didn't propose any significant new regulations, either. He and his old paymasters at the Big Five seemed very much to be playing a delaying game, hoping that the Enron controversy would blow over so that they could get back to business. On Capitol Hill, Republican congressman Michael G. Oxley, the industry's designated waterboy, introduced a "reform" bill so weak it couldn't even be called cosmetic. The White House supported it while quietly trying to kill tougher legislation introduced by Democratic senator Paul Sarbanes.

Meanwhile, the accounting industry proudly continued its tradition of refusing to accept any responsibility for audit failures. In December the CEOs of the Big Five released a joint statement blaming Enron's collapse on the fact that it had to report its results only once every three months. "Backward-looking financial statements delivered on a periodic basis no longer are sufficient to communicate real value and risk," the firms said, as if more fake numbers from Enron would have cleared up the company's financial position. The industry's position called to mind the old joke about the kid who kills his parents and then pleads for mercy on the grounds that he's an orphan. As Floyd Norris pointed out in the *Times*, "The primary controversy has been whether [Enron's] financial reports were accurate, not whether they were sufficiently timely."[32]

The myopia and arrogance that gripped the Big Five (which would become the Final Four after Andersen crumpled) were on full display in a 2002 book by Samuel A. DiPiazza, the CEO of Pricewaterhouse-Coopers, and Robert G. Eccles, a senior Pricewaterhouse partner. In *Building Public Trust: The Future of Corporate Reporting,* DiPiazza and Eccles had lots of advice. But it was mostly directed at investors, boards of directors, and corporate executives, not accountants. "Sometimes, unfortunately, nonexecutive directors who sit on boards—even of some of the world's most prestigious companies—do not devote the time necessary to fulfill properly their obligations,"[33] DiPiazza and Eccles complained. And a few pages later: "No level of assurance, even of the highest quality, can replace investors' need for analysis of the information they receive."[34]

But DiPiazza and Eccles didn't bother to suggest substantive reforms for the industry they knew best: their own. They never took a position on whether accountants should be allowed to consult. Or whether public companies should have to switch accounting firms every few years to prevent companies and their auditors from getting too chummy. Or, heaven forbid, whether the federal government should create a national accounting regulator with the power to discipline firms that conduct bad audits, instead of leaving the job to the overburdened S.E.C. Instead, they confined themselves to the vague suggestion that auditors should "accept a broader charter that would entail wider responsibility, greater controversy, and more risk."

A similar disconnect from reality was on display at the big investment banks, where analysts remained reluctant to say a discouraging word about the companies they covered. As late as March 2002, fewer than 2 percent of all recommendations were sell or strong sell. Sixty-three percent were buys or strong buys.

—

But this time the furor would not die. The fuse that Enron had lit burned hotter each month.

The shorts no longer had problems getting their calls returned; any reporter who could read a balance sheet wanted help finding the next

Enron. So did the S.E.C.'s Division of Enforcement and state and federal prosecutors. While sell-side analysts continued to slumber, the
three major credit rating agencies, which didn't depend on investment banking fees, looked much more carefully at any company
whose accounting seemed hinky. And having seen the criticism that
Janus and other big mutual fund companies took for their investments in Enron, even the most complacent buysiders thought twice
before buying shares in companies whose accounting was under
attack.

The search for gimmickry was on. And the harder investigators
and reporters looked, the more tricks they found.

The next company to crumble was Tyco, the last great conglomerate sham. Tyco's numbers had always been dubious. Like L-T-V
a generation earlier, Tyco specialized in buying low-margin companies and magically increasing their profits. Between 1992 and 2001
its profits jumped from $95 million to $4.5 billion. At its peak in
December 2001, Tyco's market value topped $120 billion, and it had
240,000 employees. The next month *Business Week* named Dennis
Kozlowski, its chairman, one of the world's top twenty-five managers. "Kozlowski vows Tyco's earnings will once again grow by
more than 20 percent a year. That would bring him closer to his ultimate goal: inheriting the mantle once worn by Jack Welch," the magazine wrote.[35]

But Tyco wasn't G.E. Like Enron and Lucent, Tyco had obvious
weaknesses, which Wall Street had ignored in its fixation on the number. The company's growth-by-acquisition business model had been
proven a failure a generation earlier, and its financial statements were
filled with red flags. For example, in July 2001, Tyco projected sales
of $12 billion and profits of 83 cents a share for its September quar-
ter. In October it reported sales for the quarter of only $10.1 billion,
but somehow, despite the sales shortfall, Tyco's profit came in at
86 cents per share, even better than its earlier forecast. Most companies can't meet their profit goals if their sales are $2 billion below

expectations; the disconnect was a sure sign that Tyco was computing its profits from the bottom line up instead of the top line down. But instead of questioning the gap, analysts simply said it proved Kozlowski's brilliance.

In December 2001, I started digging into Tyco's numbers. (A few months earlier, Chanos had told me he thought Enron and Tyco were the two companies most likely to go down because of bad accounting; after Enron collapsed, I figured Tyco was worth a look.) I quickly found inconsistencies in its financial statements that added up to billions of dollars. Mark Maremont at the *Journal* and Herb Greenberg at TheStreet.com soon began to ask questions of their own. And then Tyco showed how little Kozlowski and his advisers on Wall Street thought of the company's investors. On January 22, at a press conference at New York's Plaza Hotel, Kozlowski said he would split Tyco into four companies, raising billions of dollars from four initial public offerings.

The breakup plan ran absolutely contrary to the strategy that Kozlowski had used for a decade in building Tyco, but it had three great virtues: It meant hundreds of millions of dollars in fees for Wall Street, ensuring that analysts wouldn't probe Tyco's numbers too closely; it allowed Tyco to raise several billion dollars to lessen its $25 billion debt burden; and it gave the four new companies the chance to bury whatever problems they had in lots of one-time charges. In other words, the breakup was financial gimmickry disguised as a business decision. And had Dennis tried it during the bubble, he probably would have gotten away with it.

But the bubble was over. Dennis could huff and puff about how good Tyco's businesses were, but he couldn't convince investors to pour billions of dollars into his coffers, not after what had happened at Enron, not when Tyco's debt was rising even though it supposedly had strong profits and cash flow.

Kozlowski's credibility was not helped when, in February, I

reported that he had used the same Form 5 trick as Kenneth Lay to sell more than $300 million in stock without publicly disclosing it. Those revelations raised the question of how many other CEOs were using Form 5s to sell stock without telling investors—and evading the spirit of the rules of insider selling that formed one of the core principles of the securities laws. In April, Kozlowski canceled his breakup plan. Tyco's stock plunged from $60 in December to $17 in late April, erasing $86 billion in wealth, more than Enron's collapse.

Tyco wasn't the only market bellwether having its financials scrutinized in the spring of 2002. In February, Gretchen Morgenson, a Pulitzer Prize–winning reporter for the *Times,* revealed that I.B.M. had met its number for its December 2001 quarter by including a $300 million gain from the sale of a business unit in its operating profits. On December 28, the last Friday before the quarter closed, I.B.M. sold its optical transceiver business to JDS Uniphase, a communications equipment company, for $340 million and booked the profit as "intellectual property income" rather than a one-time gain from a sale. The profits from the deal enabled I.B.M. to beat the consensus profit estimate by 1 cent a share—its sixteenth straight quarter of meeting or exceeding the consensus—even though its sales for the quarter were $1 billion below analysts' forecasts. I.B.M. said it had done nothing wrong, but Lynn Turner, the former chief accountant of the S.E.C., disagreed. "Accounting rules are "very clear that gains from the sale of assets have to be in the 'other income' line," not booked as operating income, Turner said.[36]

Two months later, Morgenson raised questions about the accounting practices of General Electric, the world's most valuable stock and probably the most respected company in America. To produce the consistent earnings increases investors expected, G.E. had sold assets and made optimistic assumptions about the future performance of its pension plan. The maneuvers, while legal, had significantly boosted G.E.'s reported earnings. One mutual fund manager estimated that the manuevers had increased General Electric's income by about $2.5 billion in 2001, accounting for 18 percent of the company's profits. "We went through a decade where we just accepted G.E.'s numbers," Thomas K. Brown, a hedge fund manager, said. "Now the more we look at them, the more we say, 'Wait a minute, I don't understand what's going on here, and the more I understand it, the more I'm concerned." [37]

I.B.M. and General Electric were not Enron or even Tyco; they had real sales and real profits and weren't about to collapse. But the fact that they, too, had come under suspicion proved that the financial statements of even the bluest blue-chip companies could no longer be taken on faith. Even the phrase "blue chip" seemed dated; the idea that the market's leaders had a special responsibility to set standards for the rest of corporate America had disappeared. In two years, 5 of the 50 most valuable companies in the S&P 500—Enron, General Electric, Lucent, Tyco, and I.B.M.—had faced serious questions about the honesty of their financial statements. Why should investors believe in the other 45, or the next 450?

In April, Bristol-Myers Squibb, the fifth largest drugmaker, admitted that it had inflated its earnings in 2001 by encouraging its wholesalers to buy more drugs than they needed. "Channel stuffing," as Bristol-Myers had done, is among the crudest accounting gimmicks, all but certain to fail in the long run. And Adelphia, the sixth largest cable company, revealed that its top executives had borrowed more than $2 billion in loans guaranteed by the company that hadn't been disclosed. Within months the executives would be arrested and Adelphia in bankruptcy. And after Adelphia, the federal investigations and earnings restatements and shortfalls poured down: Nvidia. Halliburton. Dynegy. Qwest. Global Crossing. AOL Time Warner. Williams. El Paso. Vivendi Universal. Every day brought a new disaster, a new and exotic scam: loans disguised as natural gas sales, telecom "capacity swaps," mark-to-market and gain-on-sale accounting,

debt hidden so far off the balance sheet that it didn't even exist—
until it had to be paid back.

—

For a decade, analysts and institutional investors had shrugged off
earnings management.

Sure, companies massaged their numbers a bit on the margins to
get through a tough quarter, or put a penny aside for a rainy day
when business was good. *So what?* Even Microsoft managed its earnings—although it managed them down by not booking all its sales as
early as it could and thus building a cushion of "unearned revenue"
it could call on if sales slowed. (In June 2002, under pressure from
the S.E.C., Microsoft agreed to stop using the unearned revenues as a
reserve fund.) "Did Microsoft manage earnings? Does G.E. manage
earnings?" one professional investor said in June. "Sure, we all know
that. If G.E. needs to make a penny this quarter, they'll take it out of
next quarter."[38]

But now Wall Street faced the reality that at hundreds of companies, in every industry, earnings management had slid into earnings
manipulation. Everything the short-sellers had said was true. A few
companies, such as WorldCom, had committed outright fraud; many
more, such as Computer Associates, had pushed the boundaries of
GAAP to report results that bore only the faintest relationship to the
reality of their businesses. And almost every company had overestimated its pension plan returns and refused to expense the cost
of options—two gimmicks that were allowable under standard accounting rules but that significantly inflated profits. The ideal of
transparency and disclosure enshrined in the securities laws had been
forgotten; 10-Qs and 10-Ks had become a funhouse mirror.

The games had started earlier, and run deeper, than anyone
thought, and they hadn't ended when the Nasdaq bubble burst in
2000. In fact, they had gotten even more egregious as companies
tried to keep making their numbers despite the unfriendly economy.

In 1997, the number of companies that restated their earnings was 92; in 2001, it was 225. An additional 125 followed in the first half of 2002, according to a General Accounting Office study in October 2002. In addition, the size of the companies making restatements had soared. Between 1997 and 2002 the average market value of a restating company quadrupled, from $500 million to $2 billion.[39]

It may never be possible to determine exactly how much companies inflated their profits during the bubble and the bust, but a reasonable estimate is that fraud and gimmickry added several hundred billion dollars to the reported profits of the S&P 500 from 1997 to 2002. Consider this: From the start of 1997 through the end of 2000, S&P 500 companies said their profits grew a total of 40 percent. Profits peaked in 2000 when companies in the index said they earned more than $500 billion. At the time, optimistic stock strategists argued that the profit growth made perfect sense; companies were running more efficiently thanks to the Internet and information technology. But a second set of earnings figures, those that all public and private companies submit to the federal government, painted a very different picture.[40] They showed that corporate profits actually fell 10 percent between January 1997 and December 2000—probably because the productivity gains were eaten up by pay increases that skilled workers commanded during the boom.

In earlier years the government's data and the S&P figures had tracked each other more closely. Between 1986 and 1996, for example, both the government and the S&P found that profits had roughly tripled. The gap between the late 1990s data offers strong evidence that much of the growth that public companies reported during the period was a mirage. Options and pension accounting, the two biggest gimmicks, each boosted profits by tens of billions of dollars a year; the collective impact of the other, more egregious games totaled tens of billions more. If those estimates seem high, consider that in 2001, Computer Associates' pro forma earnings were $3 billion higher than its profit under standard accounting rules. That's just one company for just one year.

The naysayers who said that earnings weren't growing as quickly as they appeared had been right all along. Accounting gimmicks, not productivity improvements, had driven earnings higher; investors had paid for profits that simply didn't exist.

For a decade Wall Street had fed on the number, and the number had fed on Wall Street. Investors had wanted excuses to buy. They had wanted rising profits. Companies had given them those profits. But in the end it hadn't been a fair fight. Small investors thought earnings were a little inflated, and bought; executives knew that they were hugely exaggerated, and sold, sold on the way up and all the way back down.

The implicit contract between companies and Wall Street and investors—we're all in this together, and we promise not to cheat you too much, and if we do, the S.E.C. will stop us, so stop worrying, buy some decent stocks, and you'll do fine—had turned out to be no contract at all. *U.S. markets were the fairest and most honest in the world.* Yeah, right. Tell me another.

The after-the-fact shamelessness displayed by executives such as Lay and Skilling only made matters worse. In 1933, J. P. Morgan at least had had the guts to sit in front of Ferdinand Pecora and answer the questions he was asked. This time around, America saw the sorry spectacle of dozens of executives and Wall Street analysts pleading the Fifth Amendment before congressional committees or testifying that they didn't remember what had happened at the companies they ran. Executives who had happily taken home tens of millions of dollars refused to accept even a modicum of responsibility for the losses that their investors had suffered. Skilling told a House committee that he couldn't remember the details of a crucial Enron board meeting because the lights had gone out just as Andrew Fastow was describing one of the partnerships that Fastow had created to hide the company's losses.[41] Reviewing Skilling's testimony at another hearing, Floyd Norris wrote that Enron's former CEO

> does not appear to have picked up much in the way of humility since Enron collapsed. "If I were in charge of the world," he began one answer that ended with him blaming the banks for Enron's collapse. . . .
>
> Even now, Mr. Skilling knows of nothing wrong with Enron's financial statements. So far as he is concerned, the auditors from Arthur Andersen signed off on the statements, and if other auditors disagree, that is a technical argument that he, as a nonaccountant, cannot be expected to understand.[42]

There were no midgets in 2002; none were needed.

"Main Street Loses Faith in Buying Stocks at Last," the *Journal* reported in a front-page article in May 2002. In Youngstown, Ohio, brokers told the newspaper that "months of accounting scandals and cloudy earnings forecasts are taking a toll on their clients, and contributing to a deep change in investor attitudes."[43] In April and May, stocks fell about 10 percent.

The last straw for many investors came in June when Manhattan prosecutors indicted Dennis Kozlowski for evading more than $1 million in sales tax, and WorldCom admitted it had inflated its cash flow by $4 billion, a number that later rose to $9 billion. The size of WorldCom fraud and the fact that it involved the company's cash flow shocked even the usually unflappable James Chanos. "The one touchstone that investors had was that you couldn't fudge cash flow numbers, but apparently you can," Chanos said.[44]

WorldCom, the second largest long-distance company, filed for bankruptcy less than a month later. Meanwhile, Kozlowski, who would be charged in September with stealing hundreds of millions of dollars, became a symbol of the destructive greed that so many

American CEOs had shown during the boom. (In January 2002, Kozlowski sat across a table from me and angrily told me that he had never sold a share of stock in Tyco except to pay taxes or for "estate planning purposes." Tyco's board of directors believed that he should have all his net worth tied up in the company, he said. In their September indictment, Manhattan prosecutors would allege that the truth was more or less the reverse; Kozlowski had run Tyco as his personal piggy bank, they said. Kozlowski pled not guilty to the charges.)

The losses that had begun in April accelerated in June and July. In four months the S&P 500 fell more than 30 percent, erasing $4 trillion in shareholder wealth. It was the worst drop in a generation, and combined with the decline of the previous two years, the worst since the 1930s. The Nasdaq fell to 1,114.11, down almost 80 percent from its March 2000 high. (The most aggressive mutual funds suffered even steeper losses; the Firsthand fund that had tripled in 1999 fell 64 percent in the first nine months of 2002. By September 2002 it was down 90 percent from its all-time high in 2000. So much for diversification. Still, as Jesse Eisinger wrote in the *Journal* in September, "The fund industry brilliantly has managed to avoid blame for pumping up stocks during the 1990s. Alan Greenspan, CEOs, sell-side analysts, investment bankers, all have taken their lumps. Yet it was these fund managers, who as a group underperform the indexes while charging huge fees to do it . . . who flocked to hot initial public offerings [and] washed the feet of Ken Lay.")[45]

The broadest poll of investor confidence, the UBS/Gallup index, fell to an all-time low of 46 in July; in February the index had stood at 120. Mutual fund investors, who had steadily bought shares in the months after September 11, began pulling out their money in June, and the outflows worsened in July. "I'm the type that stays fully invested no matter what the hell happens out there, but I'm concerned," an Alabama woman told *Bloomberg News*. "It's really scary, isn't it? I don't know whether you can buy a mattress large enough to put all your money in."[46] Even analysts started to get religion. Between March and September the number of sell recommendations quadrupled, to more than 7 percent.

Finally, at last, the game was over.

———

The economic consequences of the bust stretched beyond Wall Street. The initial public offering market effectively shut down, preventing young companies from raising money for growth. Even established companies reined in their capital spending, worrying that Wall Street might at any moment deny them access to new funding. Despite the lowest interest rates in forty years, the U.S. economy, which had grown strongly during the first three months of 2002, slowed dramatically the rest of the year. Unemployment crept higher as job growth stagnated.

It would be nice to be able to write that the market's plunge and the economic slowdown shook up Washington, the accounting industry, Wall Street, and corporate America, galvanizing them to examine ways to make financial reporting more honest and meet their responsibilities to investors.

It would also be a lie. As late as June, most political reporters expected that Congress would not pass meaningful legislation to strengthen the S.E.C. or oversight of the accounting industry. And even on July 9, as President Bush went to Wall Street to give a speech on "Corporate Responsibility," the White House was trying to water down a Senate proposal to tighten oversight of the accounting industry and toughen penalties for fraud. "There's no capitalism without conscience," the president said. "There's no wealth without character."[47] Meanwhile, the *Times* reported, "the Bush administration said it wanted some curbs on the power of a new accounting regulatory board. . . . The administration would also like to scale back a provision of the bill that would restrict the services accounting firms can sell."[48] But investors would no longer tolerate empty rhetoric; the Dow Jones industrial average fell 179 points the day the president spoke, and the S&P 500 dropped 2.5 percent. As stocks continued to drop, the pressure for more meaningful reform became over-whelming. On July 30, Bush signed the Sarbanes-Oxley bill, which increased penalties for fraud, authorized that the S.E.C.'s budget be increased from $430 million to $776 million, and created a new accounting oversight board.

The new board has the power to oversee audits of public compa-nies and penalize accountants who do shady work. The legislation also requires accounting firms to rotate the partners in charge of audits every five years, so that partners don't get too chummy with their clients. Bush called the legislation "the most far-reaching reforms of American business practices since the time of Franklin Delano Roosevelt."[49]

But almost as soon as the ink dried on the bill—and, probably not coincidentally, the media's attention turned from Wall Street to the potential war with Iraq—the administration and S.E.C. chairman Harvey Pitt began to gut the new legislation. In September, Pitt promised John Biggs, the highly regarded chairman of the giant TIAA-CREF pension fund, that Biggs would become the first head of the accounting board.[50] Then the accounting industry and Oxley objected that Biggs might be too tough a regulator, and Pitt withdrew his support for Biggs. Once again the industry would be allowed to choose its own boss. William Webster, whom Pitt later pushed through to head the accounting board, was seventy-eight at the time of his appointment and had no accounting experience—aside from a short stint as the head of the audit committee for U.S. Technologies, a nearly bankrupt Internet company that has been accused of fraud.

"I have tears in my eyes," John Bogle, the founder of the Vanguard Group, whose low-cost mutual funds are the best deal on Wall Street for small investors, said after Biggs was rejected. "I just don't see how this can give the markets any reassurance. It's just more of the same old political stuff."[51]

Then, astonishingly, Bush proposed that the S.E.C. not be given all the money it had been authorized in July. Instead of $776 million, Bush said the commission should get $568 million, 27 percent less than he had previously promised. Even Pitt admitted that the smaller budget would hurt the commission's effectiveness. That prospect didn't seem to bother the White House.[52] In November, following criticism that Webster was unqualified to run the board and that Pitt had not disclosed Webster's role at U.S. Technologies to the other commissioners, both Pitt and Webster resigned. The next month, Bush nominated William H. Donaldson, a former chairman of the New York Stock Exchange, to replace Pitt. Donaldson is well respected on Wall Street for his integrity, but he is the ultimate insider—a member of the Skull and Bones secret society at Yale, undersecretary of state for President Richard Nixon—and is hardly likely to bring strong momentum for reform to the S.E.C., especially at seventy-one. The commission "runs a very substantial risk of being marginalized," one securities law expert warned in December.[53]

The drive for change was slightly stronger on Wall Street, where investment banks seemed to recognize that they needed to take dramatic steps to restore investor confidence. The major firms opened negotiations with the S.E.C. and Eliot Spitzer, the New York State attorney general, to fund independent research that would be separate from their own research departments. The industry could spend as much as $1 billion on the independent research program in the next several years. But even if Wall Street firms truly split research from investment banking, analysts will still face pressure to be positive from the companies they cover and the institutions who hold the stocks they rate. For all the attention it has received, the conflict between research and banking played only a secondary role in the rise of the number; making research better won't make executives, accountants, or fund managers more honest, or improve the S.E.C.

It is easy to understand why the market's decline did not produce a more aggressive political response. In the wake of the bust, the economy is struggling, but the United States is hardly in a depression, so the public's anger has been muted. The potential war with Iraq has understandably distracted voters. Meanwhile, the power of the accounting industry and the nation's chief executives should not be underestimated. "In the Washington lobbying hierarchy, the corporation is by far the most muscular power center, followed by workers . . . and consumers," Arthur Levitt, who saw that power close up, wrote in *Take On the Street,* a memoir of his time at the S.E.C. "Shareholders, and especially individual investors, come last. There is no one, in fact, who represents individual investors full-time. They are the most overlooked and underrepresented interest group in America."[54]

Especially under the current president. Despite his speeches about the need for tough action against criminal CEOs, President Bush is hardly a fan of government intervention in the markets. In his laissez-faire attitude, Bush, for better or worse, has more in common with Reagan than with Roosevelt.

At the same time, with the creation of the accounting oversight board, the easy steps have all been taken. The obvious laws are already on the books. Congress could go further. It could limit the number of options that companies can give their CEOs, or even put restrictions on overall executive pay. It could try to end the conflict of interest that accountants face by giving the government the power to hire auditors at public companies. Instead of bidding for work directly from their clients, accounting firms would submit bids to a federal board that would pick a winner based on audit quality. Congress could even change tax policy to end taxes on dividends, a step that would encourage companies to pay dividends and thus make reported earnings less important.

But none of those proposals is likely to become law. The first two would deeply involve Washington in decisions that have historically been left to private business; the third would be a major tax break for the rich at a time when the federal government faces a $200 billion deficit. Even a relatively modest change, a proposal to limit the percentage of 401(k) accounts that workers can invest in their own company's stock, has little chance of getting through Congress.*

So unless a new wave of scandals hits, Sarbanes-Oxley will probably be the only major new law passed in the wake of the 1990s bubble. What happens now depends on the will of regulators to enforce the rules that already exist, of CEOs to fulfill their duties to their shareholders, of accountants to stand up to their clients, of analysts and fund managers to do honest work.

If history is any guide, they won't.

---

*Whether or not that law passes, employees would be well advised to pretend that it has. Putting a lot of your 401(k) in any one stock breaks the all-important rule of diversification. Putting it in your own company's stock is even worse. You already rely on your employer for your paycheck; why double your dependence by betting your retirement on your company's stock? If something goes wrong, your finances will be devastated.

Conclusion

—

LOOK BOTH WAYS

In October 2002, Michael Lewis, cynical as ever, wrote that the fraud of the 1990s "was, in the grand scheme of things, trivial. Less than trivial: expected. A boom without crooks is like a dog without fleas. It doesn't happen. . . . A healthy free-market economy must tempt a certain number of people to behave corruptly."[1] But Lewis's airy dismissal of the fraud misses a larger point. The boom wasn't healthy. The cult of the number distorted the U.S. economy in ways that will take years to fix.

By overstating their profits, Cisco and Nortel and Lucent and WorldCom and Global Crossing and Motorola and Computer Associates and Microstrategy and America Online and all the rest encouraged investors to pour trillions of dollars into other technology and telecom companies. Much of that money was simply wasted, and the U.S. economy is suffering as a result. Money that could have been invested in building more efficient cars or developing affordable housing or making small business loans was instead poured into Internet sites and telecom companies that never had a prayer of making a profit. (In his October 2002 piece, Lewis made the ludicrous argument that the United States hadn't invested enough in technology before the late 1990s, as if promising tech companies have ever had a difficult time getting funded.) Yes, the tech bubble would have happened even if companies hadn't inflated their profits; many investors were desperate to get in on the Internet and telecom. But the fake profits that technology companies reported caused the bubble to grow even larger than it otherwise would have.

And the impact of the cult of the number went far beyond the wasted investment on Internet and telecom companies. The race to make profits grow unrealistically fast touched every company. For a century, profits at public companies have grown at a nominal rate, including inflation, of around 6 to 7 percent a year. When inflation is low, as it was in the 1990s, even that figure is difficult to achieve. (Where does the 7 percent figure come from? In the long run, public companies have a very difficult time growing their sales or profits much more quickly than the economy as a whole, and the long-term nominal economic growth rate in the United States is roughly 6 to 7 percent. Productivity gains account for 2 to 3 percent, inflation for 3 to 4 percent, and population growth for 1 percent or so. In the short run, companies can grow profits faster than sales by putting a lid on salaries, but in the long run workers will usually get their share of those extra profits. As a percentage of sales, after-tax corporate profits have been flat for around seventy years.)[2]

That 7 percent figure is as close to an iron law as the market has. But in the 1990s, the explosive growth shown by Cisco, America Online, and a few other technology companies blinded Wall Street to that fact. Instead of viewing the tech sector's growth as a once-in-a-century aberration, analysts and strategists steadily raised their expectations for every company. Forecasts for the profit growth of the entire S&P 500 steadily rose, from 9 percent in 1994 to 10 percent to 12 percent to 14 percent by early 2000.[3]

Instead of trying to keep investors' expectations realistic, companies responded by ratcheting up their own internal goals for profit growth. Computers helped a little; falling energy costs helped a little. But not enough. So executives squeezed managers, and managers squeezed employees. Sell more: More books, more razors, more soda, more cars, more software. Finance clients if you have to. Book sales now and have customers pay later if you have to. And if you can't sell more, cut costs: Have managers work fifty hours a week instead of forty, or sixty instead of fifty. Hold down salaries and make up the difference with options. Squeeze suppliers if you can; move jobs overseas if you must. Buy back stock and load up on cheap debt, which will help your earnings per share because you'll have fewer shares outstanding—though heavy leverage increases your risks if the economy slows down. Hold off on research and development.

Bit by bit, the number started to run companies rather than the other way around. Executives made decisions based on the next quarter rather than the next decade. Those choices made their companies less valuable and less stable, hurting their investors, their employees, and sometimes even their customers.

In early September 2001, I saw firsthand the havoc the number can wreak—in the most unlikely of places, an abandoned trailer home in South Carolina. The home had been bought three years before with a loan from Conseco, an Indiana company whose predecessor, Green Tree Financial, was the largest lender on trailer homes during the 1990s. Bad accounting had been the key to Green Tree's growth; the company had used an accounting convention called "gain on sale" that enabled it to book a profit upfront every time it made a loan—and worry later if the loan was actually going to be repaid.

In its race to report ever larger profits, Green Tree had desperately sought out new borrowers, sparking a nationwide boom in manufactured housing. Between 1991 and 1998, annual sales of trailer homes more than doubled, to 374,000. Green Tree's profits soared sixfold between 1991 and 1997. Its stock rose thirtyfold. Overall, the company reported more than $2 billion in profits during the decade, and its CEO, Lawrence M. Coss, took home $200 million in pay.

But Green Tree's profits never really existed. Many of the people it financed had little chance of ever paying off their loans; they were working-class families who had never owned a home before and were so eager to own instead of rent that they borrowed money they could not repay. Normally, of course, financial companies try to avoid making loans to people who can't pay them back. But Green Tree didn't care. As long as it kept making new loans, it could keep booking new profits, thanks to gain-on-sale. "It was easy," a South Carolina dealer told me. "The lenders were greedy as hell." Green Tree "cared more about quotas than the quality of the loan," he said.

At least for a while. Gain-on-sale accounting or not, a loan isn't profitable if it isn't repaid. And eventually Green Tree had to admit that many of its loans were losers. Between 1997 and 2001, Green Tree and Conseco admitted that they had inflated their profits by more than $2 billion—erasing all the profits Green Tree had ever supposedly earned. In 2002, Conseco is near bankruptcy.

But by then it was too late for the company's borrowers, who were defaulting and being evicted from their homes in record numbers. The home I was walking through in September 2001 was one of those, and whoever had left it had gone in a hurry. Dirty pans filled the sink; tiny shoes, a broken stroller, and a small book called *God's Gift to Mothers* were strewn across the stained green carpet. There was no way to tell where the family had gone.

It was a small tragedy, one repeated all over the rural South and Midwest. Conseco alone repossessed more than fifty thousand homes in 2000 and 2001. By the time the hangover in the manufactured housing industry ends later this decade, hundreds of thousands more borrowers will lose their homes. Gain-on-sale accounting, and the boom in manufactured housing that it sparked, turned out to be disastrous for everyone involved: the investors who lost almost

$20 billion on Conseco stock; the trailer home industry, which hired workers and built factories to meet demand that didn't really exist; and, of course, the low-income families evicted from homes they couldn't afford in the first place. Well, not quite everyone: Larry Coss kept his $200 million.

—

Tales like Green Tree's are maddening. Why can't investors look beyond the number? Why can't executives run their businesses for the long run instead of trying to meet arbitrary earnings targets? There must be a better way, right?

Yes and no. The number is tricky. The number is the *point,* after all. In a capitalist system, profits are the way that companies and investors keep score: Should we expand the factory or scrap it? Should I put my money in Merck or Pfizer? Focusing too much on the number's quarter-to-quarter gyrations, or trying to force profits to grow more quickly than history says they can, is madness. But ignoring the number entirely is equally impossible. In the early 1990s, many American academics and business leaders argued that Japan had a crucial edge over the United States because of the "patient capital" that Japanese banks offered Japanese companies. The conventional wisdom held that long-term, low-interest loans freed Japanese companies to make investments that wouldn't pay off for many years, while U.S. companies were hampered by their short-term focus and the higher cost of capital here. Now, after a decade of economic stagnation in Japan, it is clear that an inexhaustible supply of cheap credit (and the inattention to the number that comes with it) can be a curse as well as a blessing. Japanese companies don't have to worry about profits, so they avoid making difficult decisions to fire workers or close stores and factories. They limp along indefinitely, stealing capital from younger, smaller businesses with better growth prospects. American companies can't do that, and our economy is stronger as a result.

But we go wrong when we make the number something more than

it is. Like all faiths, the cult of the number flourishes because it gives its followers certainty. *This is all you need to know,* its acolytes tell us. Admit that the number is nothing more than an assumption, one that may not fully capture a company's worth, and another piece of truth disappears from a world that needs all the certainty it can muster.

Still, it's time for all of us, investors and executives and managers and employees, to admit what we already know: Just because a company hits its earnings targets doesn't mean that it is flourishing; just because it misses for a quarter or two doesn't mean that it is failing. Just because a company has grown 15 percent a year for a couple of years in a row doesn't mean it can grow 15 percent a year forever. Only a handful of companies has earnings that can be smoothly plotted more than a few months in advance. Business doesn't work that way. Life doesn't work that way. Planes run late; meetings go badly; contracts don't get signed when they're supposed to. Hiring good people is hard; making good acquisitions is harder. Even well-run companies have a tough time keeping decent financial controls, figuring out where to invest research dollars, and satisfying investors and the media. And not every investment pays off in three months. Sometimes smaller profits now can mean a better business and bigger profits later.

The number is a lie. We need it; we can't avoid it. But it's still a lie. And as long as investors remain too focused on the number, companies will find ways to manipulate it. In *Inherit the Wind,* the 1955 play about the Scopes monkey trial in Tennessee, Henry Drummond— a stand-in for Clarence Darrow—says during his climactic cross-examination of Matthew Brady, the fictionalized version of William Jennings Bryan, that "the Bible is a book. A good book. But it's not the *only* book."[4] So too with the number.

None of this means that investors shouldn't try to find good, fast-growing companies. They do exist, and they can be great investments.

But no company is perfect, and management often has interests far different from shareholders. In any era, investors would be wise to remember that, and to know how to find the truth behind the numbers. A healthy skepticism is the best defense against fraud; only when investors demand honesty about good news *and* bad will companies respond with the truth.

Caveat emptor.

Afterword

—

THE MORE THINGS CHANGE

A year after the market bottomed in October 2002, the news was mixed for both the United States economy and stock market.

On the plus side, the American economy once again showed its amazing resilience in 2003. Helped by massive deficit spending and extraordinarily low interest rates, the economy broke out of its coma halfway through the year, expanding at an annual rate of 8 percent over the summer, the fastest in twenty years. Consumer spending and business investment rebounded strongly, with solid gains in home prices and sales of computers and cars. After three miserable years in Silicon Valley, a new wave of investment in technology appeared to have begun. Unemployment, after rising as high as 6.4 percent in the spring, dipped below 6 percent in October.

With corporate profits growing sharply, the stock market also rebounded strongly. In December 2003, the Dow closed above 10,000 for the first time in eighteen months. The Wilshire 5000 index, the broadest gauge of the American market, rose 42 percent in the fourteen months after it bottomed in October 2002. Once again, the market had rewarded contrarians. An investor who pulled out of stocks in the fall of 1999, when everyone else piled in, and put his chips back in three years later, when many investors were giving up on stocks, would have done very well indeed.

The gains in 2003 gave Wall Street back its natural optimism. On the surface, the United States seemed ready for another big expansion. The 1990s began badly and ended with the greatest economic and stock gains in American history; why couldn't this decade go the same way?

But a closer look revealed reasons for serious concern. In the short run, big government deficits are a good way to jump-start the economy. The government can borrow money more cheaply than any private business and then distribute the cash to consumers and businesses either through tax cuts or government programs. But deficit spending has limits. Eventually deficits must be paid back. Even the United States government cannot borrow to infinity. At the same time, deficits are like drugs—over time, larger and larger doses are needed to have an impact, because the absolute size of a deficit matters less as a stimulus than its year-over-year change. A deficit of $100 billion may be enough to kick-start growth one year. But the next year, if consumers and businesses have not started spending on their own, a $100 billion deficit will not do the trick, since that level of stimulus will already be built into the economy. The deficit will have to increase to $200 billion, or $300 billion.

But the process cannot continue indefinitely. Most economists think an annual deficit of more than 5 percent of the overall economy is potentially dangerous, especially if foreign investors are funding a lot of it. A deficit of that size leaves the government very dependent on the continued goodwill of its financiers. If those buyers, for whatever reason, decide they do not want to fund the deficit and stop buying government debt, long-term interest rates can soar almost overnight. In 2003, the federal deficit was almost $500 billion, or almost 5 percent of the American economy—near the danger zone. And big deficits are projected for many years to come. And short-term interest rates, which are controlled by the Federal Reserve, are also very low. If growth slows next year, Washington and the Fed will have few good options to get it back on track.

America's giant trade deficit also showed the economy's structural imbalances. Though the United States has run a trade deficit for decades, it reached gargantuan levels in 2003—nearly $500 billion. In essence, the trade deficit shows that the United States is consuming more than it can produce and is dependent on foreign manufacturers to make up the difference. The trade deficit and the budget deficit go hand in hand. We send dollars to foreign companies. They buy our government bonds and mortgages. We, or our children, will have to pay them back eventually. And in the meantime we hope that they do not decide that they have better ways to invest their money.

In contrast, the boom in the 1990s was built on business investment, not government-financed consumer spending. The last decade's growth began even as the federal budget deficit shrank, and the trade deficit remained relatively stable. The 1990s was also a time of what was in retrospect unprecedented political and social stability worldwide. Now the United States is locked in a war in Iraq that will continue for years, and a broader conflict against Islamic terrorism worldwide that may not end for decades. Meanwhile, China is emerging as a major new competitor to the United States. The odds that this decade will be as smooth as the last are slim indeed.

Still, barring another major terrorist attack in the United States or some kind of interest rate shock, the American economy will probably grow strongly for at least the next year. With his election at stake, President Bush has every incentive to pump the economy with huge deficits. We probably will not know whether the American economy is back on a strong growth track until after the 2004 election, when the president—whether Bush or a Democrat—will have to restrain the deficit whether he wants to or not.

Meanwhile, regulators and prosecutors had little luck bringing Wall Street or top corporate executives to justice for their accounting sins during the boom.

In December 2002, Eliot Spitzer, the New York state attorney general, forced Wall Street investment banks to pay $1.4 billion in fines and restitution to states and investors for failing to supervise their analysts. But like the recent economic growth, the deal is less impressive than it first appears. The analysts were far from the worst villains during the 1990s, and the fine is only a tiny fraction of the banks' annual profits.

More important, if the history of Wall Street and corporate America proves anything, it is that only prosecuting and jailing individuals will stop bad behavior. Fining companies is not enough of a deterrent. On that score, prosecutors have almost entirely failed. The corporate rogues who defined the boom and bust have largely escaped punishment.

As of this writing, none of the major offenders has been jailed, and only a handful have seen the inside of a courtroom. The most notable case to reach a jury so far is that of Frank Quattrone, a top Internet investment banker. Federal prosecutors in New York charged Quattrone with obstruction of justice for allegedly interfering with an investigation of the way his firm handed out hot public offerings to favored clients during the boom. His first trial ended in a hung jury; prosecutors say they will retry the case. The second major trial so far is taking place in a New York state courtroom not far from the federal courthouse where Quattrone was tried. The Manhattan district attorney's office has charged L. Dennis Kozlowski and Mark Swartz, the chairman and chief financial officer of Tyco, with looting hundreds of millions of dollars from their company. Prosecutors have shown that the supposedly hardworking Kozlowski spent much of his time sleeping with Tyco employees and spending shareholders' money on expensive antiques and art for an $18 million Manhattan apartment Tyco owned and used. But as the trial drags on, whether Kozlowski and Swartz will be found guilty of breaking any laws remains unclear.

At Enron, the biggest and most important of all the frauds, prosecutors have made slow progress. But whether they will be able to convict Kenneth Lay, Enron's chairman, and Jeff Skilling, its chief executive, is far from clear, despite the fortunes that Skilling and Lay made from Enron's stock before it collapsed. Andrew Fastow, the company's chief financial officer, pled guilty in January 2004 to securities fraud charges, but Fastow is far less important symbolically than Skilling or Lay. Walter Forbes of CUC, a company whose fraud was exposed in 1998, will not be tried until later in 2004. Stephen Hilbert of Conseco will probably never face prosecution, and neither will Charles Wang of Computer Associates.

The lack of successful prosecutions sends a clear signal to chief executives as they consider whether to present their results honestly, or to push accounting boundaries. Get a big accounting firm to sign off on your decisions, and you will almost never be prosecuted for them, even if they create a totally deceptive picture of your business. Discussing Enron in *The New Yorker* in October 2003, Jeffrey Toobin wrote that "in the end, prosecutors may be able to show only that Lay and Skilling presided over a culture where this kind of pervasive dishonesty flourished—which is not, in any legal sense, a crime."

For investors, that message is not reassuring.

—

And even as prosecutors struggled, two major new scandals erupted during the fall of 2003. The first came at the corner of Broad and Wall Streets, the home of more than one previous embarrassment, where Dick Grasso proved that despite his humble origins he could be just as arrogant and haughty as any of his pedigreed predecessors. In 1968, Grasso arrived at the New York Stock Exchange as a sharp-elbowed clerk from Brooklyn making $82.50 a week. A generation later, he had risen to run the Big Board, earning praise for his steady hand after the attacks of September 11, 2001. Then, in September 2003, the exchange revealed that Grasso was due to be paid $140 million, some of it from previous years. Grasso seemed to have forgotten that the Big Board was a nonprofit business owned by its members and accountable to the public; he had paid himself like the head of a Wall Street investment bank. Even Grasso's performance after September 11 could no longer be viewed without scorn; the exchange disclosed that he had gotten a $5 million bonus for reopening the Big Board, while a few blocks away, volunteers picked through the rubble of the World Trade Center.

Still, Grasso kept to the tradition of Richard "The Exchange Is A Perfect Institution" Whitney, refusing to take any blame for his actions. "I believe that I am the right person to be in the position that I'm in," he said, whining that "people now, all of a sudden, have a different impression (of me). . . . I'd be less than candid if I didn't say that hurts."

A week later, after William Donaldson, the chairman of the S.E.C., said that Grasso's huge pay package raised "serious questions" about the Big Board, the exchange forced Grasso to resign. Bitter to the end, Grasso complained he was leaving "with the deepest reluctance." But Grasso's departure did not end the exchange's problems. The generations-old complaints that the Big Board protects its members at the expense of the investors it is supposed to serve grew louder. Calpers—the California state pension fund, one of the largest and most important investors in the world—sued the exchange and its marketmakers, accusing them of cheating by trading for themselves ahead of outside investors whose orders they are required to execute first.

With institutional investors and the S.E.C. taking aim at the Big Board, and electronic trading systems calling into question its very reason for existence, a moment of reckoning for the Big Board appeared nigh. Of course, the N.Y.S.E. appeared in similarly desperate straits in 1937 and 1973, and escaped major damage both times. The exchange's floor, the imagined seat of capitalism, seems to have an almost mythical power over regulators and investors. Whether it will work its magic again in a new century is yet to be seen.

The second financial scandal of the fall was less freighted with symbolism but potentially far more important. Several mutual fund companies, including Putnam Investments, the fifth largest, admitted that they had allowed employees, including fund managers, to profit at the expense of investors by taking advantage of inefficiencies related to the way that mutual funds are priced. Other big fund companies said they had made similar deals with outside hedge funds; in return, they received extra fees from the outside investors. In both cases, mutual funds, which in theory are perhaps the only place on Wall Street that represents the small investor, appeared to be scalping their individual customers.

It will come as no surprise that the S.E.C. had little to do with unearthing the problem, which was discovered largely by Spitzer and prosecutors in Massachusetts. And as the scandal widened during the fall, it threw into relief the conflicts of interest endemic to the fund industry. In theory, the directors of mutual funds work for fund shareholders and have the power to replace fund companies with different managers if their fees are too high or their performance lags. In reality, the directors of funds are appointed and paid by the companies and almost never challenge them. As a result, fund fees have soared over the last twenty years. Investors paid fund companies fees of $35 billion in 2003, almost 1 percent of all the assets in mutual funds, and that figure does not include the upfront sales charges for funds sold by brokers. Considering that mutual funds as a group underperform the overall market, that $35 billion does not appear to be money well spent.

"Now that investors realize that their interests do not always come first with their mutual fund managers, perhaps they will focus on the sky-high fees they have been forking over for years," columnist Gretchen Morgenson wrote in *The New York Times* in December 2003. "If nothing else, this Mount Everest of money makes it even more amazing that some fund managers decided to chisel."

A few days later, the always-aggressive Spitzer pushed the limits of his power, forcing Alliance Capital, a huge fund company, to cut its fees to investors 20 percent to settle his investigation. "This is tantamount to saying that our managers don't add value," one analyst told the *Times*. Exactly. Prosecutors generally should not be encouraged to interfere with the prices set by free markets, but in this case, Spitzer's arm-twisting looks like a necessary corrective for an industry that seems to have been exempt from market forces for decades. (In part, the lack of price competition occurs because fund companies quote their fees as a percentage of assets, rather than a dollar figure, so investors rarely realize exactly how much they are paying.) If Alliance's price cuts lead to a fee war across the fund industry, small investors will save billions of dollars and Spitzer will deserve all the praise he gets.

—

Looking at Wall Street in 2003, a cynic could wonder whether investors had learned anything at all from the previous three years. The biggest gainers in 2003 were money-losing Internet, telecom, and biotech stocks. The Nasdaq as a whole nearly doubled from its lows of October 2002. The few profitable Internet companies, like eBay and Amazon, traded at price-earnings multiples of more than 100, levels that both distant and recent experience suggested could not be justified. Some of the gains were undoubtedly justified, a realization that companies like Lucent and Nortel were not going to disappear.

Still, much of the runup stank of desperate greed, as investors punished during the bust tried to make back their losses with the same blind hunger that had gotten them into trouble to begin with. During the bust, spam e-mails offering tips on hot stocks largely disappeared. But in the fall of 2003, penny stock schemers rejoined the spammers who promised a glimpse of Paris Hilton at her best. No one who studied Wall Street's history could be surprised that greed had once again replaced fear as the market's dominant emotion. But the speed with which investors forgave and forgot came as something of a shock. The buyers remained as blissfully unaware as ever.

ACCRUAL VERSUS CASH ACCOUNTING

Here's a hypothetical example of why accrual accounting makes more sense than cash accounting for big companies. Suppose Ford builds a Taurus for $20,000. Jane buys it the next day for $23,000. If she pays the full price in cash for the car, Ford's profit is obvious: $3,000.

But Jane is more likely to finance the Taurus, making a down payment of, say, $5,000 and paying the rest over time. If Ford simply uses cash flows to measure its profits and losses, it will book a loss of $15,000 ($5,000 minus $20,000) up front as it sells the Taurus, then a profit each month as Jane pays back her loan.

And the more Tauruses Ford sells, the more it will lose up front.

Measuring profit that way doesn't make sense. Whether Jane pays cash for the car or takes out a loan, the sale is what counts to Ford. So what Ford should do—and does, under accrual accounting—is book the $23,000 in revenue and $3,000 in profit as soon as Jane signs on the dotted line and drives off the lot. Whether the company gets paid in full immediately or over time is irrelevant, at least in theory.

Unfortunately, what makes sense in theory offers lots of opportunities for abuse in practice.

Take Jane and her Taurus. Suppose it's September 30, and Ford needs to sell just one more Taurus to hit its earnings target for the quarter.

In walks Jane. She'd love a new Taurus. But she really can't afford one. Ford's going to wind up owning that Taurus again next year after Jane defaults on her loan.

Well, next year is next year. And this quarter is now. If Jane signs, the car's sold, and Ford gets to book $3,000 in profit today. Sign here, Jane.

On the cost side of the ledger, the picture can be equally murky. Again, consider the Taurus. Ford can't just start building Tauruses one sunny day. Years before the first car rolls off an assembly line, the company must spend billions of dollars to build a plant, buy equipment, and pay engineers and designers. But not all of that spending is created equal. Some of it, like the new machinery Ford buys, is classified as a "capital expense," an investment for the future that doesn't count immediately against the company's bottom line. Instead, Ford will charge the cost of the machinery over time, as it slowly wears out. On the other hand, engineers' salaries are an ongoing expense for Ford even if they are working on projects that will take years to finish. Under accounting rules, salaries should usually be expensed immediately.

For big companies, the distinction between capital investment and operating expense is crucial. If a company can figure out how to classify its ongoing costs as capital investments, it can hide those expenses from its financial statements and make its bottom line look better.

BALANCE SHEETS AND INCOME STATEMENTS

The core principle in accounting is that a company's assets and liabilities must always balance. Assets are cash, property, and other items of value to a company, such as accounts receivable, or sales for which customers have not yet paid. Liabilities are bonds, loans, and other debts, such as accounts payable—supplies that a company has ordered but still hasn't paid for.

For accounting purposes, a company's equity also is listed as a liability on the balance sheet. But equity is a very odd kind of liability, one that is not owed to anyone. Equity belongs to the company itself, and thus to the company's shareholders.

So: Assets = Liabilities = Debt plus Equity. Hence the term "balance sheet." For example, consider the balance sheet of Aprilfirst.com, an imaginary Web design firm, at the moment of its creation. Its shareholders have put in $1 million in cash, and the firm has borrowed another $1 million from the local bank.* Aprilfirst.com's balance sheet is perfectly pure:

---

*For the sake of simplicity, assume the loan is interest-free.

ASSETS
Cash: $2 million

LIABILITIES
Debt: $1 million
Equity: $1 million

Five minutes later, Aprilfirst.com buys an old office building for $250,000 in cash and spends $250,000 on Aeron chairs and computers, payable interest-free in six months. It is ready for business, with a new, slightly more complicated balance sheet:

ASSETS
Cash: $1.75 million
Property, plant, and equipment: $500,000
Total: $2.25 million

LIABILITIES
Debt: $1 million
Accounts payable: $250,000 (the money it owes for the chairs and computers)
Equity: $1 million
Total: $2.25 million

Aprilfirst.com's assets and liabilities have risen, but its equity has not changed, because it has not actually made or lost any money.

But a balance sheet offers only part of the picture of a company's financial health. A balance sheet is a snapshot of a particular moment, not a view of whether a company is making or losing money over a period of time. For that, companies use an income statement comparing their sales and expenses.

The income statement first lists a company's revenues—the "top line." Then come the expenses, beginning with the direct cost of creating the product or service—the "cost of goods sold." Broader over-head costs, such as legal expenses and executive salaries, follow, under the heading of "selling, general, and administrative expenses." Depending on the industry, different line items follow. Drug companies break out their research and development costs; airlines their fuel costs; consumer products companies their advertising expenses. All those costs are subtracted from the top line, leaving (hopefully) an operating profit.

But the expenses don't end there. There are interest payments, taxes, depreciation and amortization costs, and possibly "one-time" charges for extraordinary events such as a merger. Only after all those items are subtracted does the company find out its net profit or loss.

On the surface, the income statement and the balance sheet don't seem to have much to do with each other. One reveals the company's assets and debts at a single moment; the other is a running tab of sales and expenses. But—and this is the reason that accounting, believe it or not, can be deeply satisfying intellectually—the balance sheet and the income statement are actually two sides of the same coin. If a company spends money, it must either count the spending as an expense on its income statement or add an asset to its balance sheet in place of the cash. The money can't just disappear.

Here's a concrete example. Imagine Aprilfirst.com has gotten off to a slow start. After three months all it has done is hire and fire five employees, costing it $250,000 in severance expenses. Its income statement for the period:

> Revenues: $0
> Cost of goods sold: $0
> Selling, general, and administrative expenses: $250,000
> Operating loss: $250,000
> Net loss: $250,000

That $250,000 loss is subtracted from the equity on the Aprilfirst
.com balance sheet. Its new balance sheet:

ASSETS
Cash and equivalents: $1.5 million (was $1.75 million)
Property, plant, and equipment: $500,000
Total: $2 million (was $2.25 million)

LIABILITIES
Debt: $1 million
Accounts payable: $250,000
Equity: $750,000 (was $1 million)
Total: $2 million (was $2.25 million)

If Aprilfirst.com wants to hide how badly things are going, it may
try to disguise the severance payments by putting them on its balance
sheet as an asset instead of flowing them through its income statement. The revised income statement:

Revenues: $0
Cost of goods sold: $0
Selling, general, and administrative expenses: $0
Operating loss: $0
Net loss: $0

Behold: The loss has vanished. Aprilfirst.com has "capitalized" the
payments. But the cash has still been spent. So Aprilfirst.com must put
a nonexistent asset on its balance sheet to hide the missing money and
keep its equity at $1 million. Its revised, fraudulent balance sheet:

ASSETS
Cash and equivalents: $1.5 million
Property, plant, and equipment: $500,000

Goodwill and intangibles: $250,000
Total: $2.25 million

LIABILITIES
Debt: $1 million
Accounts payable: $250,000
Equity: $1 million
Total: $2.25 million

Aprilfirst.com has kept the loss off its income statement, but it has had to distort its balance sheet to do so. It is now overstating its equity by $250,000.

The first law of thermodynamics says that energy cannot simply disappear from the universe. It can go from one form to another or even be converted into matter, but it always continues to exist. The first law of accounting says the same about cash. It can't just vanish. It leaves a trail.

NOTES

PROLOGUE: ONE OF MANY

1 Mark Harrington, "Upbeat Report for CA: A Rise in Earnings," *Newsday*, January 23, 2001, p. A36.

INTRODUCTION: SYSTEM FAILURE

1 Kate Zernike, "Stocks Slide Is Playing Havoc with Older Americans' Dreams," *The New York Times*, July 14, 2002, p. A1.

CHAPTER 1: BOOM AND BUST

1 Sherwin D. Smith, "Thirty Years Ago: A Midget Sat on J. P. Morgan's Lap and Showed the Great Banker Was Only Human," *The New York Times Magazine*, May 26, 1963, p. 50.

2 Graf's story had a tragic ending. In 1935, tired of the publicity from her encounter with Morgan, she returned to her native Germany. Lya Graf was her stage name; her given name was Lia Schwarz. Half-Jewish and a midget, she was arrested by the Nazis in 1937 as a useless person. She died in the gas chambers at Auschwitz.

3 Vincent Carosso, *Investment Banking in America: A History*, Harvard University Press, 1970, p. 252.

4 Robert Sobel, *The Great Bull Market: Wall Street in the 1920s*, W. W. Norton & Company, 1968, p. 73.

5 Benjamin Graham, *The Memoirs of the Dean of Wall Street*, McGraw-Hill, 1996, p. 150.

6 Association for Investment Management and Research, *From Prac-*

tice to Profession: A History of the Financial Analysts Foundation and the Investment Profession, p. 13.

7 Benjamin Graham and David Dodd, Security Analysis, McGraw-Hill, 1934, pp. 44–45.

8 From Practice to Profession, p. 13.

9 B. Mark Smith, Toward Rational Exuberance, Farrar, Straus & Giroux, 2001, p. 76.

10 Benjamin Graham, The Intelligent Investor: Fourth Revised Edition, HarperCollins, 1973, p. 317.

11 Graham and Dodd, Security Analysis, p. 307.

12 Ibid.

13 John Brooks, Once in Golconda, Harper & Row, 1969, p. 97.

14 Carosso, Investment Banking in America, p. 254.

15 Sobel, The Great Bull Market.

16 Robert Shaplen: Kreuger: Genius and Swindler, Alfred A. Knopf, 1960, p. 76.

17 Graham and Dodd, Security Analysis, p. 617.

18 Graham and Dodd discuss these gimmicks in detail in Chapters 31 through 48 of Security Analysis.

19 Sobel, The Great Bull Market, p. 127.

20 Ibid., p. 138.

21 Shaplen, Kreuger, pp. 225–26.

22 Joel Seligman, The Transformation of Wall Street, Houghton Mifflin Company, 1982, p. 38.

23 Carosso, Investment Banking in America, p. 346.

24 Brooks, Once in Golconda, p. 198.

25 Charles R. Geisst, One Hundred Years of Wall Street, McGraw-Hill, 2000, p. 19.

CHAPTER 2: FOUNDATIONS

1 Seligman, The Transformation of Wall Street, Houghton Mifflin Company, 1982, p. 41.

2 Carosso, Investment Banking in America: A History, Harvard University Press, 1970, pp. 362–63.

3 Seligman, The Transformation of Wall Street, p. 114.

4 Brooks, Once in Golconda, Harper & Row, 1969, p. 273.

5 Seligman, The Transformation of Wall Street, p. 198.

6 Ibid., p. 200.

7 Mark Stevens, *The Big Eight*, Macmillan Publishing Company, 1981, p. 7.

8 Gary John Previts and Barbara Dubis Merino, *A History of Accounting in the United States: The Cultural Significance of Accounting*, Ohio State University Press, 1998, p. 78.

9 Ibid., p. 157.

10 The Cohen Commission Report, in Stevens, *The Big Six*, Touchstone, 1991, p. 7.

11 Previts and Merino, *A History of Accounting in the United States*, p. 132.

12 Ibid., p. 207.

13 Ibid., p. 291.

14 Reaction to the tour as well as the comments by Fred Allen are from Robert Sobel, *N.Y.S.E.*, Weybright and Talley, 1975, p. 5–8.

15 Gilbert Edmund Kaplan and Chris Welles, eds., *The Money Managers*, p. iii.

16 Sobel, *N.Y.S.E.*, p. 131.

17 Carosso, *Investment Banking in America*, p. 458.

18 Benjamin Graham and David Dodd, *Security Analysis*, McGraw-Hill, 1934, p. 315.

19 Peter L. Bernstein, *Capital Ideas: The Improbable Origins of Modern Wall Street*, The Free Press, 1992, p. 154.

20 John L. Carey, *The Rise of the Accounting Profession*, American Institute of Certified Public Accountants, 1970, Vol. 2, p. 23.

21 Benjamin Graham, *The Intelligent Investor: Fourth Revised Edition*, Harper Collins, 1973, p. 2.

22 Ibid., p. 22.

23 Sobel, *N.Y.S.E.*, p. 170.

24 Janet Lowe, *The Rediscovered Benjamin Graham: Selected Writings of the Wall Street Legend*, John Wiley & Sons, 1999, p. 130.

25 Sobel, *N.Y.S.E.*, p. 172.

26 B. Mark Smith, *Towards Rational Exuberance*, Farrar, Strauss & Giroux, 2001, p. 143.

CHAPTER 5: BUBBLING UNDER

1 Robert Sobel, *The Last Bull Market*, W. W. Norton and Company, 1980, p. 19.

2 Ibid., p. 20.

3 Leslie Wayne, "Gerry Tsai Builds His Dreamhouse," *The New York Times,* June 13, 1982, p. C1.

4 Gilbert Edmund Kaplan and Chris Welles, eds., *The Money Managers,* Dell Publishing, 1969, p. 84.

5 Jeremy J. Siegel, *Stocks for the Long Run: Third Edition,* McGraw-Hill, 2002, p. 344.

6 Robert Sobel, *N.Y.S.E.,* Weybright and Talley, 1975, p. 242.

7 Sobel, *The Last Bull Market,* p. 66.

8 Ibid., p. 32.

9 Association for Investment Management and Research, *From Practice to Profession,* p. 36.

10 Sobel, *The Last Bull Market,* p. 106.

11 Benjamin Graham, *The Intelligent Investor: Fourth Revised Edition,* Harper Collins, 1973, p. 237.

12 John Brooks, *The Go-Go Years,* Allworth Press, 1973, p. 167.

13 Ibid., p. 162.

14 Ibid., p. 305.

15 Joel Seligman, *The Transformation of Wall Street,* Houghton Mifflin Company, 1982, p. 422.

16 Brooks, *The Go-Go Years,* p. 161.

17 Kaplan and Welles, eds., *The Money Managers,* introduction, p. 2.

18 Ibid., p. 33.

19 Chris Welles, *The Last Days of the Club,* E. P. Dutton & Co., 1975, p. 24.

20 Wayne, "Gerry Tsai Builds His Dreamhouse."

21 Sobel, *The Last Bull Market,* p. 191.

22 Kaplan and Welles, eds., *The Money Managers,* p. 74.

23 Carosso, *Investment Banking in America: A History,* Harvard University Press, 1970, p. 390.

24 Seligman, *The Transformation of Wall Street,* p. 213.

25 Ibid., p. 264.

26 Ibid., p. 416.

27 Sidney Cottle, Roger E. Murray, and Frank E. Block, *Graham and Dodd's Security Analysis: 5th ed.,* McGraw-Hill, 1988, p. 21.

28 Graham, *The Intelligent Investor,* p. 245.

CHAPTER 4: THE DEATH OF EQUITIES

1 Raymond L. Dirks and Leonard Gross, *The Great Wall Street Scandal,* McGraw-Hill, 1974, p. 35.

2 Ronald L. Soble and Robert E. Dallas, *The Impossible Dream: The Equity Funding Story,* G. P. Putnam's Sons, 1975, p. 286.

3 Dirks and Gross, *The Great Wall Street Scandal,* p. 10.

4 Soble and Dallas, *The Impossible Dream,* p. 158.

5 Joel Seligman, *The Transformation of Wall Street,* Houghton Mifflin Company, 1982, p. 550.

6 Ibid., pp. 553–54.

7 Lee Seidler, speaking in prepared testimony before a House committee oversight hearing on "Accounting and Investor Protection Issues Raised by Enron and Other Public Companies," March 6, 2000, Washington, D.C.

8 Mark Stevens, *The Big Eight,* Macmillan Publishing Company, 1981, p. 134.

9 Ibid., pp. 215–16.

10 Ibid., p. 213.

11 Ibid., p. 220.

12 Ibid., p. 207.

13 Brooks, *The Go-Go Years,* Allworth Press, 1973, p. 305.

14 Seligman, *The Transformation of Wall Street,* p. 410.

15 Ibid., p. 483.

16 Ibid., p. 485.

CHAPTER 5: COUNTDOWN

1 Records from the National Weather Service station in Brooklyn, New York, show a high of 85 degrees and very light rain for August 17.

2 Alexander R. Hammer, "Dow Soars by 38.81; Volume Near Peak," *The New York Times,* August 18, 1982, p. D1.

3 Warren Buffett, "The Superinvestors of Graham-and-Doddsville," in Graham, *The Intelligent Investor,* p. 298.

4 Charles R. Morris, *Money, Greed, and Risk,* Random House, 1999, p. 111.

5 Ibid., p. 113.

6 Jeffrey A. Leib, "Mobil Plans to Divest Ward Unit," *The New York Times,* May 7, 1985, p. D1.

7 Floyd Norris, "Milken's Plea Reflects Ethics of Drexel in 80s," *The New York Times,* April 25, 1990, p. D1.

8 Jeremy J. Siegel, "Stocks Are Still an Oasis," *The Wall Street Journal,* July 22, 2002, p. A10.

9 Lawrence J. DeMaria, "Stocks Plunge 508 Points, a Drop of 22.6%; 604 Million Volume Nearly Doubles Record," *The New York Times*, October 20, 1987, p. A1.

10 Ibid.

11 Diane K. Shah, "Riding the Bull for a Day," *The New York Times Magazine*, December 1, 1996, p. 99.

12 Warren Getler, "Stock Market Skids as Fed Applies Brakes; Investors Shift to Growth," *The Wall Street Journal*, January 3, 1995, p. R4.

13 Jeffrey M. Laderman, "The Earnings Boom That Can't Budge Investors," *Business Week*, November 7, 1994, p. 127.

14 Dave Kansas, "Dow Industrials Close Above 5000 Mark," *The Wall Street Journal*, November 22, 1995, p. C1.

CHAPTER 6: THE NUMBER IS BORN

1 Gilbert Edmund Kaplan and Chris Welles, eds., *The Money Managers*, Dell Publishing, 1969, p. 184.

2 Welles, *The Last Days of the Club*, E. P. Dutton & Co., 1975, p. 69.

3 Joseph Nocera, "Picking the Winners," *The New York Times Magazine*, September 20, 1987, p. 26

4 Ann B. Fisher, "Can You Trust Analysts' Reports?" *Fortune*, October 1, 1990, p. 195.

5 Raymond L. Dirks and Leonard Gross, *The Great Wall Street Scandal*, McGraw-Hill, 1974, p. 256.

6 Michael Siconolfi, "Under Pressure: At Morgan Stanley, Analysts Were Urged to Soften Harsh Views," *The Wall Street Journal*, July 14, 1992, p. A1.

7 Jeffrey M. Laderman, "How Much Should You Trust Your Analyst?" *Business Week*, July 23, 1990, p. 54.

8 Nocera, "Picking the Winners," p. 26.

9 Siconolfi, "Under Pressure," p. A1.

10 Fisher, "Can You Trust Analysts' Reports?" p. 195.

11 N. R. Kleinfield, "The Many Faces of the Wall Street Analyst," *The New York Times*, October 25, 1987, p. C1.

12 Stuart Weiss, "Hell Hath No Fury Like a Surprised Stock Analyst," *Business Week*, January 21, 1985, p. 98.

13 Bill Barnhart, "Blood, Sweat, Tears, and a Few Pennies," *Chicago Tribune*, October 31, 1994, p. C1.

CHAPTER 7: OPTIONS

1 "For Whom Were the Golden Eighties Most Golden?" *Business Week,* May 7, 1990, p. 60.

2 Warren Buffett, "Who Really Cooks the Books," *The New York Times,* July 24, 2002, p. A19.

3 From an unpublished letter by Graham that Buffett quoted in his 1990 letter to Berkshire Hathaway shareholders.

4 World Accounting Report, *Financial Times,* April 11, 1994.

5 "For Whom Were the Golden Eighties Most Golden?" p. 60.

6 Justin Fox, "The Next Best Thing to Free Money," *Fortune,* July 7, 1997, p. 52.

7 J. Carter Beese, "A Rule That Stunts Growth," *The Wall Street Journal,* February 4, 1994, p. A18.

8 "Big Six Accounting Firms Urge FASB Chairman to Withdraw Stock Option Plan," *Securities Week,* July 25, 1994, p. 1.

9 Justin Fox, "The Next Best Thing to Free Money," p. 52.

10 Ibid.

11 David Leonhardt, "Stock Options Said Not to Be as Widespread as Backers Say," *The New York Times,* July 18, 2002, p. C1.

12 Fox, "The Next Best Thing to Free Money," p. 52.

13 David Leonhardt, "Why Is This Man Smiling? Executive Pay Drops Off the Political Radar," *The New York Times,* Week-in-Review, April 16, 2000, p. 4.

14 Peter G. Gosselin, "Fed Official Urges Execs to Trim Their Pay," *Los Angeles Times,* September 12, 2002, p. C1.

15 Leonhardt, "Why Is This Man Smiling?" p. 4.

16 Gretchen Morgenson, "As Pressure Grows, Option Costs Come Out of Hiding," *The New York Times,* Money and Business, May 19, 2002, p. 3.

17 Roger Lowenstein, "Heads I Win, Tails I Win," *The New York Times Magazine,* June 27, 2002, p. 102.

CHAPTER 8: ACCOUNTANTS AT THE TROUGH

1 Mark Stevens, *The Big Eight,* Macmillan Publishing Company, 1981, pp. 23–24.

2 Ibid., p. 31.

3 Ibid., p. 42.

4 Previts and Merino, *A History of Accountancy in the United States*, p. 372.

5 Stevens, *The Big Eight*, p. 9.

6 Ibid., p. 62.

7 Lee Berton, "Total War: CPA Firms Diversify, Cut Fees, Steal Clients in Battle for Business," *The Wall Street Journal*, September 20, 1985 p. A1.

8 Flynn McRoberts et al., "The Fall of Andersen: Greed Tarnished Golden Reputation," *Chicago Tribune*, September 1, 2002, p. 1.

9 McRoberts et al., "Civil War Splits Andersen: Consulting Conquers, Traditions Wither," *Chicago Tribune*, September 2, 2002, p. 1.

10 Stevens, *The Big Six*, Touchstone, 1991, p. 210.

11 Ibid., p. 210.

12 Jill Andresky, "But I'm Just the Piano Player (Laventhol & Horwath)," *Forbes*, May 4, 1987, p. 56.

13 Stevens, *The Big Six*, p. 21.

14 McRoberts et al., "The Fall of Andersen."

15 Emily Nelson and Joann S. Lublin, "Buy the Numbers," *The Wall Street Journal*, August 13, 1998, p. A1.

16 Floyd Norris, "Market Place: Cendant's Share Price Plunges 46% on 'Accounting Irregularities,'" *The New York Times*, April 17, 1998, p. D1.

17 Silverman's quotes in footnote: Reed Abelson, "The Road to Reviving a Reputation: Cendant Chief Tries to Recover from a Deal Gone Very Bad," *The New York Times*, June 15, 2000, p. D1.

18 Floyd Norris, "Editorial Observer: Wall Street Turns Hostile to Chainsaw Al," *The New York Times*, June 3, 1998, p. A24.

19 Reed Abelson, "Market Place: As the Accounting World Shifts, Conflicts Are Items to Audit," *The New York Times*, November 25, 1997, p. D10.

20 Melody Petersen, "Consulting by Auditors Stirs Concern," *The New York Times*, July 13, 1998, p. D1.

21 Arthur Levitt, *Take On the Street*, Pantheon Books, 2002, p. 128.

22 Statistics from Opensecrets.org, an Internet site that compiles data on political contributions.

23 Jane Mayer, "The Accountants' War," *The New Yorker*, April 22, 2002, p. 70.

24 Floyd Norris, "A War the Accountants Will Lose Even If They Win," *The New York Times*, July 28, 2000, p. C1.

25 Mayer, "The Accountants' War," p. 72.

CHAPTER 9: ARCHAEOLOGISTS AND DETECTIVES

1 Arthur Levitt, "The Numbers Game," speech before New York University's Center for Law and Business, September 28, 1998.

2 *SEC Operations: Increased Workload Creates Challenges*, General Accounting Office, March 2002, p. 3.

3 *Securities and Exchange Commission: Human Capital Challenges Require Management Attention*, General Accounting Office, September 2001, p. 24.

4 Ibid., p. 18.

5 Ibid., p. 8.

6 *SEC Operations: Increased Workload*, General Accounting Office, p. 23.

7 Ibid., p. 19.

8 Scot J. Paltrow, Greg Ip, and Michael Schroeder: "Beat Cop: As Huge Changes Roil the Market, Some Ask: Where Is the SEC?" *The Wall Street Journal*, October 11, 1999, p. A1.

9 Herb Greenberg, "Herb's Hotline: A Swift Response from Dan Borislow," TheStreet.com, December 12, 2000.

10 Joel Seligman, *The Transformation of Wall Street*, Houghton Mifflin Company, 1982, p. 565.

11 Ibid., p. 568.

12 Floyd Norris, "3 Big Accounting Firms Assail S.E.C.'s Proposed Restrictions," *The New York Times*, July 27, 2002, p. C9.

13 Marshall E. Blume and Irwin Friend, *The Changing Role of the Individual Investor*, John Wiley & Sons, 1978, p. 203.

14 Jerry Knight, "GOP Begins Bid to Revamp Securities Laws," *The Washington Post*, July 19, 1995, p. F1.

15 Roger Lowenstein, "House Aims to Fix Securities Laws, But Indeed, Is the System Broke?" *The Wall Street Journal*, August 10, 1995, p. C1.

16 Michael Schroeder, "Guess Who's Gunning for the S.E.C," *Business Week*, August 14, 1995, p. 40.

17 Paltrow, Ip, and Schroeder, "Beat Cop."

18 Jane Mayer, "The Accountants' War," p. 66.

19 Michael Lewis, "Jonathan Lebod's Extracurricular Activities," *The New York Times Magazine*, February 25, 2001, p. 25.

20 Clifton Leaf, "It's Time to Stop Coddling White-Collar Crooks. Send Them to Jail," *Fortune*, March 18, 2002, p. 66.

21 Ibid., p. 64.

22 Dean Rotbart, "Market Hardball: Aggressive Methods of Some Short Sellers Stir Critics to Cry Foul," *The Wall Street Journal*, September 9, 1985, p. A1.

23 Gary Weiss, "Sure-Shot Shorts: Short Sellers Are Hitting the Right Stocks at the Right Time," *Business Week*, November 16, 1992, p. 101.

24 E. S. Browning, "Short Sellers Lose Big, but Some Say Their Day Is Due," *The Wall Street Journal*, November 2, 1995, p. A1.

CHAPTER 10: FRENZY

1 Molly Baker, "Pixar IPO Underscores Changes in the IPO World," *The Wall Street Journal*, December 11, 1995, p. C1.

2 Craig Torres, "Pricing of Hot Stock Offerings Sparks Concerns," *The Wall Street Journal*, March 4, 1992, p. C1.

3 Molly Baker and Joan E. Rigdon, "Netscape's IPO Gets an Explosive Welcome," *The Wall Street Journal*, August 9, 1995, p. C1.

4 Joan E. Rigdon, "Netscape's Market for Future Growth May Not Be Big Enough for Wall Street," *The Wall Street Journal*, August 11, 1995, p. A3.

5 Baker and Rigdon, "Netscape's IPO Gets an Explosive Welcome," p. C1.

6 Reed Abelson, "A Guide to the Goofs of Wall Street's Wizards," *The New York Times*, December 1, 1996, p. C1.

7 Gretchen Morgenson, "How Did So Many Get It So Wrong?" *The New York Times*, December 31, 2001, p. C1.

8 Floyd Norris, "Stormy Weather?" *The New York Times*, January 2, 1997, p. C21.

9 Securities Industry Association 2002 fact book, p. 49.

10 David Barboza, "On-Line Trade Fees Falling Off the Screen," *The New York Times*, March 1, 1998, p. C4.

11 Gregory J. Millman, *The Day Traders: The Untold Story of the Extreme Investors and How They Changed Wall Street Forever*, Times Books, 1999, p. 29.

12 Matthew Klam, "Riding the Mo in the Lime Green Glow," *The New York Times Magazine,* November 21, 1999, p. 70.

13 Securities Industry Association fact book, p. 58.

14 Investment Company Institute Mutual Fund fact book, p. 3, section 2.

15 Suzanne McGee, "Quest for Security: Money Managers Seek Places to Park Cash Until Market Calms," *The Wall Street Journal,* January 19, 1998, p. C1.

16 Diane K. Shah, "Riding the Bull for a Day," *The New York Times Magazine,* December 1, 1996, p. 99.

17 Statistics courtesy of Barra, a financial risk management company based in Berkeley, California.

18 Jeffrey Bronchick, "We Need Better Stock Analysis, Not More Info," *The Wall Street Journal,* August 6, 2002, p. A20.

19 Christopher Oster and Ken Brown, "First Call Changes Last Word on Earnings," *The Wall Street Journal,* August 22, 2002, p. C1.

20 Joan E. Rigdon, "H-P Posts 25% Net Gain, but Stock Falls Due to Missed Forecasts," *The New York Times,* May 17, 1996, p. A3.

21 Greg Ip, "Traders Laugh Off the Official Estimate on Earnings, Act on Whispered Number," *The Wall Street Journal,* January 17, 1997, p. C1.

22 Jack Ciesielski, "More Second Guessing: Markets Need Better Disclosure of Earnings Management," *Barron's,* August 24, 1998, p. 47.

23 Nanette Byrnes and Richard A. Melcher, "Earnings Hocus-pocus— How Companies Come Up with the Numbers They Want," *Business Week,* October 5, 1998, p. 134.

24 Bernard Condon, "Pick a Number, Any Number," *Forbes,* March 23, 1998, p. 124.

25 Jesse Eisinger, "Why Accounting Matters," TheStreet.com, September 21, 1998.

26 Condon, "Pick a Number," p. 124

27 David Wessel and Jacob M. Schlesinger, "Fed Cuts Interest Rates a Quarter-Point in a Surprise Move to Shore Up Markets," *The Wall Street Journal,* October 16, 1998, p. A3.

28 George Melloan, "Global View: Fed's Silver Lining Hides Some Clouds," *The Wall Street Journal,* November 24, 1998, p. A23.

29 Steve Johnson, "These Days, TV Is Bullish on Business," *Chicago Tribune,* January 24, 2000, p. T1.

30 Susan Pulliam, "At Bill's Barber Shop, In Like Flynn Is a Cut Above the Rest," *The Wall Street Journal*, March 13, 2000, p. A1.

31 Maria Atanasov, "Share and Share Alike," *Newsday*, August 30, 2000, p. C8.

32 Floyd Norris, "The Year in the Markets, 1999: Extraordinary Winners and More Losers," *The New York Times*, January 3, 2000, p. C17.

33 Greg Ip, "High Anxiety: Techs Keep Rising Despite Fears—Dow Industrials, Nasdaq Ascend to New Peaks," *The Wall Street Journal*, December 27, 1999, p. C1.

34 Shawn Tully, "Has the Market Gone Mad?" *Fortune*, January 24, 2000, p. 80.

35 Robert D. Hershey Jr., "Down and Out on Wall Street," *The New York Times*, December 26, 1999, p. C1.

36 Stacey I. Bradford, "The Future Is Now," *SmartMoney*, February 2000, p. 106.

37 James J. Cramer, "The Winners of the New World," TheStreet.com, February 29, 2000.

38 Statistics courtesy of Thomson First Call, which compiles analysts' estimates.

39 Andrew Marks, "Nasdaq Express Just Rolls On and On," *Business Times* (Singapore), March 11, 2000, p. 3.

CHAPTER 11: TRUTH

1 Alex Berenson and Patrick McGeehan, "Amid the Stock Market's Losses, a Sense the Game Has Changed," *The New York Times*, April 16, 2000, p. A1.

2 Alex Berenson and Kevin Petrie, "Cracking the Books II: Lucent's Growing Fast but Desperate to Keep Up with the Ciscos," TheStreet.com, October 18, 1999.

3 Simon Romero, "Compressed Data; Lucent to Sell Its Golf Complex at a Profit," *The New York Times*, July 30, 2001, p. C4.

4 Seth Schiesel, "New Warning, and Deeper, from Lucent," *The New York Times*, July 21, 2000, p. C1.

5 Justin Baer, "Lucent Inflated Sales, Hurting Future Revenue, Executives Said," *Bloomberg News*, November 20, 2002.

6 Mark Maremont, Jesse Eisinger, and John Carrerou, "Muffled

Voice: How High-Tech Dream at Lernout & Hauspie Crumbled in Scandal," *The Wall Street Journal*, December 7, 2000, p. A1.

7 Ibid.

8 John Markoff, "Cisco Results Come In Short of Forecast," *The New York Times*, February 7, 2001, p. C1.

9 Susan Pulliam, "Hair Today, Gone Tomorrow: Tech Ills Shave Barber," *The Wall Street Journal*, March 7, 2001, p. C1.

10 Bethany McLean, "Enron's Power Crisis," *Fortune*, September 17, 2001, p. 48.

11 David Cay Johnston, "A 1995 Executive Pay Plan Led to Big Bonus This Week," *The New York Times*, May 23, 1998, p. D15.

12 Raju Narisetti, "CA's CEO Vows Growth Prospects Remain Strong," *The Wall Street Journal*, August 12, 1998, p. B6.

13 Computer Associates press release, *PR Newswire*, October 25, 2000.

14 Jerry Guidera, "Nobody Is Too Sure Why Charles Wang Is Buying Up a Village," *The Wall Street Journal*, June 27, 2001, p. A1.

15 Jesse Drucker, "Motorola's Profit: Special Again?" *The Wall Street Journal*, October 15, 2002, p. C1.

16 Jonathan Weil, "Deals and Deal Markets: Pro Forma Figures May Stay in Reports, but Must Be Explained, Panel Suggests," *The Wall Street Journal*, April 27, 2001, p. C16.

17 Mark Harrington, "Upbeat Report for CA: A Rise in Earnings," *Newsday*, January 23, 2001, p. A36.

18 Bethany McLean, "Is Enron Overpriced?" *Fortune*, March 5, 2001, p. 122.

19 Laura Goldberg, "Enron Posts Loss After Writedowns; Core Businesses Considered Solid," *Houston Chronicle*, October 17, 2001, p. 1.

20 Susanne Craig and Jonathan Weil, "Most Analysts Remain Plugged In to Enron," *The Wall Street Journal*, October 26, 2001, p. C1.

21 Bethany McLean, "Why Enron Went Bust," *Fortune*, December 24, 2001, p. 58.

22 Leslie Wayne, "Before Debacle, Enron Insiders Cashed in More than $1.1 Billion in Shares," *The New York Times*, January 13, 2002, p. A1.

23 Floyd Norris and David Barboza, "Ex-Chairman's Finances: Lay Sold Shares for $100 Million," *The New York Times*, February 16, 2002, p. A1.

24 Joe Berardino, "Enron: A Wake-Up Call," *The Wall Street Journal*, December 4, 2001, p. A18.

25 Michael Rapoport, "In the Money: Enron Auditor's Complaints Don't Wash," *Dow Jones News Service*, December 4, 2001.

26 Flynn McRoberts et al., "Ties to Enron Blinded Andersen: Firm Couldn't Say No to Prized Client," *Chicago Tribune*, September 3, 2002, p. 1.

27 Kurt Eichenwald, "Andersen Misread Depths of the Government's Anger," *The New York Times*, March 18, 2002, p. A1.

28 Richard L. Berke and Janet Elder, "Poll Finds Enron's Taint Clings More to G.O.P. than Democrats," *The New York Times*, January 27, 2002, p. A1.

29 Jeff Gerth and Richard W. Stevenson, "Bush Calls for End to Loans of a Type He Once Received," *The New York Times*, July 11, 2002, p. A1.

30 David E. Sanger and David Barboza, "In Shift, Bush Assails Enron over Handling of Collapse," *The New York Times*, January 23, 2002, p. A1.

31 Michael Schroeder, "As Pitt Launches S.E.C. Probe of Himself, Criticism Mounts," *The Wall Street Journal*, November 1, 2002, p. A1.

32 Floyd Norris, "The Big Five Comment on Accounting Practices and the Fall of Enron," *The New York Times*, December 5, 2001, p. C1.

33 Samuel DiPiazza and Robert Eccles, *Building Public Trust: The Future of Corporate Reporting*, John Wiley & Sons, 2002, p. 156.

34 Ibid., p. 100.

35 "The Top 25 Managers of the Year," *Business Week*, January 14, 2002.

36 Gretchen Morgenson, "As It Beat Profit Forecast, I.B.M. Said Little About Sale of a Unit," *The New York Times*, February 15, 2002, p. C1.

37 Gretchen Morgenson, "Wait a Second: What Devils Lurk in the Details," *The New York Times*, April 14, 2002, p. C1.

38 Alex Berenson, "Tweaking Numbers to Meet Goals Comes Back to Haunt Executives," *The New York Times*, June 29, 2002, p. A1.

39 "Financial Statement Restatements: Trends, Market Impacts, Regulatory Responses, and Remaining Challenges," General Accounting Office, October 2002, p. 17.

40 Statistics from Bloomberg analytics, a data service for professional investors.

41 Steven Labaton and Richard A. Oppel Jr., "Testimony from Exxon Executives Is Contradictory," *The New York Times*, February 8, 2002, p. A1.

42 Floyd Norris, "Enron's Many Strands: The World According to Enron's Ex-Chief," *The New York Times*, February 27, 2002, p. C1.

43 E. S. Browning, "Main Street Loses Faith in Buying Stock at Last," *The Wall Street Journal*, May 7, 2002, p. A1.

44 Simon Romero and Alex Berenson, "WorldCom Says It Hid Expenses, Inflating Cash Flow $3.8 Billion," *The New York Times*, June 26, 2002, p. A1.

45 Jesse Eisinger, "The Power of Analysts Is Still Strong on Street," *The Wall Street Journal*, September 9, 2002, p. C1.

46 Randy Whitestone, "Investors Lose Interest in U.S. Stocks as Shares Fall," *Bloomberg News*, July 11, 2002.

47 David E. Sanger, "Corporate Conduct: Bush, on Wall St., Offers Tough Stance," *The New York Times*, July 10, 2002, p. A1.

48 Richard A. Oppel Jr., "Corporate Conduct: Bush and Democrats Still Deeply Split on What Needs to Be Done," *The New York Times*, July 9, 2002, p. C5.

49 Elisabeth Bumiller, "Corporate Conduct: Bush Signs Bill Aimed at Fraud in Corporations," *The New York Times*, July 31, 2002, p. A1.

50 Stephen Labaton, "Bitter Divide as Securities Panel Picks an Accounting Watchdog," *The New York Times*, October 26, 2002, p. A1.

51 Ibid.

52 Stephen Labaton, "Bush Tries to Shrink S.E.C. Raise Intended for Corporate Cleanup," *The New York Times*, October 19, 2002, p. A1.

53 Stephen Labaton, "Can a Bloodied S.E.C. Dust Itself Off Now and Get Moving?" *The New York Times*, December 16, 2002, p. C2.

54 Arthur Levitt, *Take On the Street*, Pantheon Books, 2002, p. 236.

CONCLUSION: LOOK BOTH WAYS

1 Michael Lewis, "The Vilification of the Money Class (and the Triumph of the Mob)," *The New York Times Magazine*, October 27, 2002, p. 94.

2 Jeremy J. Siegel, *Stocks for the Long Run: Third Edition,* McGraw-Hill, 2002, p. 113.

3 Statistics courtesy of Thomson First Call.

4 Jerome Lawrence and Robert E. Lee, *Inherit the Wind,* Random House, 1955, p. 96.

ACKNOWLEDGMENTS

With thanks to:

Ellen and Harvey, my parents

Heather Schroder, my agent, who encouraged me from proposal to final draft

Jonathan Karp, a wise and experienced editor

Andrew Ross Sorkin, who offered keen suggestions on the first draft

Jodie Allen, a friend in word and deed

Matthew Kaminski, who read this manuscrpt at a time he had far more important things to worry about

Winnie O'Kelley and Glenn Kramon, my editors at the *Times,* who gave me the time to write this book

Floyd Norris and Gretchen Morgenson, who have seen everything on Wall Street and are always generous with their knowledge

Chuck Hill of Thomson First Call, the master of financial statistics

And a special thanks to the boys and girls of 4446 Finley, especially Nora and Matt, who looked the other way as I dug a hole in their couch.

—*Written in Los Angeles, CA, and New York, NY*

INDEX

ABOUT THE TYPE

This book was set in Sabon, a typeface designed by the well-known German typographer Jan Tschichold (1902–74). Sabon's design is based upon the original letter forms of Claude Garamond and was created specifically to be used for three sources: foundry type for hand composition, Linotype, and Monotype. Tschichold named his typeface for the famous Frankfurt typefounder Jacques Sabon, who died in 1580.

Printed in the United States
by Baker & Taylor Publisher Services